INDIAN PETROGLYPHS

INDIAN PETROGLYPHS

of the Pacific Northwest

Beth and Ray Hill

Library of Congress
Catalog Card Number: 74-78344
ISBN 0-919654-07-x

Designed and first produced in 1974
HANCOCK HOUSE PUBLISHERS

DESIGN:
NICHOLAS NEWBECK

Published by:

 HANCOCK HOUSE PUBLISHERS LTD.
3215 Island View Road,
Saanichton, B.C., Canada.

Contents

Foreword

by Donald N. Abbott, Curator of Archeology, British Columbia Provincial Museum

Recent years have seen an explosion of interest in native rock art throughout the world and specifically in British Columbia. This has been brought home to us at the Provincial Museum by the increasing number of requests to search the central archaeological site record file for pictograph and petroglyph records. Studies by professional-level archaeologists and art historians have been a relatively minor part of this phenomenon. What have been more significant are the many amateur enthusiasts who are "collecting" these fascinating sites by means of their own notes, sketches, rubbings and photographs — or merely by visiting them. Increased interest creates an increase in knowledge so that a reciprocal result has been many previously unrecorded rock art sites added to our central inventory.

No doubt the current fascination with such ancient monuments is related to trends such as the ecological movement — a realization that we are part of the land upon which we live. Yet the majority of us in North America are at a great disadvantage in finding the empathy with nature that we seek. For not only has the major thrust of modern culture until now been to insulate man from nature, our very culture is a transplant from other environments altogether and we ourselves are very recent biological transplants here. The only people who have truly deep roots in this land are the Indians whose ancestors had, over many millenia, worked out advantageous terms of inter-existence with each of this continent's environments. An essential part of these contracts involved interaction with the spirits of the place and doubtless most petroglyphs and pictographs document certain of these interactions. A concept of "spirits" is really a means of personifying a sense of identity so that in meditating over these ancient depictions each one of us, native or immigrant, is capable of sharing some of the same mystery that motivated the artist.

It is unlikely that we can hope now to regain from most rock art much more detailed information than this about the myths and experiences they portray. Like totem poles, pictographs and petroglyphs are illustrations but not writing. Since they are not writing, they cannot be "read" even though they may refer to stories which were once known verbally. Once those unwritten stories have ceased to be told — as, sadly, most have — they can never be reconstructed confidently however much we study the art.

Another frustration with petroglyph studies has been our inability so far to find any means of dating most of them. Indeed, from the scientific point of view, the most we have been able to expect is some insight into culture-historical relationships among them and with other aspects of the prehistoric cultures based upon studies of distribution, and stylistic and technical analysis.

These kinds of study obviously require detailed, accurate, and as far as possible complete records. We attempt to maintain such records for British Columbia at the Provincial Museum — depending heavily upon people like the Hills and many amateur and professional archaeologists as well as ordinary members of the public to provide information. Obviously files such as this are of limited help and accessibility to people whose interest is more casual. For them, books like this one, like Ed Meade's **Indian Rock Carvings of the Pacific Northwest** and like John Corner's **Pictographs** (Indian Rock Paintings) **in the Interior of British Columbia** are important services. Yet it must be emphasized that each of these books has been a major research accomplishment as well, providing a compendium of new and existing data for the scholar and artist as well as the amateur and the general visitor or admirer of ancient art.

Building on the work of Meade and others, Beth and Ray Hill have expended an amazing amount of productive energy during the past two years visiting the known sites, discovering new ones, relocating some whose location had been lost and even finding more or less portable petroglyphs which had been removed years before. Most of these were recorded by means of the superb rubbings reproduced herein and now stored together with full records at the Provincial Museum. The technique of reproducing the rubbings as illustrations here adds another dimension to the aesthetic quality of outstanding photographic reproductions emphasized by Meade. Many rock carvings simply do not photograph well but a skillfully made rubbing brings out clearly every detail. Another problem with photography is that camera angles introduce distortion, giving different relationships between lines on the plane of the print from what is actually found on the planes of the rock. With the Hills' rubbing techniques one can scale from these illustrations in confidence.

In her text Mrs. Hill has also included all available information from many scattered sources about each site including, where such exist, any myths or traditions associated with it. The book is thus an invaluable research tool for anthropologists, art historians and people of many other motivations who share the fascination of these carvings.

Another thing which this book does by describing the locations is to make all of the sites more accessible to its readers and, through them to others. It is certain to inspire many to visit the petroglyphs themselves. Unfortunately, this fact exposes many more petroglyphs to the same thoughtless damage and vandalism which is evident at some of the previously publicized sites such as Nanaimo's Petroglyph Park. Since many are on private property, including

Indian reserves, it also raises the possibility that owners may be subjected to increasing annoyance by trespass.

On both these points, of course, there are specific laws of which potential visitors must be aware. Protecting the petroglyphs themselves, whether they are on private property or crown land, is the Archaeological and Historic Sites Protection Act which sets a maximum penalty of $1000 fine and six months jail for anyone who should "destroy, deface or alter an Indian painting or carving on rock".

A much more effective protection for this heritage from the past, however, is a sense of value and of courtesy within all of us, directed to the landowners, to the land itself, and above all to the petroglyphs, to the ancient cultures they represent, and to the Indian people whose ancestors created those cultures. It is obvious that people like John Corner, Ed Meade and the Hills feel such a reverence for it is communicated in their writing and in the sensitivity of their illustrations. Anyone reading these pages is certain to come away sharing it as well.

Introduction

by DORIS LUNDY

To many residents and visitors of the West Coast, the term "petroglyph" brings to mind a small provincial park located a short distance south of the city of Nanaimo, British Columbia. This site, Petroglyph Park, is perhaps the best known and most visited of the carved rock sites of the Northwest Coast. Here, a short, steep path leads to a shady ridge where groups of figures have been abraded into smooth sandstone bedrock. The visitor who looks closely will see carvings of men, fish, birds, and the unusual wolf-like creatures which dominate the largest group. The work appears crowded and crude, yet the grooved lines are regular and smooth, the technique sure, and a curious feeling of arrested motion is well conveyed. Although the ridge is said to have been the home of one Thochwan who lived "in the beginnings of time" and who is supposed to have made the carvings, little is actually known regarding the history of the site, and the visitor, left with only the sight of these strange creatures and his own speculations, usually takes his photographs and returns to his car wondering at the purpose behind it all. Yet, much time and patient effort went into each line and figure.

The Northwest Coast is one of the outstanding rock art areas of the world with well over five hundred known sites of both painted (pictographs) and carved (petroglyphs) sites. The actual designs may be anthropomorphic, zoomorphic or geometric, all three types being regularly encountered along the Northwest Coast. One of the most common, however, is the "circle-face", which is simply a pair of single or concentric circles representing eyes. Sometimes a third circle indicating a large mouth, is also present, but among the Tlingit of the northern coast it is said that the eyes were all that was needed in order to represent "the spirits". Other common design elements are human figures, whales and fishes, and those strange creatures which, resembling no living animal, are considered as mythical beings. One of the most striking facets of Northwest Coast rock art is the frequent recurrence of such similar designs along the length of the coast. Although the very simple geometric designs, such as circles, have an almost world-wide distribution it should be noted that as the carvings of this coast become more complex, so they also tend to reveal more hints or traces of the classical art style for which the Northwest Coast is famous. Relatively speaking, stone is a difficult, laborious artistic medium and rock carvings often appear as crude and less detailed when compared to other forms of carved art. However, most petroglyphs are characterized by curvilinear forms, inner structural detail and emphasized heads, all of which are to be found in the historic art style.

Considerable care was taken in selecting the particular rock face on which to work as it is commonly noted by recorders that while one face may be covered with designs, neighbouring surfaces remain bare. Perhaps the portion used gained greater significance as each design was added. With very few exceptions most rock art sites are located near villages, or the mouths of streams and are within view of the ocean. The designs are usually to be found on the seaward faces and are often washed or submerged by the tides. Sandstone on the coast and basalt on the Columbia River seem to have been preferred over the less easily worked granites.

Perhaps because we know so little about petroglyphs (when compared with other remnants of native culture) we are inclined to view them with much mystery and grant them a greater age than they probably warrant. Those few petroglyphs which can be (approximately) dated have tended to fall within the early historic period. In most such cases subject matter is the best clue, as for example, the "recent" sailing ships and horse at Blowhole Beach. Sometimes, too, there are native legends or traditions concerning the carvings, as at Angaish River which was carved by a chief of some two hundred years ago. But what of the vast majority of petroglyphs that have no such helpful clues? In other parts of the world the superposition of later carvings over older ones has proven to be a useful means of establishing relative dates; but there is no clear case of superposition in coastal rock art. Thus, the researcher is forced to fall back on such unsatisfactory "evidence" as appearance, that is, the degree of erosion present. This is unsatisfactory because while one would expect older carvings to exhibit more signs of erosion, the location (and other factors) of the site can make all the difference in its appearance. For example, a recent site located openly on a storm beach is likely to be more eroded than an actually older, but protected site. There are, however, a few coastal sites so eroded as to be almost invisible and these may indeed be indicative of great age. Tentatively, the age range given for most Northwest Coast petroglyphs is Late Prehistoric through Early Historic. This is not to say that some sites could not be considerably older, only that we as yet lack accurate methods for determining such ages.

When we come to why these carvings were made we are on slightly firmer ground. Often, there are native traditions to provide information, more rarely, a European observer. While all petroglyphs are a sort of record (of persons, privileges or events), they seem to have served a wide variety of purposes. Some carvings were part of the winter ceremonials, or recorded the activities of secret societies. Several of the mythical creatures or the "spirit faces" so frequently encountered may also have been concerned with the ceremonial life of native people. At Jack's Point a carved and painted group of fish figures was part of the economically important First Salmon Ceremony where supernatural aid was enlisted in ensuring a productive salmon run. One Alaskan researcher has suggested that the carver's choice of rocks submerged by the tides was in fact a constantly renewed appeal to the "salmon people" to favour certain rivers. Possibly, the numerous whale and seal carvings may have been concerned with the hunting of these creatures. Others may mark productive or dangerous fishing places. Records of local history may have been a factor as a few sites are concerned with warfare, shipwrecks or deaths. At several sites carvings were made to indicate hereditary property rights, marking hunting or fishing territories. These sites frequently contain as designs, the crest signs of the owners. A few sites may have been concerned with marking fresh water springs while others may have recorded the dreams, rituals or spirit aids of shamans. Possibly too, some carvings may have been records of personal experiences, their meaning known only to those who carved them. In most cases we don't really know enough to support even speculation.

Rock art is a never-ending field of study, for "new" sites are continually being discovered especially as the wilder portions of the coast become better known. Such sites need to be accurately recorded before they are damaged or destroyed. Most are photographed, sketched and left. However, photography doesn't always capture important details and sketching is often highly subjective. One of the best ways of recording rock carvings involves the making of rubbings. By this method exact images can be transferred to cloth or paper with little or no subjective interpretation on the part of the recorder and no damage to the carvings. All of which leads to the main portion of this volume, an excellent record of the petroglyphs of the Northwest Coast.

Prologue

Petroglyphs . . . ten years ago I didn't know what a petroglyph was. Why did we stop at Petroglyph Park in Nanaimo that summer day so long ago? Curiosity, I suppose. I can't remember why we went to see the petroglyphs, but I remember well the moment when I first looked at the pictures carved into the rock. Strange animals — dragons? — made with flowing, curving lines. Flat fish and birds and little human stick figures in a brittle dance, the tensions of the human angularity a sharp contrast to the flowing power of the mythological animals. What do these pictures mean? I wondered. Who made them? How long ago? I suppose one might say that this book began at that moment and is an attempt to answer my own questions.

I began the search for information at the British Columbia Provincial Museum. Research led me to books and reports, to archaeological excavation and finally to formal study at Cambridge where I was particularly interested in prehistoric art. But the leg work really began when a Local Initiatives Grant (sponsored by the B.C. Provincial Museum) was awarded to Marg Simons, Bob Simons, Les Patterson, and myself to make rubbings and photographs at all the petroglyph sites of Vancouver Island. During cold wet spring months we managed to reach all sixty sites, some of them easily accessible but many sites difficult to find. We slept in strange places, back-packed along wet muddy trails, hired a variety of boats at different times (including a long cold journey down Nitinat Lake against a driving rain, hunched in the wet bottom of a dug-out canoe), were frequently rain-drenched, exhausted, cold . . . and exhilarated! The petroglyph places are sublime. Perhaps visiting the sites could be compared to a tour of mediaeval cathedrals.

When the time ran out on the L.I.P. grant, much interesting and useful material had been collected for the Museum. Many yards of white cotton sheeting had been covered with the recorded impressions of the carvings. The next task was to put the 150 rubbings, the site reports and some of the hundreds of photographs into a report. As the L.I.P. grant covered neither the costs of publication nor the research involved, my photographer husband and I decided to do it on our own. Ray stretched each rubbing inside a calibrated frame and photographed it, printing the pictures by a reversal process so that in this book the white lines of the rubbings become black. I wrote the text, Ray produced pictures and we both struggled with design and layout. But before the report was quite ready to print, another exciting complication arose.

Upon receiving an application from the B.C. Provincial Museum, the Koerner Foundation approved a grant towards the extension of the work of recording petroglyphs. This time just Ray and I were involved. The second petroglyph expedition was to study the petroglyphs between the northern end of Vancouver Island and Prince Rupert. Since very few of these sites can be reached by road, we became the owners of a 38 foot west coast gillnetter which was everywhere recognized up coast as the Birdland II even though we gave her a coat of paint and renamed her the *Liza Jane*. In the eighteen hundred miles of coast we travelled that summer, the *Liza Jane* never failed us. When the seas came crashing down on the tiny cabin, she merely shrugged off the water and plunged on, her deafening gas motor never missing a heartbeat.

How did we know where to look for petroglyphs? Before departure much time was spent going carefully through the files at the B.C. Provincial Museum to collect all the petroglyph information deposited there by those who had been on the coast before us — the Indians, fishermen, government inspectors, archaeologists, anthropologists, loggers and earlier petroglyph enthusiasts . . . Ed Meade of Campbell River, Alfred Williams of Sointula, Dick Pattinson of Alert Bay . . . the list would be very long if we tried to be complete. With this information in hand we then spent hours on our knees, dozens of marine charts spread around the floor, matching written site descriptions to the jig-saw coast line. The person to whom we are particularly indebted, our unseen companion on the journey, was the late Harlan I. Smith of the National Museum, whose many published petroglyph reports were with us aboard the *Liza Jane*. His love of the wild coast and his interest in the Indian people are imbedded in the carefully accurate records he made of his own tenacious, persistent and enthusiastic petroglyph search. We made good use of his reports. For example, the Noeick River site would be forever lost except for his note about the Indian families using the forty-five degree slope of the rock as a slide; we had to clear trees to uncover the petroglyphs at this site and only recognized the spot by the angle of the slope.

The coast seems emptier now than in the 1920's when Harlan I. Smith passed this way. Where he was guided to the sites by Indian villagers, we usually found only deserted places, guarded by the raucous ravens and the high wheeling eagles. We called at all the inhabited villages of the coast, introducing ourselves, explaining our mission and asking permission of the Band Councils to trespass on Indian land. To each Band whose territories have petroglyph sites we have sent separate reports and photographs. This book serves as our report to the Indian people about the project as a whole. We were made aware of their anger towards non-Indians and some felt that we were exploiting their culture. However, beginning with that first long look at the petroglyphs in Nanaimo and the questions that flooded into my mind, I'm not sure that I could have prevented my own strong interest in learning more about the carvings. And when I knew some of the answers, so many other people were interested in sharing this knowledge that this book seemed almost inevitable. The search that I am making reaches back into my own cultural beginnings, not just the prehistoric world of the Indian people. I want to know about the relationship of man and his world before the comparatively recent technological advances of Western society, and I want to understand the beginnings of religion and art, which are as much a part of the economics of prehistory as breathing is inseparable from eating. In these uncertain times of violent change, when we observe ourselves fouling our own home, the Earth, and greedily destroying the resources that enable us to live, we look back with sharpened interest to the harmonious physical and psychical ecology of earlier times. There were other Indians who shrugged off our quest as irrelevant to the modern Indian. And there were those primarily concerned that the Indians should be the ones to make money from petroglyphs, if there was money to be made. But for the most part the warmth of our encounters with the Indian people reflected their growing interest in the preservation of their history and a pride in the strength of past and present Indian ways.

After completing the Vancouver Island and northern coast surveys, it became obvious that the survey had to be further extended to include the north and south limits of our particular petroglyph style area, the Northwest Coast. As coastal Washington State and the lower reaches of the Columbia River had to be examined, we set off again. For the northern territory, we have been grateful to accept the study of Alaskan coast petroglyphs contributed by Michael Kennedy, Director of the State Museum of Alaska.

Two people who have given unfailing support are Ed Meade and Doris Lundy. Meade's book, *Indian Rock Carvings Of The Pacific Northwest*, was a first publication in this field and much of our work has been only to fill in the details of his broad survey. We are also grateful to Doris Lundy whose thesis for Simon Fraser University is a survey of all the "rock art" sites of the Northwest Coast, both petroglyph and pictograph. Happily our work complements hers, our field work providing much information for her thesis and her detailed study of publications helping us to locate and understand the petroglyphs.

The complex of theories and facts that goes by the name "archaeology" is a vast, collective enterprise. The bibliography appended to this book is in no way a complete expression of our dependence on others. Nor can we even list all those to whom we're indebted for assistance during the past two years of petroglyph research. However, I wish to thank Don Abbott and the members of the British Columbia Provincial Museum Archaeological Division for their patience and assistance. I am agrateful to Marg Simons, Bob Simons and Les Patterson, co-workers on the first petroglyph recording project, Lilo Berliner of the University of Victoria Library, Del McBride of the State Capitol Museum in Olympia, Malcolm and Louise Loring of Portland. And now I am remembering all the people we encountered on our journeys ... the man who helped us recover the outboard motor from forty feet of water at a little harbour called God's Pocket . . . the friendly people at the Oregon Museum of Science and Industry . . . the Band Managers of the coastal villages . . . and people like Mr. King of Canyon City. We can't name all those who gave us help but you will be remembered with gratitude as we turn the pages of this book.

Thousands of miles have given us not only the petroglyphs but also the privilege of tuning in to the world of the Indian people. I hope this book expresses our interest and appreciation. Though the petroglyphs are from the Indian past, they speak to all of us.

1. Some Petroglyph Problems

Once, at an almost-deserted village on Vancouver Island's west coast, near the petroglyph of the 19th century paddlewheel steamer *Beaver,* I talked to an Indian woman who took me in from the rain to dry by her fire. As the daughter of a Chief, she grew up only a few miles from the carved pictures which could have been made by her great grandfather, but she could tell me nothing about them.

The Beaver   Clo-oose

Our questions are too late. Even the first Europeans did not ask about the pictures on the rocks, probably because they did not see them. Most petroglyphs are not easy to find. With the exception of the well-signposted Petroglyph Park site in Nanaimo, how many of the approximately one hundred and fifty petroglyph places on this coast are known to the modern residents? Lewis and Clark, those discerning observers and chroniclers of Indian life, stopped in 1805 near one of the continent's most dramatic petroglyph sites at The Dalles on the Columbia River ... and failed even to notice the rock pictures. Newcombe[1] in 1907 was too late; he writes despairingly that "It seems impossible to decipher these inscriptions satisfactorily as it is not likely that anyone except the makers and those living at the time the work was done could tell what was meant by them."

Though archaeologists and artists have given serious attention to the study of primitive art in some other parts of the world, most North American archaeologists have left the subject of petroglyphs to the amateurs. Trained to feel uneasy about the subjective world of art and unable to relate the rock carvings to the precise and objective study of dated excavation levels, many scientists have just ignored the rock pictures. However, their neglect has been more than matched by the enthusiastic interest of amateurs.

Along the Columbia River especially, we must be grateful to the many non-professional workers whose efforts have preserved at least a small fraction of the original wealth of carvings now submerged behind the great dams of the river. There were workers who frantically made rubbings of the petroglyphs as the rising waters of the new lakes lapped at their legs. Unfortunately neither neglect nor enthusiasm protected the petroglyphs at The Dalles, one of the finest petroglyph sites in North America. And in the same area, many archaeologists are now afraid to publish information about archaeological sites lest voracious vandals with shovels and dynamite destroy them. In southern California, rock art sites have been subdivided for housing lots and the pictures bulldozed out of existence. Since 1960 in British Columbia and since 1971 in

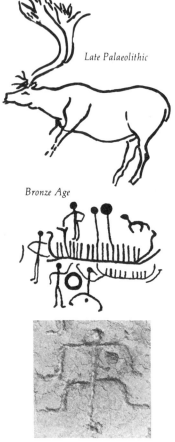

Late Palaeolithic

Bronze Age

Hawaii, Edward Stasak Photo

Fisher's Landing

Alaska, archaeological sites have been protected by legislation. The State of Washington also has legal provisions to protect cairns, graves and rock art, but the law does not cover all archaeological sites and in any case does not appear to be enforced. A site protection law is an important first step. Now amateur and professional must work together to save rock art from those ignorant of the law or willing to break it. A systematic survey is a necessary preliminary to both the protection of the sites and the analysis of the art, and this book is a contribution to these ends. But whether the publication will also be a factor in the destruction of the petroglyphs by unscrupulous and ignorant people has been a matter of great concern. Certainly the lover of primitive art who buys a book as a guide to the sites is not likely to deface the petroglyphs. Nor has the lack of publicity saved the rock art along the Columbia River. We would suggest that public understanding and appreciation are necessary to support the enforcement of protective laws. Also, to prevent casual and thoughtless vandalism, petroglyph sites should not be made into public parks unless there is adequate supervision.

Rock art may be found in many places around the world. The earliest is in the caves of the Late Palaeolithic peoples in Europe about 30,000 years ago. Although petroglyphs everywhere are somewhat similar, being usually the simple outlines of basic forms and symbols, each area has rock art with a separate identity, a recognizable style. Most of the petroglyphs of our distinct style area lie on the very rim of the northwestern edge of the North American continent. Washed by the Pacific tides, the petroglyphs begin abruptly among the Aleutians and end, with some confusion of styles, along the lower Columbia River separating Washington and Oregon. Wherever there are rivers breaking through the coastal mountain wall, there is an interaction of coastal and interior cultures which tends to blur the boundaries of the petroglyph region. We include the lower reaches of the Skeena, Stikine, Fraser and Columbia rivers.

In North American rock art we can distinguish certain basic traditions. The pit and groove type of petroglyph is not only the easiest to make but is also the most widely disseminated around the world. As a widely distributed feature is generally older than one with a limited range, we may consider the pit and groove type of petroglyph to be our oldest tradition, probably brought in by the immigrants from Asia. Central American civilizations influenced many aspects

California Design Elements

of the Indian cultures of North America and were probably the stimulus for some nonrepresentational geometric rock art forms. The animal images seem to be part of a general tradition of the interior of North America. In our petroglyph region there is some evidence supporting the possibility of an art tradition generated by the ancient civilizations in China, diffused around the Pacific Ocean, a complex subject only briefly mentioned in later chapters of this book.

The Dalles

Although we may look at the petroglyphs of the Northwest Coast first in terms of the world's rock carvings and then in the context of their North American setting, we must then recognize that the representations at any one site are the product of the specific group of people who produced them. In searching for meaning in the pictures we must concentrate on the specific rather than the general area. Cox and Stasack[2] show that the small round holes of many Hawaiian petroglyph sites are frequently *piko holes* in which the umbilical stump of a new-born child was placed, the practice being associated with long life for the infant. There is absolutely no hint of any similar purpose for the many round petroglyph holes of the Northwest Coast. Heizer's[3] conclusions concerning the use of petroglyphs as hunting magic in Nevada, and Colton's[4] account of the petroglyphs associated with the perilous journey for salt in Arizona, also illustrate the importance of specific and detailed study to determine the function of petroglyphs.

Where, precisely, are the petroglyphs of our area found? They are usually between the tide lines on the coast, or (less frequently) along the shores of lakes and rivers. Although there are many isolated single carvings, petroglyph sites more commonly have a number of designs. Sometimes they are similarly positioned in relation to the sea and at other sites the designs have haphazard alignments. Superimposition rarely occurs, but at certain sites (at Dean River canyon, for example, and at some of the Venn Passage sites) the very uneven surface is possibly the record of ancient eroded carvings. The available rock appears to control quantity and quality of carvings: designs tend to be larger, more elaborate and more carefully executed where there are large expanses of sandstone, and limited in size and number and more crudely carved where the local stone is roughly textured and harder.

A petroglyph outside a cave at Pachena Point demonstrates one method of making the designs. There one can still see and feel the line of pecked holes which in most carvings has been abraded into a smooth groove. Near petroglyph sites we have picked up small hard stones which could be used as hammers to peck rock pictures. Strong and Schenck,[5] on their visit to Petroglyph Canyon on the Columbia River in 1924 when the site was almost unknown, found a hammerstone lying where the petroglyph maker had put it down:

"On the ledge underneath one of the largest figures we found one of the rock tools used in making the pictures. It was a small, irregular boulder of hard green stone naturally conforming at one end to the grip of a hand and worn down at the more pointed end. A little experimentation showed that these pictures were not pecked into the rock but were ground out by constant rubbing which was carried on until the dark surface of the basalt was entirely removed and a gray solid body for the design formed."

The photographs of carvings from this site (Chapter 6) show how shallow pecking removes the dark cortex of the rock to make lighter coloured designs. Strong and Schenck's description of both tool and technique is undoubtedly accurate. However, the Pachena Point petroglyph is an example of another method of making the designs. Where the stone is softer, the petroglyph

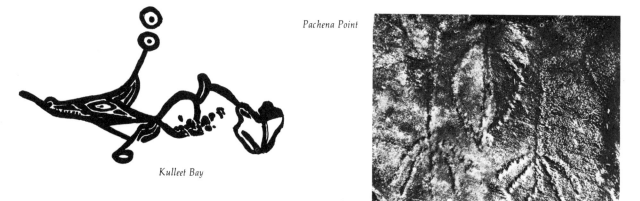

Pachena Point

Kulleet Bay

channels are usually deeper, the most deeply cut petroglyph being the "rain god" figure near the village of Kulleet Bay, where the grooves are an inch deep and about one and a half inches wide. The Kulleet Bay figure is also an example of the use of natural holes and rock fissures as part of the design. The pattern of holes along the bottom of the body oval is composed of natural round pits in the sandstone.

Along the Strait of Juan de Fuca the nature of the rock requires a different technique again. There the petroglyphs are made by bruising lines in the rock. The natural surface of the stone consists of large hard crystals weathered out in relief, like a very coarse sandpaper. As the crystals throw shadows and the intervening spaces hold dirt and lichens, the stone appears dark in contrast to the smooth bruised line of the petroglyph figures, which from a distance resembles a faint chalk mark. In fact some of the petroglyphs of the Juan de Fuca coast are so faint that they can hardly be seen at all, but must be felt with the fingertips. Whether the designs were clearly visible when they were first

Aldridge Point

made cannot now be determined, but possibly it is the making of the design which has significance and the degree of visuality is not important.

On two occasions Indians have been observed actually at work on petroglyphs. Boas[6] records the ceremonial carving of a petroglyph to commemorate the ritual eating of a slave at Fort Rupert, before 1882, with Hudson's Bay Company officials as witnesses. In 1952 Leechman[7] tells of being out in a canoe with an Indian friend near Seattle. They had to go ashore to wait for slack water before venturing through narrow Agate Pass.

"We sat down on the beach and had a smoke and then my companion, Jack Adams, selected a pebble from those at his feet and stood up. He began to peck at a large boulder which lay just behind us. I watched him and discovered that he was just finishing a face pecked in the stone. I asked him if he had made this face and he answered that he had carved this one and some of the others and that his father had done the rest. I asked what their purpose was and was told that they were done merely to pass the time while waiting for the tide to change, which they often had to do at this point."

Agate Pt.

One must immediately comment that Mr. Adams is a man of our own times, and that he could not have the same spiritual or religious motivation as petroglyph carvers may have had before the impact of European civilization. The carving of petroglyphs seems generally to have ceased in the early historic period. The Indian people of today know little about them and associate them with a time in the remote past "before animals were turned into men" (as the Fort Rupert people told Boas, when describing the antiquity of older carvings on that site). Though Mr. Adams was certainly doodling to pass the time, it would not necessarily be correct to apply this rationale to other petroglyphs. Mrs. Florence Sigo, an elderly Squaxin lady, is reported to have said that as a child growing up in the Puget Sound area, she was told by her elders not to walk in front of the petroglyph figures. Apparently the carvings still held some spiritual power for the Indians of that generation.

Agate Pass

Englishman River

We examined the large boulder at Agate Point confirmed by Dr. Leechman as the one pecked by Mr. Adams. We also saw a second smaller petroglyph stone found in 1968 at the west end of Agate Pass, again at a place where one would pause on the return trip if the tide was adverse. The Bremerton Sun[8] tells us that the stone found in 1968 was lying with "its ancient face pressed into the sand". However, if this particular stone is also a product of Mr. Adams' work then its ancient face is only about twenty-five years old. It is wise to keep Agate Point in mind when examining petroglyphs.

The Agate Pass petroglyphs introduce the problem of the age of the carvings, invariably the first question asked. Obviously some petroglyphs can be roughly dated by their subjects: the carving of the *Beaver*, the paddlewheel steamer, must have been made after 1850, and the two petroglyphs of horses must date after 1700. The only historical account of the making of a petroglyph, a face on the beach below old Fort Rupert, gives us a date for that carving between 1849 when the fort was built and 1882 when it was abandoned. During our petroglyph search we met Mr. Tranfield of Parksville, B.C., an elderly man whose father worked on the construction of the first bridge across Englishman River in 1886. There are petroglyphs carved on the sandstone only a few inches from the surviving footings of the old bridge. At the time of the construction of the bridge, Mr. Tranfield Sr. questioned the Indians fishing at this spot. When he asked who made the pictures, they pointed to a deaf-mute Indian and said that he had made the petroglyphs.

Although we may therefore say that a few petroglyphs were made in the 19th century, most rock carvings cannot be dated. McIlwraith,[9] who studied the people of Bella Coola a generation ago, tells us that "The meaning of the designs is not known to any of the present inhabitants." They could only tell him that some of the petroglyphs were made, in the remote past, by chiefs composing tunes. "They picked out the rock in time to the music forming in their minds." The Indians cannot help us with the problem of dating the petroglyphs. Nor can we use radiocarbon dating, that remarkable new tool of the archaeologists, for it can only be used to date plant or animal remains. Even if there were a method, possibly geological, of assigning a date to a rock, we cannot expect to date the depression made in the stone.

It has frequently been suggested that we could estimate a date from the fact that many of the petroglyphs are covered by the rising tide. Meade[10] thinks it unreasonable for the ancient carver to wait for a low tide in order to begin his work, and to be interrupted by the fluctuating tides when higher nearby rock surfaces were completely dry and obviously more suitable as petroglyph surfaces. Evidence from many geologically stable areas of the coast shows that the level of the sea has been slowly rising for the past 6000 years, with a total rise of about six metres.[11] This would mean that most petroglyphs would have been well above the reach of the sea if they were carved before 4000 B.C. However, once we assume that petroglyphs were carved above reach of the tides, would not their altitude have been more random? If the petroglyphs had not been intentionally placed between high and low tide, would we find so many of them confined to this narrow band at the edge of the sea? In writing of the petroglyphs of the Alaskan coast, Keithahn[12] gives plausible arguments for their position between the tidelines, which will be discussed in a later chapter. Though some petroglyphs may well belong to a time earlier than 4000 B.C., the postulated change of sea level cannot with certainty be correlated to the age of the carvings.

It has also been suggested that we could at least determine relative age by the degree of erosion of the carvings, the more eroded being the older. Such an argument can be applied to the Venn Passage sites, where frost erosion has damaged some carvings more than others. However, as the schist rock of that area is fragile and flakes easily, it is not likely that any of the petroglyphs are very old. We observed no sites where wind erosion had caused any perceptible difference between one carving and another. As for the action of the tides, the general situation is that the lower petroglyphs, being subjected to more washing by the waves, are usually the most worn. One exception to this is a site on North Return Passage, where a lower design is less eroded than higher ones. That the lower petroglyph is probably more recent is further supported by the fact that the lower design has the curved ovoid shape associated with the comparatively recent Northwest Coast wood carvings. Again, at sites along the coast of Alaska, Emmons[13] distinguished older more eroded designs from more recent petroglyphs where "the marks of the pecking implement are still clearly visible". Different degrees of erosion of a single design may be observed on the sloping surface of a hard granite boulder at Lizard Point where the carved eyes are still visible but the lines of the mouth have almost disappeared. Since such hard stone erodes slowly we may consider this petroglyph to be fairly ancient. But how old? Determining the precise age by erosion is impossible.

Return Channel

Some writers have thought that a change of style at a site was a method of relative dating, the cruder petroglyphs being considered older and the more sophisticated and carefully executed designs younger. But one may quite logically argue that the differing styles were executed on the same day by two different workers, one more competent than the other. At the Meadow Island site, the finest carvings appear to have been made first, in the prime location along the ridge of the stone, while the rough carvings seem to have been fitted into empty spaces at a later time. We must also consider the point that the technique may have been unimportant to the petroglyph carvers: a crucifix has the same meaning whether exquisitely carved or crudely made.

Lizard Point

It might be possible to draw some conclusions about age from the depth of soil cover over one newly discovered petroglyph site. On the Nanaimo River, heavy logging machinery was used to remove some trees from a building lot and subsequently the removal of about a foot of soil revealed the carvings on the smooth sandstone bedrock below. Thorough research by soil scientists could tell us whether this site was purposely covered over, or whether the soil layer was slowly built up over a period of time. When the site was discovered in 1969, government experts guessed at an age of one thousand years for the formation of this depth of soil, but a careful study has not been made.

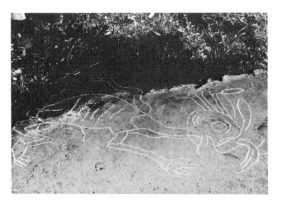

Nanaimo River

Spearfish, Wash.
B. Robert Butler Photo

Petroglyph Park

National Museum of Canada photo

Another way in which we may in the future make some progress in the problem of dating petroglyphs is by the study of changing art styles, using carved objects dated from their provenience in archaeological levels of known age. For example, Butler[14] considers some of the petroglyphs at The Dalles to be quite similar in style to the stone and antler carvings found in association with cremation burials carbon dated at about 1400 - 1800 A.D. A bone comb, two thousand years old, found near Prince Rupert, is stylistically like the petroglyph animals at Nanaimo. Such finds underline the importance of careful excavation of archaeological sites. The looting of sites by collectors destroys important evidence, for objects torn from their dateable context are of little use in working out the chronology of art styles and petroglyphs.

With regard to the age of the petroglyphs we can only say that some are comparatively recent while others may be as old as the history of men on this coast. How old is that? Carbon 14 dates from the lowest levels of archaeological excavations at The Dalles tell us that men have lived there since 8000 B.C. Further north early dates presently known include 7050 B.C. at the Milliken site in the Fraser River Canyon, 4300 B.C. at Port Hardy, 5850 B.C. at Namu, 6350 B.C. at Millard Creek near Courtenay and 8230 B.C. at Ground Hog Bay in Glacier Bay, Alaska. We can learn something about the petroglyphs by examining the lives and ideas of these people who made them, which we shall do in the next two chapters. We can also learn much from an examination of the petroglyphs themselves, the main object of this book. So that they may be studied and compared we have brought together, from thousands of miles of travel, these pictures cut into the immovable rock. The petroglyphs are artifacts which have not been removed from their original locations to the museums and private collections. For the most part they remain where they were made, and in this they are unique among artifacts. When you stand in front of them, your feet press the earth where the carver once stood and you feel the air on your face as he did. And possibly, if you are patient in contemplation when the slanting rays of the sun deepen the shadows in the shallow grooves cut into the stone, you may begin to know something of his involvement in nature, his world-view, from which the image on the stone emerged. But first we must know something of the people who made the petroglyphs.

2. The People of the Northwest Coast

The western edge of North America is rimmed by a long chain of high mountains. Along the northern coast, the Pacific Ocean has flooded in, drowning the valleys and creating thousands of islands and the long fiords which funnel the fierce winds. How often in our fishboat we have sought a ledge to which our anchor could cling, as the mountains rose sheer out of the sea and the bottom dropped away to two hundred fathoms or more. The Indians could pull their dug-out canoes onto the shore, but the sudden summer gales buffetted us for hours as we struggled towards a harbour where our boat would lie gentle in the night. It is this **precarious** unpredictable sea which dominated the life of the coast people. It was at the very edge of the sea that they carved most of their petroglyphs, facing away from the land and washed by the rising tides.

Fifty miles off the coast, lying like a faint blue cloud on the horizon, the Queen Charlotte Islands are part of another submerged mountain chain which reappears to the south as the long mountain backbone of Vancouver Island and as the Olympic Mountains in Washington. Westward across the vast Pacific Ocean, the Japanese current circles north against the rim of Asia, turns along the Aleutians and flows against our coast. The warm moist air of the prevailing westerlies is pushed upward by the mountain ranges and as it cools, drenching rain falls. In the summer the blinding fogbanks may suddenly appear. Once, while we were travelling in the Moore Islands in August, the fog crept in and obliterated all the world, except for the blurred outlines of the tiny lagoon where we lay for days. And when the fog persisted, we finally set compass courses with care and groped our way out through kelp beds and the unseen submerged pinnacles of drowned mountains.

The heavy rainfall and the moderate temperatures produce thick impenetrable rain forests of spruce, hemlock, fir and cedar, growing to the water's edge. Where the shore is not precipitous there are clams, mussels and crabs, and in the ocean is a plentiful supply of fish. Five species of Pacific salmon come to spawn in the coastal streams. Anchored one evening in Lowe Inlet we sat on deck and watched with delight as the salmon lept from the water all around us, arching in the golden evening light and falling back with a bright splash into the black waters. On our petroglyph quest we also saw seals and killer whales, and porpoises came to swim under the keel of our boat, escorting us northward up Grenville Channel. We even saw the sea otter, almost exterminated by the voracious fur trade of the early historic period.

On land there were deer, and twice we encountered the grizzly bear. On one occasion we were trudging up the river bed of the Pa-aat River (Pitt Island) and were far from the safety of the boat when a large black bear rose up out of the swampy meadow edging the stream. We couldn't run, neither on the slippery smooth river stones nor on the soggy shore and we had no weapon. The bear eyed us and ambled away. Reflecting on this experience, we talked of the days past when man was both hunter and hunted. Frank Waters, author of *The Book of the Hopi*, says that we do not yet grasp the psychical ecology underlying physical ecology. He writes,

"To Indians the earth is not inanimate. It is a living entity, the mother of all life, our Mother Earth. All her children, everything in nature is alive: the living stone, the great breathing mountains, trees and plants, as well as birds and animals and man. All are united in one harmonious whole."[1]

It is difficult to grasp this underlying principal when we stand before a petroglyph which has been carted to the green lawn of a museum. We can be diligent in our field work and clever in analysing the "art" and its cultural associations, but we cannot begin to understand the petroglyphs until we know something about the relationship of man and the raincoast world.

Although the boundaries of our particular petroglyph style area fit fairly well into the limits of the North Pacific Coast Culture Area as defined by anthropologists, the peoples of this area have different languages and physical attributes. They did not recognize the unity of their region nor have any name for it. Yet we can perceive that in spite of their differences they have a common identity which is reflected in the unity of the petroglyph style. What is the reason for this unity? Is it that they all lived in a special environment, poised between the mountains and the sea, and that this environment imposed certain controls on their culture? Drucker argues against such a theory of environmental determinism, pointing out that there is no abrupt change in landscape, climate, flora or fauna at the north and south borders of the region even though the culture terminates in Alaska and in northern California. He says we must consider historic and other factors. It is not easy to study the history of the coast because it has not yet been written by the archaeologists, but there is much unsynthesized information in scientific publications.

Archaeologists have not dated precisely the arrival of the first men entering North America from Asia and the evidence will not be easy to locate. They must find the remains of a camp fire buried perhaps 40,000 years deep, kindled by a small family group moving with the game herds which fed it. Certain large crude tools (the Pebble Tool tradition) may represent an early migration from north east Asia any time between 40,000 and 20,000 years ago. During that time the ice of the last Glacial Epoch had locked up so much of the world's water

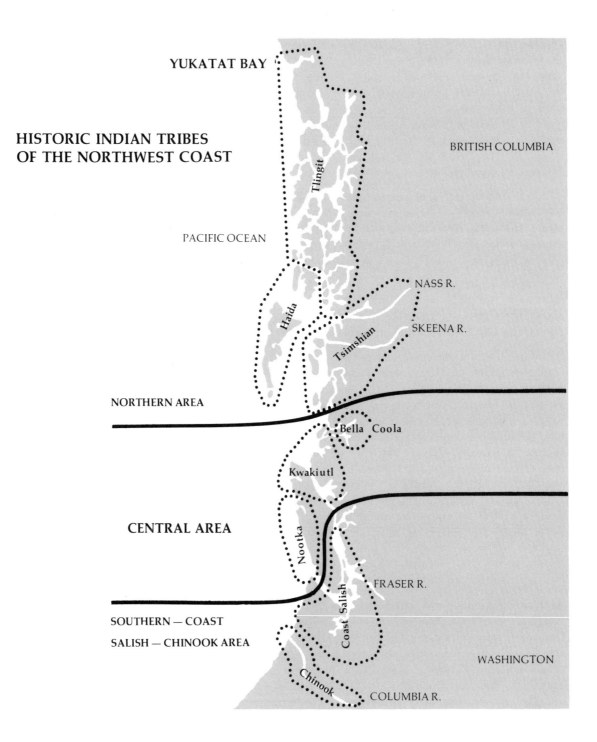

HISTORIC INDIAN TRIBES
OF THE NORTHWEST COAST

YUKATAT BAY

BRITISH COLUMBIA

Tlingit

PACIFIC OCEAN

NASS R.

Haida

Tsimshian

SKEENA R.

NORTHERN AREA

Bella Coola

Kwakiutl

CENTRAL AREA

Nootka

FRASER R.

Coast Salish

SOUTHERN — COAST

SALISH — CHINOOK AREA

WASHINGTON

Chinook

COLUMBIA R.

that the sea level was lowered to expose a land bridge to Asia across the Bering Sea. At the same time the two glacial ice masses of the North American continent (spreading out from two centres in Canada) had not yet grown together to close the route south from Alaska. Through the time of the glaciers, a low precipitation kept Alaskan valleys ice free and here have been found the remains of the mammoths and other mammals which may have fed human hunters.

It is thought that parts of the Queen Charlotte Islands may also have been unglaciated. Between 23,000 B.C. and 9,000 B.C., British Columbia was covered with Cordilleran ice to a thickness of perhaps 1500 metres. But gradually the climate changed and the ice began to shrink, diminishing from both the south and north towards its surviving stronghold on the high peaks of central British Columbia. The melting of the glaciers was accompanied by a rising sea level which ultimately closed the land bridge from Asia, and a drying up of the centre of the continent moved the game (and the human predators) into the mountain and plateau regions and through the river valleys to the Pacific coast. As the ice shrank, plants, animals and people gradually occupied the new land, moving in from both north and south. Carbon 14 dates from peat in the southern interior of British Columbia show that the ice was gone and vegetation growing by about 8000 B.C.

So the disappearance of the ice gave men a new land to occupy. When we examine the inhabitants of the coast thousands of years later, we find not only a unified cultural area but also that there are distinctly different languages and physical attributes among coast dwellers. The people of our petroglyph province can be separated into three culture areas:

a) The Northern Area: Haida, Tlingit and Tsimshian people

b) The Central (or Wakashan) Area: Kwakiutl and Nootka, plus the Salish Bella Coola.

c) The Southern Area: Salish and Chinook, and others.

If distinctly different groups of people occupied the coast, why do we find a unified culture from Alaska to northern California?

The complete answer to this conundrum still awaits the work of the archaeologists, whose summer digging during the past few years is at last providing some archaeological facts to buttress speculation based on anthropological observations. Drucker[2] suggested, many years ago, that there

was an early culture, extending along the entire coast, which was a sea hunting and fishing North Pacific culture related to Northeast Asia. The people of the Northern Area (Haida, Tlingit and Tsimshian) and the southern tribes (Salish and Chinook) all have connections with peoples in the interior of the continent. Drucker suggested that they came to the coast after the North Pacific people, adapting to the marine environment by absorbing or being absorbed by the first arrivals. Drucker considers the Wakashan people (Kwakiutl and Nootka), as well as the Eskimo and Aleut, to be descended from the original coast occupants; but these groups have been so long separated by the intrusive Northern peoples that they have evolved into distinct and separate entities. It is Drucker's view that the ancient underlying North Pacific culture has provided the basic patterns from which the Northwest culture developed.

Some groups recall their origins in legends. The Haida and the Tlingit, whose language is related to that of the Athapascan-speakers of the Yukon and Mackenzie drainages, say that they came from the interior by way of the Skeena River. When the present Haida people came to the Queen Charlotte Islands they found the "Old Haida" who, according to tradition, had lived on the islands so long that they had no memory of coming from anywhere else. Coast Salish is closely related to Interior Salish spoken in parts of interior British Columbia and east of the Cascade Mountains in Washington. The Chinook language is part of the Penutian language family, spreading through Idaho. The two outlying groups of Salish are the Bella Coola in the Kwakiutl area and the Tillamook of the Oregon Coast, perhaps cut off from the main Salish area by expansion of the Chinook people down the Columbia.

Whatever the route by which they came, whether they were sea people moving along the Pacific Coast, or big-game hunters adapting to fishing and moving to the Pacific shore by way of the rivers which cut through the mountain wall, or early Columbia River people expanding northwards into the newly ice-free land, or people moving south through the interior of British Columbia, whether they were early or late arrivals, or whether (as is most probable) all these routes were used at different times over a period of about ten thousand years, the resulting coastal tribes while maintaining their separate identities, have produced a culture which is clearly distinctive and unified. The petroglyphs reflect both the separate identities and the unity.

The coast people lived by exploiting the resources of the sea and it was the annual run of the salmon which is the real key to their way of life. Caught in huge numbers and dried for the winter, the salmon provided the surplus food wealth which gave coastal people the time to elaborate their complex cultural patterns. The first salmon rites and the taboos associated with fishing for salmon indicate not only the importance of this food resource but also the tensions associated with the mysterious ways of the migratory fish. They appeared annually in a somewhat miraculous and unpredictable fashion, thronging into the rivers to spawn, pushing relentlessly upstream against all obstacles, throwing themselves on the stony shores and dying there. During

this sacrificial journey they were easily caught by the thousands. Surely the Indians asked why they chose to die this way, and where did they come from? Why did their numbers differ from years of good runs to the years when few salmon appear? Will they always come again? The underlying mystery associated with their major food resource must have been an important factor in the world-view of the people whose wealth and life depended upon the apparent sacrifice of their brother, the salmon. It is not surprising to find petroglyphs associated with salmon spawning streams and with legends of fish who became human beings. We shall discuss this subject more fully in the next chapter.

A resource second only to the salmon in importance is the cedar, which was worked with a variety of fine stone tools to provide houses, boats, dishes, clothes, ropes and the famous wood carvings of the area. Large rectangular plank houses in the winter villages sheltered many families, each occupying separate areas around the perimeter platforms of the house. A central firepit gave heat and light. At Alert Bay and at the 'Ksan village in Hazelton and elsewhere, these fine houses have been recreated, in smaller dimensions than the originals. We can enter the great long houses through carved totem posts and experience the massive grandeur of the interiors. Nowhere is the artistry of the Northwest Coast Indian better demonstrated than in their fine canoes. With a limited number of tools but with a sure eye and hand they shaped the curving craft in perfect symmetry, so that it would slide smoothly through the seas. These too have been preserved, and may be seen in museums where we have all examined collections of tools of stone, bone and antler; but the pictures the Indians carved in stone, the petroglyphs, lie where they have always been, for the most part in lonely, secret and deserted places where the sea washes over them.

The cedar was also used for clothing. As the west coast climate would cause skin clothing to be either soggy and stretched or dry and hard, the women used cedar bark and spruce roots to make cloaks and conical hats like small umbrellas. On warm days the men wore nothing and the women had fibre aprons. They were barefooted. Their clothing seems inadequate for the bitter winds of winter but, like the Eskimos, their high oil consumption fortified them against the cold. They were a hardy people. Barnett[3] tells us that in every large house there were one or two men who routed the young boys out of bed at dawn for a cold swim, and while standing in the icy water the boys would rub their bodies vigorously with bundles of cedar or hemlock switches, to make their skin tough and insensitive.

In a narrative of a Spanish voyage to Vancouver Island in 1792, Espinoza y Tellow[4] wrote that he saw Chief Maquinna's brother go with two servants to a deep lake where he took a piece of pine bark in each hand and then hurled himself into the lake. Lifting his face from the water he rubbed his cheeks with the bark until the blood flowed. Such rigorous exercises were also part of the training for spiritual power associated with puberty and were especially strenuous for those individuals seeking the power of the shaman or medicine man. Some petroglyphs may be a part of this important aspect of life on the Northwest coast. The petroglyph-rimmed "shamans' pool" at Kulleet Bay is still used by young initiates into the winter ceremonials.

The lively village of Kulleet Bay and the petroglyph site which still plays a part in tribal ceremonials, stand in contrast to the many deserted and overgrown villages of the coast. Only the tell-tale trace of clamshell above the shore marks the place where once the huge houses faced the sea and people played their roles in life's drama, controlled by the well westablished patterns of custom and tribal law. As a discussion of the social organization of the coastal people involves a complex unravelling of the meaning of band and tribe, clan and phratry, as the terms are applied by different anthropologists to the different groups of the area, we can only briefly examine the subject here.

The basic unit of society is the extended family, although kinship is defined differently in the various tribes. The extended family group owned certain resources and shared a house or houses, common ancestors and certain names, privileges, songs and dances. In the winter village several such family groups might live together to form a band or tribe. Within each family there were nobles and commoners. The third class in society, the slaves, were mere chattels. High rank was determined by birth, whether in the male or female line depending on tribal custom. However inheritance was traced, the guiding principal was the inheritance of status and privilege. "Nowhere in America," states Sapir,[5] "is the idea of the grading of individuals carried to such an extent as among the West Coast Indians, but it applies only to the nobility, not to the commoners." Each noble person had a precise rank, determined by birth, and as kinship units were not large, each person's specific place in the social scale was known to all. At feasts and ceremonials the nobles wore the finest costumes and had the most spectacular roles in the dancing. They were deferred to in daily life, had the best seats at feasts and occupied the most comfortable part of the houses. They had greater wealth and power. But although high rank carried a high degree of personal power, it had to be validated at intervals by displays of wealth and the distribution of property which was primarily derived from a particular family and house.

Because of the stress on the acquisition of wealth, the west coast culture has been compared with modern western society. A major difference is that the entire extended family group had certain rights with regard to the food resources, the houses and the family history. The public display of wealth at the potlatch was a matter of family prestige as well as individual pride. Another difference is that the mere possession of wealth did not confer prestige. The individual was less important than the tradition and the man bearing the name of an ancestor, either real or legendary, was spurred to great efforts to maintain prestige lest he suffer the shame of letting down his predecessors. "To make my name good" was the preoccupation of his life.

Much has been written of the potlatch which was an important institution everywhere on the coast except in the extreme south. Basically the potlatch was a ceremony given by a chief and his group to another group for the purpose of validating a title or status, to announce a marriage or birth, or to mourn the death of a chief, at which time the guests or witnesses to the event were given gifts. Rigid protocol controlled every aspect of the event: the issuing of invitations, the seating around the fire, the serving of food, and the order and contents of speeches, songs and dances which related to the reason for the potlatch. In the 18th and 19th centuries however, the sudden wealth from the European fur trade and the movement of bands to new homes at trading centres were responsible for the spectacular rivalry potlatches of the Kwakiutl, when vast quantities of goods were given away or destroyed in prestige competitions. Further contributing to the breakdown of traditional customs and inheritance patterns were the terrible scourge of smallpox and the epidemics of measles, influenza and tuberculosis.

Because of its possible association with the petroglyphs, one further aspect of social organization requires a brief outline: the phratries and clans. Among the Tlingits every person belonged either to the Raven or Wolf phratry and must marry a person of the opposite group. The children belonged to the mother's side. The main crest of the Raven phratry was Raven, the most important mythological being of the Tlingits, whom we will meet later in a myth associated with the petroglyphs of Alaska. Each phratry was divided into many clans, each with its own crest or crests. The two phratries of the Haidas were the Ravens and the Eagles. The Tsimshian had four phratries: Ravens, Eagles, Wolves and Grizzly Bears. The Kwakiutl were not divided into phratries but had many clans, each of which probably originated as a separate village community of one family group. It is possible that clan crests were used to mark ownership of certain areas or fishing streams. Chief Wright[6] of the Kitselas people relates in *Men of Medeek* that:

"Before they left to resume their up-river journey Neas Waias took the native paint, powdered red rock compounded with the oil from the salmon roe. With this paint the Chief marked rocks on the shore that all who saw might know that here was a land claimed and possessed; a land that would, in due time, become the site of a new town and its activities."

The petroglyph boulder now at the Prince Rupert Museum, originally from Observatory Inlet, is reported to have been carved by a chief who lived some two hundred years ago to mark his hunting and fishing rights in the area.[7] In a later chapter we shall see that specific petroglyph figures on the Arizona plateau are the crests of certain clans, but on our coast a clan does not have the sole right to a crest. The grizzly bear crest, for example, is claimed by twelve Haida clans of the Raven phratry. We cannot therefore identify petroglyphs as the crests of specific clans. Crests were of course used in the carving of totem poles and in decorating many other objects. Sapir[8] notes that crests have a tendency to be thought of in concrete terms, as carvings, and that the Kwakiutl term for crest denotes primarily a carving. Of the petroglyphs at Etoline Island, Emmons[9] plainly states that "The animal designs, which largely predominate, are all totemic in character, representing the principal emblems of the family divisions of the Stikine tribe that inhabits this locality."

In oversimplifying the story of the people who lived between the mountains and the sea we are perhaps misled by the ethnographically recorded flowering of the culture which followed the first contact with Europeans. The conundrum of the petroglyphs and perhaps the reason why they have been neglected by scientists is that we cannot be certain where, precisely, they fit into the evolution of the Northwest Coast culture. When we look back, a fog of time blurs our view of these proud people who lived so richly and ceremoniously on this stormy shore. To know more of the ceremonials, some of which are associated with the petroglyphs, we may learn from the anthropologists and ethnographers who have so well served us on this coast.

3. The Religion
of the Northwest Coast Indians

On a summer morning there are fires burning on the beach below the Indian village. The people have come down from their houses to the shore where they stand expectantly, looking across the calm water to watch fishermen. A man whom we will call the ritualist and several assistants are fishing for salmon with a reef net. Now they have pulled in their nets and are coming towards the shore. The people divide to form an avenue from the edge of the water to the place where the fires are burning. Some children, their faces painted red with ochre and white eagle down sprinkled on their heads, come to meet the fishermen. The ritualist carefully hands the children the fish he has caught and they carry it between the two lines of villagers, stroking the fish gently and taking care that the fish's head is pointed inland (upstream). The ritualist follows, singing and shaking his rattle. At the fires he directs the cutting and roasting of the fish. After another ritual song, everybody eats his share of the fish off split-cedar planks. When the fishbones are thrown back into the water, the ceremony is over.

This account of a first-salmon ceremony in the Gulf Islands is summarized from Boas.[1] Though there are many variations of the rite, the feature common to all is the tenderness with which the fish is handled and the reverence and gentleness of the people.

It has been easier for archaeologists to describe the tools found in the middens and the fishing techniques associated with them than to understand the attitudes of the fishermen themselves. The surviving bones and stones can tell us little about the way the Indians saw the world in which they lived, or what meaning they attached to life itself. We see the carved picture on the rock but we cannot see into the mind that envisaged it and directed the hand that pecked it out. It is the work of the early ethnographers that must guide us here, and the myths so diligently collected offer clues but we must go carefully for there is little firm ground when we begin to examine the minds of prehistoric people. What happened to a man after death? Did he linger nearby, jealous of the living and dangerous to them, or did he turn into a salmon, or an owl hooting in the forest at night?

The coast people do not seem to have believed in a 'heaven', although the myths tell of a world above, inhabited by immortals, into which certain men have climbed. Is there a God-Creator up there? There appears to be a deity commonly linked with the sky or sun, but remote and vaguely known and of relatively little importance in the daily routines of life. Drucker[2] tells us that

"More important to the Indians were the supernatural beings who inhabited their own world: the forests, the mountains, the beaches, the waters and the nearer reaches of the skies. These were the gods with whom human beings might come in contact, to their benefit or disaster. A great many of these were guardian spirits, familiar to most American Indians — beings who could confer blessings, good fortune. and even a measure of supernatural power on man. Many were animal spirits, at least they assumed the form of animals; others were monsters of weird and terrifying aspect. It seems that monsters were more numerous on the North Pacific coast than in other parts of western North America. There were huge cave-dwelling man-eating birds with tremendous sharp beaks; there were frightful sea monsters in the ocean deeps. On the highest mountain peaks dwelled thunderbirds, who kept live whales as easily as an eagle flies away with a trout in its talons. Ogres and malevolent dwarfs shared the forest with animals and animal spirits. A huge hand emerged from the ground, shaking a rattle, but no one dared to imagine to what horrendous form it was attached. Giant quartz crystals possessed a life of their own; they glowed with a blinding white light, vibrated with a humming sound, flew through the air, and killed ordinary men and animals with a mysterious charge. These are but a few of the myriad of terrifying supernatural beings who peopled the native environment. All were dangerous to mortals, but most of them could confer valuable gifts too.

Animal spirits of a special class were believed to live in groups similar to those of human beings. The core of this belief related to the salmon, who dwelled in a huge house, similar to the houses of the Indians, far under the sea. In their home, the salmon went about in human form. When the time came for the annual runs, they put on their robes of salmon skin and converted themselves into the fish that were the staple of the area. The run was thus conceived to be a voluntary sacrifice for the benefit of mankind, and when the bones of the fish were returned to the water, they washed down to the sea where each fish became reassembled and came back to life."

It is E.L. Keithahn's[3] opinion that the petroglyphs, carved on boulders which were covered every day by the rising tide, were for the purpose of calling the fish. He noted that they were at the mouths of spawning streams, that they faced out towards the sea in the direction from which the salmon would come, and that they were regularly submerged and became part of the undersea world where the fish lived. He also included as support for his views a Tlingit myth collected in 1909 by J.R. Swanton,[4] a story about the activities of Raven, the most important mythological personage of the Tlingit people:

"... after a while he came to an abandoned camp where lay a piece of jade half buried in the ground, on which some design had been pecked. This he dug up. Far out in the bay he saw a large spring salmon jumping about and wanted to get it but did not know how. Then he stuck his stone into the ground and put eagle down upon the head designed thereon. The next time the salmon jumped, he said, 'See here, spring salmon jumping out there, do you know what this green stone is saying to you? It is saying, 'You thing with dirty, filthy back, you thing with dirty, filthy gills, come ashore here.'"

"Raven made this jade talk to the salmon," the legend tells us. Boas[5] reports that "if the fish do not come in due season, and the Indians are hungry, a Nootka wizard will make an image of a swimming fish and put it into the water in the direction from which the fish generally appear. This ceremony, accompanied by a prayer to the fish to come, will cause them to arrive at once."

According to Barnett,[6] when the salmon ran poorly or late, the Indians resorted to magic to call the fish. We have already spoken of the inevitable tension associated with the mystery and uncertainty of this major food resource, and the Tlingit legend suggests the way in which the petroglyphs may have functioned in magic rites. The fine petroglyph called the "rain god" is carved on a large boulder which lay originally between the tide lines at the entrance to Kulleet Bay. It was discovered by loggers who moved the stone to the top of the beach because it was interfering with the movement of log booms. When the carving was found, the Indians of Kulleet Bay promptly named it the "rain god"

Kulleet Bay

The name seems strange on this wet coast and among a non-agricultural people. However, Keithahn[7] informs us that the salmon, returning to spawn in the streams, will school up in the deep water and will not swim into the streams until after a heavy downpour of rain has raised the water level of the rivers. On the shores of the streams are the waiting Indians, their weirs and spears ready. They can see the spring salmon jumping out there, as in the Tlingit legend. Probably the petroglyph was used in a ceremony to induce the rain which would bring the salmon within their reach.

The Jack Point petroglyph boulder has similar associations. When the salmon run was late, the ritualist painted over the carved figures of fish with red ochre.[8] He also put ochre on pieces of four different substances (goat wool and a grass are the two Barnett identifies) and these are burned at the foot of the petroglyph boulder. The Jack Point petroglyph is associated with a myth about a dog salmon who became a man and took the chief's daughter into the sea as his wife. In Barnett's version of the tale, her father went to the far north to search for her where the dog salmon live beyond the other salmon but there he

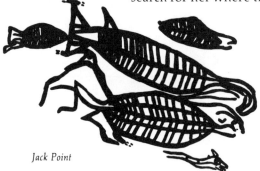

Jack Point

was told that although she could not go home, she and her husband would come to Nanaimo each year and would swim up the river, leaping out of the water together. No one but the chief and his descendants should touch them. Each year the Nanaimo people could eat roasted whole dog salmon but could not cut them up for drying or smoking until the ritualist invited all the people of the village to a ceremony at his house. There a male and female dog salmon were painted with ochre and sprinkled with eagles' down. Then the ritualist shook his rattle and started his song over the fish and everyone joined in. After the ceremony the villagers were free to smoke the dog salmon.

These legends show us the Indian way of functioning in a world of unknown and dangerous powers. The Indian recognized his total integration in the world of nature and his dependence on the powerful spirits of the universe. To live he must kill the salmon, his brother. To live he must both propitiate and exploit the spirit world. The basic prerequisites were ritual cleanliness and the acquisition of spiritual power.

"As a young man, Johnny Louie's father was always swimming and purifying himself. One night a wolf appeared in the village and howled. It came there seeking Louie's father and it spoke to him by howling. After that the wolf was 'just like a dog for him' and he never had any trouble getting deer. The wolf rounded them up and drove them toward him."[9]

Writing of the Salish, Barnett tells us that men aspiring to be hunters trained to seek power from the wolf, the best hunter in the animal world. Similarly, hunters of sea mammals sought power from the killer whale, the most successful of the hunters in the world of the sea. These two animals were propitiated. When an Indian saw a killer whale he would throw eagle down on the water. Wolves were considered to be humans as the salmon were.

Connected with this was the idea that land hunters became wolves when they died, and sea hunters became killer whales.

The training of the hunter involved ritual cleanliness achieved by fasting, emetics and purges, by bathing and scrubbing the body with branches, and by sexual continence.

"The goat and bear hunter steamed himself at dawn every day for a month in the spring, and after each steaming he dived into a creek of cold water. He also scrubbed first the right side of his body, then the left with hemlock branches dipped in sea water. When his training period was over, he secretly painted his face in the way directed by his 'power' (i.e. spirit helper) and set out ... If his first hunt was unsuccessful, the goat and bear hunter went through the regimen again, this time using cedar branches to rub his body raw."[10]

In Alaska informants told de Laguna[11] that whale hunters made paintings in secret places to bring them luck. She writes that the Cook Inlet pictures were also made in secret places, probably in connection with whaling rituals or other hunting magic. At Kodiak Island, our most northerly petroglyph site, the whale hunters of the Koniag people were a small, hereditary, wealthy prestige group. Heizer[12] reports that they jealously guarded their whale hunting secrets and "resorted to caves where mummified bodies of dead whalers were kept." Although there is no firm evidence connecting petroglyphs to whaling ceremonies, it is quite possible that the Kodiak Island carvings were associated with hunting or fishing magic.

Although there are many variations according to the tribal area and the specific purpose of each power quest, the basic patterns of attitude and method are constant. Among some groups, power is sought mainly during the time of puberty. Adolescent boys were urged to go into the woods alone and to stay away, using their own resources while they trained for the expected spirit encounter. They were instructed to eat and sleep little, to sleep near a lake where they could swim and scrub themselves with branches, and eventually they would have a spiritual encounter. The animal spirit usually appeared in a dream or trance and spoke to the boy, offering him symbolic objects. Some spirits were stronger than others and the strongest of all was the mythical serpent, associated with the training of shamans. An encounter with the serpent caused the person to become unconscious and to bleed from all the apertures of his body. The boy was given two warnings: he must never run away from the spirit encounter and he must not talk about it afterwards.

The anthroplogist James Teit[13] tells us that the Salish-speaking Thompson people, both in puberty rites and as an adult practice, recorded their dream figures on rock. Leechman[14] also reports puberty rites associated with rock art. We know that primitive people object to having their photographs taken because the picture steals some power from them. In the same way the pictures on the rocks are imbued with power from the spirit or animal they represent.

The changes at adolescence are mysterious and a person is filled with a dangerous spiritual strength at puberty. Similarly women have a potent magic and can produce new life, so menstrual blood is a frightening agency and the mere touch of a woman's hand can sometimes spoil the hunter's weapons and keep the game beyond his reach. The hunter's wife must lie relaxed on her bed so that the deer in the forest will stand quietly while the hunter shoots. There is a flow of power between the woman and the quarry, between man and nature, between the faces carved on shoreline boulders and the salmon jumping in the bay, between petroglyphs and spirit powers.

Most important to the average Indian was the power from his guardian spirit, who gave him also a song and a dance. Jenness[15] says the majority of the people acquired their guardian spirits through the power breathed into them by old dancers rather than through individual dreams and visions, and he describes the dancers seizing a youth, rendering him unconscious with their breath and giving him one of their own guardian spirits. Such power was slight and was associated mainly with the winter dance ceremonies. There were two kinds of guardian spirit relationship, the first very intense, resulting from long and arduous training or serious illness and enabling the individual to do extraordinary things such as healing, and the second relatively slight, conferring little more than a song and dance. To cope with life the Indian sought power — power to hunt or fish, or to dance and sing, power over illness or misfortune, against his enemies or to attain wealth, and at puberty young people were specifically trained in the guardian spirit quest. But at its most intense level, the search for power is associated with the shaman.

Isaac Tens, a Gitksan shaman, told Barbeau[16] of his experiences:

"Thirty years after my birth was the time when I began to be a swanassu (shaman). I went up into the hills to get fire-wood. While I was cutting up the wood into lengths, it grew dark towards the evening. Before I had finished my last stack of wood a loud noise broke over me, CHU . . ., and a large owl appeared to me. The owl took hold of me, caught my face, and tried to lift me up. I lost consciousness. As soon as I came back to my senses I realized that I had fallen into the snow. My head was coated with ice, and some blood was running out of my mouth. I stood up and went down the trail, walking very fast, with some wood packed on my back. On my way the trees seemed to shake and to lean over me: tall trees were crawling after me, as if there had been snakes. I could see them. Before I arrived at my father's home, I told my folk what had happened to me, as soon as I walked in. I was very cold and warmed myself before going to bed. There I fell into a sort of trance. It seems that two halaaits (shamans) were working over me to bring me back to health. But it is now all vague in my memory. When I woke up and opened my eyes, I thought that flies covered my face completely. I looked down, and instead of being on firm ground, I felt that I was drifting in a huge whirlpool".

Although the shamans told him that he is to become a shaman also, Isaac Tens did not begin training until after he had a second hallucinatory experience and was ill. For him the fasting period then lasted a year, in seclusion at his father's house and out of touch with other people except for four relatives who watched over him as he gradually acquired power. Finally he was called to cure his first patient, the wife of a Chief. She had been ill for a long time and had been treated without success by other shamans. We must imagine the huge house thronged with people, lit only by the flames leaping on the central hearth, the patient laid out in a couch with the anxious family hovering near, the drums and the chanting. Then the shaman enters, wearing his tall crown of carved horns . . .

"As I began to sing over her, many people around me were hitting sticks on boards and beating skin drums for me. My canoe came to me in a dream and there were many people sitting in it. The Canoe itself was the Otter. By that time about twenty other halaaits were present in the house. To them I explained what my vision was, and asked, 'What shall I do? There the woman is sitting in the canoe, and the canoe is the Otter.' They answered, 'Try to pull her out'. I told them, 'Spread the fire out into two parts and make a pathway between them.' I walked up and down this path four times, while the other shamans kept singing until they were very tired. Then I went over to the couch on which the sick woman was lying. There was a great upheaval in the singing and the clapping of drums and the sticks on the boards. I placed my hand on her stomach and moved round her couch, all the while trying to draw the canoe out of her. I managed to pull it up very close to the surface of her chest. I grasped it, drew it out, and put it in my own bosom. This I did." The woman was cured and Isaac Tens' prestige as a shaman was greatly enhanced. He said fees might be ten blankets or one, but if the patient died the blankets were returned.

A study of shamanism among the various tribes of our coast reveals many differences in the shaman's role and function. Sometimes he is the sole specialist in the spirit world and sometimes there are also ritualists or magicians, whose contact with the spirit world is not as strong and who manipulate events by the use of magic formulas. Sometimes these formulas are inherited and the original spiritual experience may have belonged to a mythical ancestor. Some shamans can cure, some cannot. But irrespective of cultural variations, the shaman is an individual publicly acknowledged as having a high degree of power from spirit beings; the shaman acts as a public intermediary between ordinary men and the spirit world.

The connection between shamanism and the petroglyphs is tenuous. Lommel[17] considers shamanism to be associated with the very beginning of human art, first in the cave art of France and Spain and then in primitive art around the world. The long and arduous training or the recovery from illness of the shaman is accompanied by a psychological process in which the representation of the spirits is an essential part. Malouf[18] writes that the painted animals are 'spirit animals' not copies of real animals, and the psychological technique of the shaman is to make obsessional ideas conscious. Imaginings are transposed to images. The Kulleet Bay 'shaman's pool' is particularly interesting in this regard. When we first visited the site in the spring of the year, the water of the little stream filled the smooth sandstone basin, which is about fifteen feet long, six feet wide and perhaps five feet deep. We could see the frieze of carvings along the top rim of the pool but the spring runoff flowed over them. Later in the year the water had fallen to the level of the darkened band below the carvings, the usual winter water level, but we waited until midsummer, when the pool was completely dry, before we made the rubbings. At that time of year the carver would have had a very large canvas of smooth sandstone on which to work. But since the petroglyphs are carved along the narrow rim above the band marking the winter water level (and unless the pictures were carved upside down), it seems likely that they were made by a person partly submerged in the icy water of the pool. When this petroglyph site was discovered in 1931, Newcombe[19] was told by the Chief of the Kulleet Bay people that the petroglyphs were probably carved by shamans during their training. An alternative interpretation argues that the carvings were made between the high spring and winter water levels so that they would be annually submerged to release spirit power.

Hoebel[20] writes that the subjective element of religion is always given external form and that art transforms the imagined spirit into an object of art that can be seen. In this transformation, the human steals some of the spirit's power. Basic in these considerations is the perception of a profound connection between human life and the rest of the universe, a wisdom that modern technology has obscured. The anxiety induced by dependence on the environment is dealt with by a search for spiritual power, by a complex of beliefs concerning benign and malevolent beings, by rituals of atonement in which man makes retribution for the killing of animals, and by the performance of rituals and ceremonies in which men reassure themselves of spiritual support by the performance of dances and songs. Many such performances are of a public character and are no doubt partly motivated by prestige and pride considerations, or are entertainments, but they are still fundamentally related to the supernatural spirit quest. The basic pattern of ceremonial dancing on the northwest coast has three variations, each an elaboration of the same underlying theme. At the Spirit Singing ceremonies, each performer displayed the songs, dances and sometimes the supernatural powers which he has acquired from his guardian spirit. The second variation is the Crest Dance, in which were shown the songs, dances, ceremonial masks and other paraphernalia which has been given to an ancestor of the family by a supernatural being. Lastly there are the Dancing Society complexes in which the entire history of the ancestor's power quest experience is re-enacted. In the southern part of the coast the Spirit Dancing is the general form of ceremonial dance whereas in the north, although all categories existed, the performances by Dance Societies at the Winter Dances were the engrossing activity of the rainswept winter season. Duff[21] considers the elaborate masked dances of the Kwakiutl and northern tribes to have been mostly stagecraft, in contrast to the Coast Salish Spirit Dances which were more truly religious and where the dancers were "possessed" by their own guardian spirits as they danced. Spirit Dancing still survives in the southern Gulf of Georgia and Puget Sound areas. At Kulleet Bay we were told that part of the initiation and training of new dancers involves a ritual immersion in the petroglyph-rimmed pool near the village. Modern long houses are fine large structures with dirt floors, tiers of benches around the walls, and heated and lit by the fires burning in the central fire pits around which the dancers move. The dancing may begin after midnight and continue until daylight, with possibly a hundred dancers each taking their turn, with the spectators drumming and singing the dancer's song. The costumes are still spectacular. To see the strange masks and costumes displayed in the world's museums is to catch only a glimpse of the frightening and beautiful power of West Coast dancing; the modern shows which tourists may view at Alert Bay and the 'Ksan village at Hazelton are pale imitations.

Possibly the most powerful dance of all was the performance of an initiate of the hamatsa order, the cannibal society. We must again imagine the long house at night, the firelight flickering on the faces of the expectant audience closely seated around the walls. In Barnett's[22] description of a cannibal society dance at Comox, the first to enter was an attendant who backed in carrying a desiccated corpse partly wrapped in branches, and followed by a maddened hamatsa, naked or covered with branches, tied by a rope around his waist to two attendants with their faces painted black and wearing black blankets. It was the attendants duty to control the possessed hamatsa dancer. The crowd occupying the platforms around the walls watched in awe and fear as the hamatsa half danced half lunged at the corpse. Sometimes he cried "Ha:p! ha:p!" and leaped towards the watching people and had to be restrained by the blackened attendants. Occasionally he did bite a person in the crowd but Barnett says that it was prearranged and the person later compensated. Both dancer and attendants had whistles operated by bellows concealed in their armpits. After a while the corpse was laid on a plank and torn apart and eaten by the dancer and other members of the hamatsa society coming from the audience. Sometimes the whole hamatsa society might be involved in a frenzied orgy over the corpse. Barnett writes, "It is a matter of opinion whether these men ate human flesh. It seems that sometimes they did. Not all of the frenzy was a sham. Corpses sometimes were stolen from grave boxes or were those of slaves killed for a purpose." We must add that the maddened cannibal scene (representing the wild untamed aspect of human nature) is followed by gradually more controlled dancing until finally the tamed hamatsa dances with the full regalia and dignity of a responsible leader in society.

At Fort Rupert, before 1882, a slave was killed for the performance of the hamatsa dance. We are able to link this dance with the petroglyphs on the beach at Fort Rupert for the event was witnessed by Mr. Hunt and Mr. Moffat of the Hudson's Bay Company, who then described it to Franz Boas.[23] Boas records that in memory of the event the face of a powerful spirit was carved on the rock on the beach at the place where the slave had been eaten.

Now it is time to look at the petroglyphs.

All dimensions shown are approximate.

4. Petroglyphs from Puget Sound to Prince Rupert

Agate Point

45 KP 15

2′6″ x 5′6″

In the first chapter of this book we discussed the incident when Jack Adams was observed by his friend Dr. Leechman.[1] Mr. Adams stated that he had carved some of the figures on this petroglyph boulder and his father had done the rest. In the light of this information it is somewhat surprising to find this information in Hunt's History of Tacoma,[2] published in 1916:

"Another interesting 'hieroglyph' rock was found a number of years ago at Agate Point on the northeast corner of Bainbridge Island. It is three or four feet across and Indians are much afraid of it. Dr. Charles Buchanan of the Tulalip Indian School, while travelling with Indians in that neighbourhood found that they would not approach this rock."

Marian Smith,[3] writing of the petroglyphs of the Columbia-Fraser region in 1946, is discussing the religious significance of petroglyphs when she states:

"Certainly, the situation among the Coast Salish of Puget Sound is quite clear: all petroglyphs were the work of children or of 'long ago' adults and in neither case was there any religious significance. The Suquamish (Agate Point) boulder was said to have been marked by Kitsap, a famous Suquamish warrior long dead, and Sam Wilson, a Suquamish, said in 1941 that once he too 'put his mark on it'. Sam Wilson never used such a phrase in describing religious power."

Yet Hunt in 1916 said that the Indians "venerated" the Tacoma petroglyph and were "much afraid of" the Agate Point stone. Alice Cross, the Duwamish informant in the Smith paper of 1946, spoke of the Youngstown petroglyphs as "power figures". It is difficult to sort out the truth of these varied reports, but certainly it would appear that Jack Adams and his father were not the only people to peck at the Agate Point stone, and the petroglyphs seem to have had religious power for Indians of an earlier time.

Agate Pass

The Bremerton Sun[4] provided an account of the finding of this stone. The site is a small cove with sandy beach on the west shore of Agate Passage, a short half-mile southwest of the bridge across the narrowest part of the pass. The find was made by Mr. William Lane while building a bulkhead to help shore up a constantly receding shoreline. The stone was lying face down on the shore, the uppermost side covered with barnacles.

1'4" x 1'4"

Miami Beach

This stone was found on the east side of the Hood Canal at Miami Beach by Dr. Roy L. Carlson, who contributed the photograph.

R.L. Carlson photo

1'4" x 1'8"

Victor

45 MS 49

The granite boulder is imbedded in the sand not far below the present high water mark on the shore of Case Inlet at Victor. The exposed part of the rock rises about five feet above beach level, but the visible part of this petroglyph boulder is only the tip of the iceberg. In 1909 a serious but unsuccessful attempt was made to move it. According to an account written by Rowena and Gordon Alcorn,[6] the directors of the Alaska Yukon Exposition sent a steam tug with a scow to move the stone to the fair at Seattle. In charge of the operation was the Captain of the tug "Favorite", a tall man with handlebar mustaches, known as "Hell Roaring Jack". He had expected to hoist the rock aboard the scow without too much trouble, but as the digging went on to expose the boulder, the rock grew wider and thicker. At a depth of about fifteen feet the base of the boulder was not yet in sight and the carved pictures had continued on down the entire western side. Hell Roaring Jack attached lines from the tug's winch to the stone and logs were brought to serve as levers. With shouted orders from the Captain, the tug's engines pulled and the workers pried, but the boulder never moved. Again and again they tried, churning the sea into a froth, but the rock did not budge an inch. The project was finally abandoned and Hell Roaring Jack steamed back to Seattle towing an empty scow. Perhaps some day the petroglyph will again be dug up, not for the purpose of moving it but only so that we may know what carvings fill the western face and how big the boulder actually is.

Eneti

The only source of information about this petroglyph, now missing, is a note by an early pioneer missionary, Rev. F. Eels.[5] He reported an irregular basaltic rock about 3' by 3'4" and 1'6" high, with a design consisting of two eyes, each six inches in diameter and a nose or beak nine inches long. He called it the thunder bird. He had been told that it was made by some man a long time ago who felt very badly and went and sat on the rock and with another stone hammered out the eyes and nose. The Indians said that if the rock were shaken, rain would fall.

1'6" x 9"

Present day Enetai lies east of East Bremerton, on Sinclair Inlet. We interviewed old-time residents along this shore but no memory of a petroglyph boulder exists. Rev. Eels gave the petroglyph location as "at Eneti on the Twana Reservation", but the present Twana-Skokomish area is some distance to the west, on both sides of the Hood Canal. Possibly future research will re-discover this petroglyph, which can then be positively identified from Rev. Eels' sketch.

Hartslene Island   45 MS 28

We found this granite boulder at Tumwater Falls Park, in Olympia, Washington. A sign identified it as having originally been located at "The Maples" on the west shore of Hartslene Island, twelve miles north of Olympia. The sign also stated that the central figure was a bear and that several of the smaller figures depicted the mountains, the sun, a bow and arrow and "lesser animals". It seemed just as likely that the mountains were the initials V.W. and H.W. The small animals were crudely and shallowly pecked and were lighter in color than the round-eyed faces, suggesting that they were more recent and the grooves had not yet darkened with weathering. There was also a shallow foot-shaped depression, with "toes" pecked at one end so that the depression appeared to be a large foot-print, sasquatch-size. It would appear that the depression itself was natural, because there is a second, shallower and smaller depression a few inches away, without the pecked toes.

8'0" x 4'0"

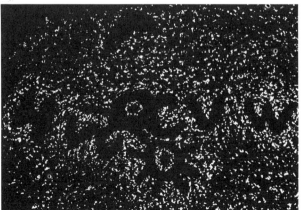

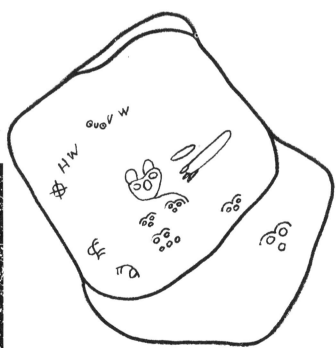

Hartslene Island

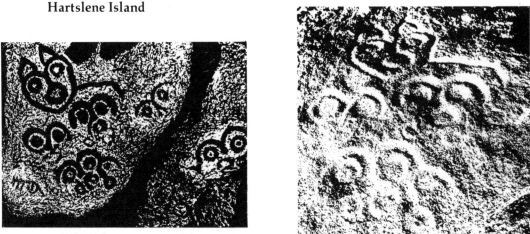

5′0″ x 5′6″

Mrs. Joyce Cheeka,[7] an elderly Indian lady, told us that she had played on this stone as a child. She said the old Indians thought the petroglyph boulders were used as landmarks for travelling. When asked if the petroglyphs had been carved by people of her tribe, she replied that they had been carved long ago and the meanings of the figures had been lost to memory. Mrs. Florence Sigo[8] is reported to have said that as a child she was told not to walk in front of the petroglyph figures, which suggests that the stone still held some power in the minds of some of the Indians of the previous generation.

Tacoma

All we know of the petroglyph boulder at Tacoma is recorded by Herbert Hunt[9] in his History of Tacoma:

"Prized among the Indians was a great rock, some seven or eight feet in height, which lay on the beach now covered by the Half Moon yards, and which carelessly was covered when the railroad company made the fill there. Its surface bore the figure of a man, not clear in places, to be sure, but distinct enough for the Indians to declare that it was the work of 'The Changer' — the mythical almighty who sometimes in the far past, had worked among inanimate, as well as animate, things, wonderful miracles. Men had been turned into birds and trees and stones. A human being had been converted into Mount Tacoma. The stone on the beach once had been a man. The Indians venerated it."

The stone is thought to be at about 15th and Pacific in Tacoma, the site of the former Pullyap Indian village, buried fifteen to twenty feet deep under the railroad grade. Originally it stood upon a beach.

Eld Inlet 45 TN 6

This carved boulder, originally located on the gravel beach of Eld Inlet (also known as Mud Bay), was placed in the State Capitol Museum in Olympia through the cooperation of the Squaxin Island Tribal Council whose ancestors lived in this area. The seventeen ton sandstone boulder measures 3'6" by 2'2" by 1'6" high. The small round figure below the large face is somewhat more crudely pecked, with a line that is slightly shallower and narrower than those of the large face adjacent. The outline of the face crosses the line of the smaller figure and is bent out of its curve by the crossing, suggesting that the large face was made after the small figure.

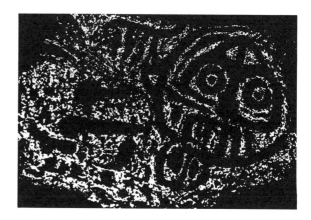

Youngstown

South of West Seattle and at the south end of Elliott Bay is that section of Seattle known as Youngstown. It is the site of a missing petroglyph boulder. Marion Smith,[10] discussing whether or not the petroglyphs of the Columbia-Fraser region have religious significance, illustrates her article with pictures of the 'power boards' of the central Puget Sound are and says that the animals painted on them were patterned after supernatural powers.

"Thus, a shaman who 'had' a one-eyed bear 'for power' would paint a one-eyed bear on his board. Alice Cross, a Duwamish informant who worked with Arthur C. Ballard, told of a boulder which stood near Youngstown adjoining West Seattle. She spoke of various animals pecked on the rock and related them definitely to power figures. The first person to mark the boulder was the father of one of her older contemporaries and, like the Suquamish (Agate Point) boulder, it was used by more than one person."

This petroglyph boulder cannot now be found and may be buried in the construction of some city building.

Lake Whatcom

We photographed this petroglyph in a private garden in Bellingham. According to the present owner it was originally under an overhanging sandstone shelter on the south shore of Lake Whatcom on property known as Rocky Ridge, about one hundred feet above and two hundred feet back from the lake. He writes that he had purchased the property and was developing waterfront sites

"when one morning I noticed that vandals had been trying to remove the carving by splitting the stone along seams in the wall, so I removed it to its present location. The old timers here have advised me that the carving was for a chief's burial site, and the cave does have flat stone benches that might have held a body or bodies. When I first viewed the stone it was solid in original live sandstone in the back wall of the cave."

The stone is now protected from further weathering or vandalism and is available for study, but how much better it is to preserve the petroglyphs in their original sites. Rock carvings are now protected under the laws listed in the Addenda of this book, and all people interested in archaeology must assist the police and the archaeological boards in the enforcement of the new laws making vandalism of petroglyphs a serious offence.

1'6" x 2'1"

Consolidation Road, Bellingham

This petroglyph is located on private property on Consolidation Road in Bellingham and we have been unable to obtain permission to examine it.

Whiterock

The petroglyphs have been cut into the dark portion of this black and white granite boulder. Originally found below the Great Northern Railroad tracks, on the beach above Semiahmoo Bay, it has been moved to a small park area located where the Crescent Beach Road crosses the railroad.

9'3" x 5'0"

9'3" x 5'0"

Crescent Beach

This petroglyph stone, found in 1957 at the foot of North Bluff Road, Crescent Beach, is now in the Surrey Museum at Cloverdale.

2'0" x 2'0"

Jack Berry photo

Hastings Mill Museum

Nothing is known of the provenience of this petroglyph boulder now lying in the Hastings Mill Museum in Vancouver. Its size is ten by fourteen by four inches.

Aldridge Point   DbRv 5

In the British Columbia Provincial Museum report for the year 1928 W.A. Newcombe relates this legend of the[11] Aldridge Point petroglyph as told to him by Henry Charles of Becher Bay: "Long years ago a great supernatural animal like a sea-lion killed many of the Becher Bay Indians when canoeing. The tribe became nearly extinct; the remaining members were afraid to go on the water until one day a mythical man caught the sea-lion and turned him into the stone representation as seen on Aldridge Point."

Aldridge Point

In contrast to most of the petroglyphs of Vancouver Island which are pecked and abraded to some depth into sandstone or granite, the lines of the petroglyphs of the seven Juan de Fuca area sites are shallowly bruised into a hard sandstone whose surface is made rough by the sharp crystals weathered out in relief. These throw shadows and hold dirt. Where the petroglyph has been made by pounding or grinding off the rough crystals, the surface is smooth and appears lighter. It is not possible to make rubbings of the petroglyphs produced by this technique.

Large Bedford Island

DbRv 6

These two petroglyph faces are on the high southern cliffs of the largest Bedford Island but they could not be seen from the sea and were difficult to find when clambering along rock ledges sheer above the water. We have sketched the face which could not be photographed because of its cliff location.

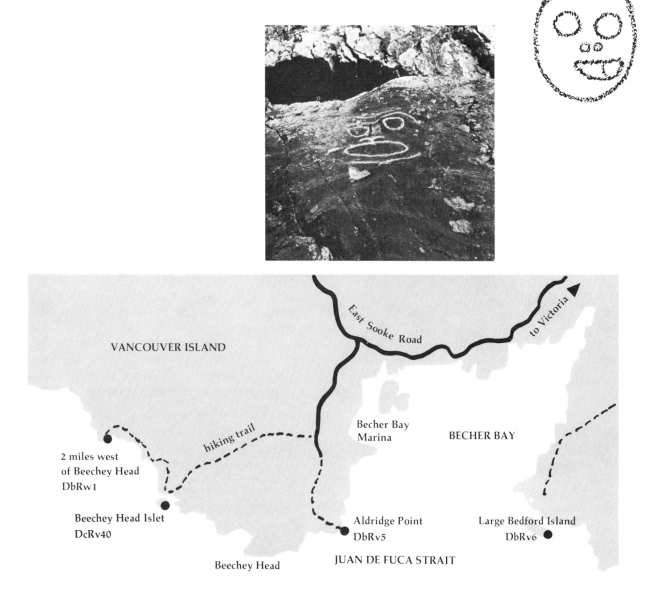

Point 2 Mi. West of Beechey Head DbRw 1

The hiking trail from Becher Bay Marina to the Beechey Head Islet continues west, little used and marked only with red plastic ribbons. After about a mile of cliff-hanging on this spectacular coast, the trail reaches a point marked by a large splash of white paint, a marine marker. The petroglyphs are on the east side of this point. The site has been called Hohap Point on some reports but no reference can be found for this name.

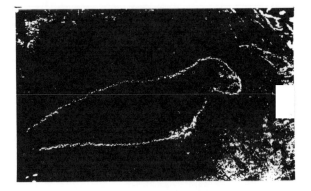

Beechey Head Islet

A hiking trail which starts near the Becher Bay Marina leads across Beechey Head and descends to a delightful small beach where a freshwater stream flows into a cove. Sheltering this bay is Beechey Head Islet, separated from the Vancouver Island shore by a deep pass only ten feet wide at the narrowest point but difficult to cross except at low tide. The petroglyphs are on the south end of the islet on rocky cliffs above the sea. According to Mr. Percy Brown, a long time resident of Becher Bay, the islet was once a burial site.

Beechey Head Islet

According to Jenness,[12] the Coast Salish people of this area first had masks when Khaals, a mythical figure, gave them the wooden mask at Sooke, "where one can be seen today pecked into a rock". The first masks represented Khaals himself, Jenness states. There is no certainty that the Beechey Head Islet petroglyph face is the mask of Khaals, but no other petroglyph face closer to Sooke has been reported.

Half Mile West of Otter Point

DcRw 18

The fish petroglyph is on a flat vertical sandstone face above steep high basalt rocks, sea-smoothed. Directly below the petroglyph, which faces south towards the Strait of Juan de Fuca, is a large flat rock. Local people say that the Indians used to spear fish from this rock. They report that Japanese fishing floats frequently appear on the beach just west of the petroglyph and that the current makes this point an excellent fishing spot. Near the petroglyph is a narrow crevasse from which a deep cave opens.

Point no Point

DcRx 1

The whale and fish petroglyphs are found at the extreme tip of the rocky point where the Strait of Juan de Fuca joins the wide Pacific. The manager of the Point No Point Resort stated that when she first came to the resort about 1952 many blackfish were seen, some in pods several miles long comprising twenty to forty whales.

Otter Point

Where Highway 14 makes an abrupt turn at the end of Otter Point, a few miles west of Sooke, a gravel-filled gulley leads down to the rocky shore. East of the gulley above the tide line and approximately three metres below the vegetation line, an exceedingly faint petroglyph is abraded on the rock, facing south toward the Strait of Juan de Fuca. The glint of sunlight may show first the teeth of the sea creature and the other lines must then be found by a close examination of the surface. The lines feel smooth in contrast to the toughness of the bedrock on which they have been rubbed.

Otter Point is an excellent fishing spot and until a few years ago it was the site of a commercial fish trap.

Cape Alava

During the winter storms of 1970, high tides and waves undermined a bank in part of an old village site at Cape Alava, exposing a house that had been buried by a clay-mud slide hundreds of years earlier. Since the spring of 1971, year round excavations have been continuing at this site, one of the most significant archaeological projects of the coast. It is interesting not only because of the wealth of the Makah people and their complex ceremonial life, but also because the clay virtually stopped all bacterial action and oxidation, thus preserving intact implements of wood, and plant materials. To have entire houses and contents preserved is very unusual indeed. It is to be hoped that a study of the finds will possibly give us further information about the petroglyphs at Wedding Rocks, three miles south of the village site. The petro-

Cape Alava

glyphs are carved on a few of the boulders at the base of a very high rocky pinnacle. To reach the site, the visitor must drive to Ozette Lake, hike a three mile trail to the beach, then walk a mile south along the shore to Wedding Rocks. On our visit to Cape Alava we missed seeing petroglyphs on the beach in front of the excavation site. On the spit joining Cannonball Island (shown in the photograph) to the mainland at low tide is a simple face with three holes and an encircling outline. We also missed a small fish on the rock where the trail from Lake Ozette reaches the beach and a possible bird shape on a nearby granite rock.[13]

5" x 6"

20" x 13"

3'11" x 2'10"

Cape Alava

1'6" x 1'0"

1'0" x 1'0"

4'0" LONG

1'0" x 9"

2'0" x 2'6"

3'0" x 3'0"

Whales 30" long
Faces 14", 9" dia.

The five petroglyph whales of the site reflect the importance of sea mammal hunting at Ozette and other Makah villages. Though a rich ceremonialism was attached to their sea mammal hunting, particularly to the hunting of whales, we have no evidence that the petroglyphs were a part of such ceremonies. The petroglyph whales are marked by a double diagonal line across the body, and two short lines are carved diagonally downwards from the eyes. One of the fish figures appears to be a pregnant whale. At this site a divided oval figure, which may be a female fertility symbol, is found seventeen times.

Clo-oose, Blowhole Site

DdSf 1

The two Clo-oose sites are about three hundred and fifty feet apart, half-way between Clo-oose and Whyac. They are accessible by a fairly strenuous twenty-mile hike along the West Coast Trail south from Pachena Bay, with the crossing of the swift Nitinat River an obstacle; or it is possible to hire a boat for the two hour journey to Brown's Landing or Whyac and a hike of several miles to the sites.

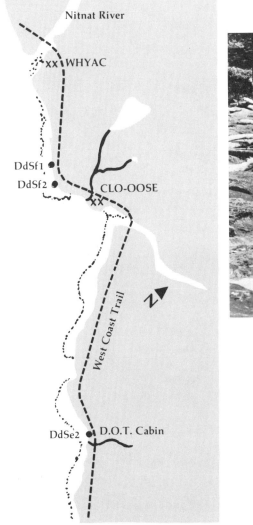

Clo-oose Blowhole Site

6'0" x 4'0"

D.W. Higgins,[14] in "The Passing of a Race", suggests that some of the petroglyphs of the Clo-oose site recorded a shipwreck in 1869 of the barque "John Bright". The captain, his wife, their baby and a nursemaid reached shore only to be killed by the Indians. A second ship, the "Sparrowhawk", was sent out and several Indians were captured and hung. Higgins thought the ships and some of the figures represented the "John Bright" and her unfortunate passengers.

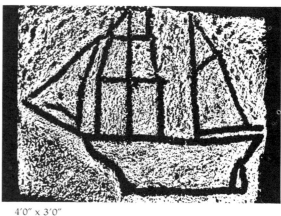

4'0" x 3'0"

1'3" x 9"

4'6" x 3'6"

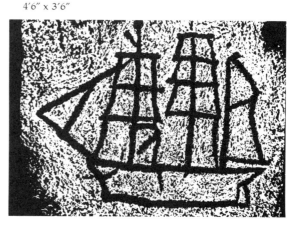

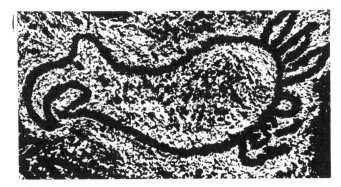

3'5" x 1'9"

4'0" x 3'3"

3'8" x 2'0"

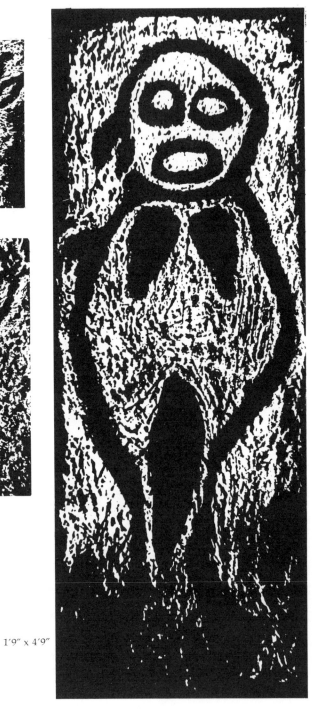

1'9" x 4'9"

1'8" x 3'9"

6'6" x 12'0"

Clo-oose Blowhole Site

7'3" x 4'8"

6'7" x 4'11"

The Beaver

The BEAVER was the first steamship on the Pacific Coast of North America. She was built for the Hudson's Bay Company in 1835, with a hull of British oak, elm, greenheart and teak, copper fastened and sheethed with copper, length 101'4", 20' beam, 109 tons, her engines rated at seventy horsepower, with a speed of nine knots. She crossed the Atlantic under sail, rounded the Horn in a snow storm, stopped at the Hawaiian Islands en route to Vancouver, Washington, where the paddle wheels were installed. On June 19, 1836 she started her first voyage under steam and on June 30th ran up Milbanke Sound and anchored opposite Milbanke Fort, which she saluted with seven guns.[15] In this first voyage under steam she passed the petroglyph site at Clo-oose where her image is carved. We have found no record, except the petroglyph, of the Nootkan Indians' reaction to her arrival but a Monterey newspaper[16] gives an account of the consternation caused by her first appearance there. The Beaver made the trip south in 1838 aiming to land at Monterey for a cargo of hides, but by some error of navigation in the fog, she got into Carmel Bay instead. What a sensation her arrival caused! Paddle wheels churning and black smoke belching, she looked to the Indians like a huge sea monster and it is reported that many fled to the hills. We would expect that she was a frightening spectacle on Vancouver Island's west coast on that June day of 1836.

3'0" x 2'4"

Clo-oose, Hill Site

Although the Blowhole site is well-known, the Hill site, about three hundred and fifty feet east, is rarely found by hikers. The petroglyphs are on a sandstone ledge well above high tide and show no evidence of erosion. On the west side of the site is a huge beaked bird, eleven feet in length. Thirty feet to the east is the unique petroglyph of a copulating couple.

10'0" x 6'0"

3'0" x 3'9"

2'6" x 6'6"

Clo-oose Hill Site

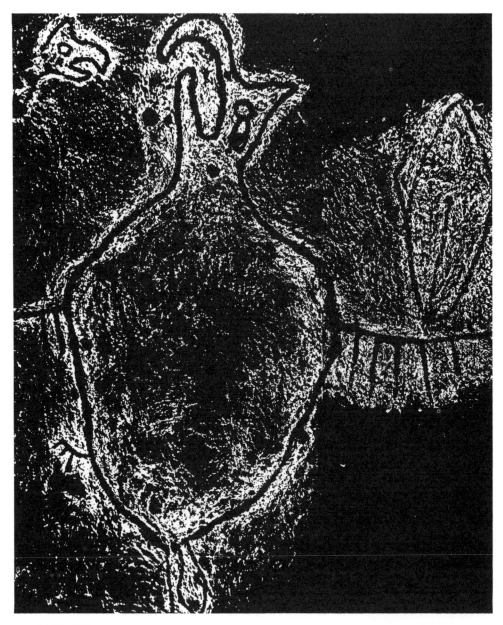

11'0" x 9'6"

Near Carmanah Point

Southeast from Clo-oose abour six miles along the West Coast Trail there is a cabin built by the Department of Transport and used by hikers on the trail. It is the only landmark by which one may locate petroglyphs site DdSe 2. The petroglyphs are about eighty-five feet east of the cabin, at the top of the beach, part of the site covered by the bank and its thickly twined salal roots. Driftwood is piled on the spot and when the winter storms bury it under sand it may be very difficult to find. About three hundred feet from the petroglyphs there is a small winter stream and a short distance further east a large creek is crossed by a high bridge on the West Coast Trail above. The petroglyph figures are clearly pecked and abraded in smooth bedrock sandstone and show no signs of erosion.

2'0" x 4'0"   2'7" x 4'0"

2'0" x 4'0"

81

Near Carmanah Point

This petroglyph, a short distance from the carvings designated DdSe 2, is usually covered with drift sand and is rarely found. The photograph, taken by D.R. Foskett, shows a small figure within a larger figure.

D.R. Foskett photo

Pachena Point

Less than a mile southeast of the lighthouse at Pachena Point along the West Coast Trail there is a rough sign which says 'Dead End' and points to a trail which descends steeply to a small cove. High tide cuts off the hiker's route around the rocky promontory which separates this 'Dead End' cove from Michigan Beach to the southeast. In the cove are two caves. The larger cave (DeSg 7) is above the winter high tide and is roomy and dry, about fifty feet deep and twelve feet high. There is a midden deposit on the cave floor and a scattering of modern glass and tin garbage left by hiders. The petroglyphs are pecked in a panel on the outside face of a sandstone boulder standing inside the cave. On the cave wall behind the boulder are three 'hour-glass' figures. Outside the cave, on the flat vertical rock face next to the cave opening, is the square petroglyph figure with the five-toed- feet.

The local Indian name for this cave is "Bad Woman".

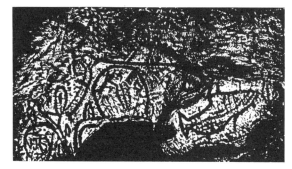

6'5" x 3'5"

6'0" x 2'0"

Pachena Point

The second cave at Pachena Point is a small, narrow opening about eight feet wide at the base and fifteen feet deep. It is below winter high tide and drift logs have been thrown into it during winter gales. Having been exposed to sea wash and bumping logs, the petroglyphs carved on one wall are badly chipped, flaked and eroded. Large sections of the designs are missing and no figures are complete. This drawing is an attempt to record the surviving fragments at a site where both rubbing and photography were impossible.

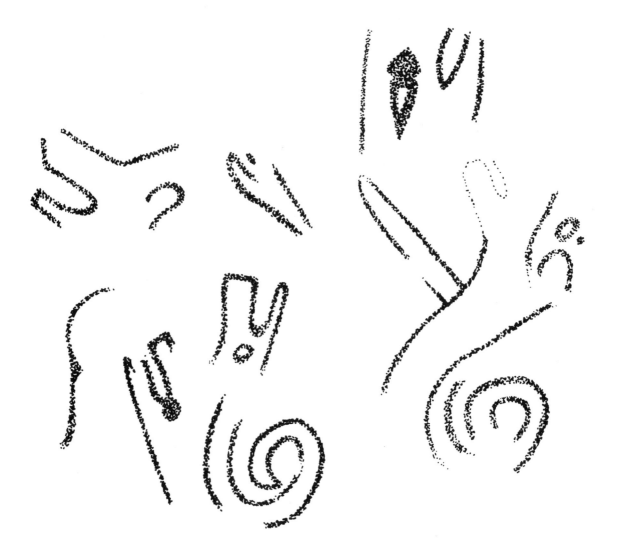

Quisitis Point

DfSj 2

It is a strenuous cliff hike to this site, from Florencia Bay around Quisitis Point. The petroglyphs are only a few feet from the 49th Parallel Marker, at the edge of the cliff. The fish and the strange spotted bird, on a vertical rock face which is at right angles to the coast line, gape towards the surging Pacific Ocean below the cliff.

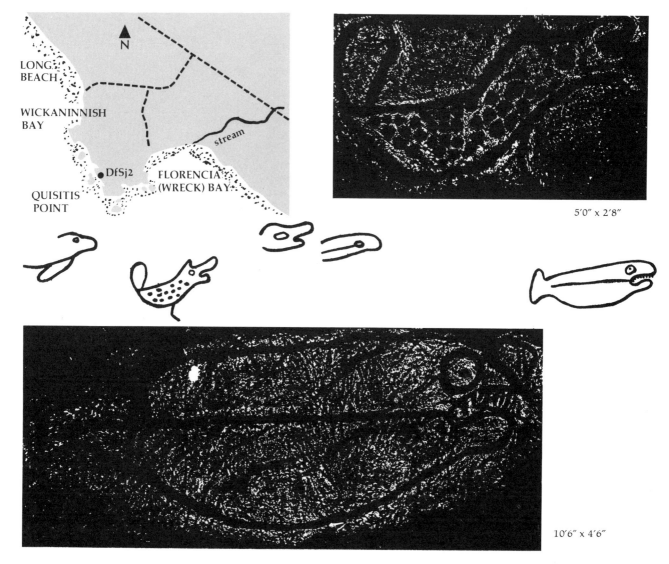

5'0" x 2'8"

10'6" x 4'6"

Hesquiat

Two miles east of Estevan Point, the boulder lies amid the drift logs on the beach.

Hesquiat Band photo

Fulford Harbour, Salt Spring Island   DeRu 45

The large petroglyph boulder, five feet wide and five feet high, was bull-dozed from the harbour floor at an extreme low tide, in the construction of the Cudmore Log Dump in 1963 and now stands at the foot of the log dump, just off Isabella Point Road. Two smaller boulders with petroglyphs, discovered at the same time, have unfortunately disappeared. Anyone knowing their present location should inform the Provincial Museum.

According to local tradition, an old shoreline (now submerged) stretched from Mr. Cudmore's log dump to the present Fulford Harbour ferry dock and the ancient village stood on an area of upper harbour which is now dry only at low tides. If this is true, the petroglyph boulders once stood on the shoreline at the seaward end of the village.

3'7" x 3'2"

Helen Point, Mayne Island

DfRu 33

Harlan I. Smith included this site in his 1927 List of Petroglyphs. Subsequently the petroglyph was hidden under collapsed bank and tree roots until it was rediscovered about 1946 by a resident of Sidney who transferred the boulder to her home. Petroglyphs are now protected by the Archaeological and Historic Sites Protection Act of 1960 and cannot be moved without the approval of the Archaeological Sites Advisory Board of British Columbia.

3'0" x 3'3"

Thetis Island

DfRv 6

Near the southern tip of Thetis Island on flat sandstone bedrock on the beach at high tide level is this single non-outlined face. There is a spring near the site and a much-disturbed midden where a summer home has been built.

THETIS ISLAND

DfRv6 ●

KUPER ISLAND

1'6" x 2'2"

Georgeson Bay, Galiano Island

DfRu 24

At the south end of Galiano Island, at the turbulent western entrance to Active Pass, there is a sheltered back eddy with a small beach. The petroglyph stone was found at low tide on this beach the time of the construction of the sea wall where the carving may now be seen. A face is pecked on two sides of the square boulder, with the edge of the stone flattened along the nose of the face.

1'6" x 1'6"

Parminter Point, Salt Spring Island   DfRv 6

The petroglyph boulder, lying at the extreme high tide line on Salt Spring Island's west coast, is one of a group of four sandstone boulders which now rest in such a way that they suggest a standing figure now toppled. The only stone with carving is the 'head' stone, with a face pecked on three sides of the rock.

3'7" x 2'0"

The Barrow notebook[17] states: "The boulder on which the petroglyph occurs has been split into four pieces by a pounding log since T. Iwasaki settled here seven years ago; the portion on which the carving is was inverted, the mouth being now above the eyes." However, in its present position the petroglyph stone has mouth, eyes and ears in logical places and a 'top-knot' properly placed on the top of the head. Also, if the stone had been broken off and inverted, one would expect to find it further removed from the other stones.

Hilarius Farm, Gabriola Island   DgRw 30

At the southern end of Gabriola Island, near Thompsons Road, on private land about a half-mile from the sea, a single anthropomorphic figure is carved on a small area of exposed bedrock sandstone in the middle of a large swampy meadow. The lower part of this field, near the petroglyph, may have been a shallow pond. There is a deposit of shell midden about two hundred feet to the north of the petroglyph.

1'7" x 2'0"

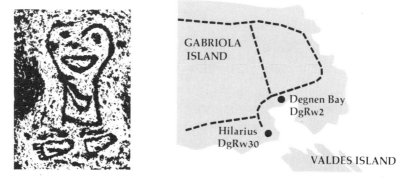

GABRIOLA
ISLAND

Degnen Bay
DgRw2

Hilarius
DgRw30

VALDES ISLAND

Degnen Bay, Gabriola Island

DgRw 2

This site has a single petroglyph of a fish, possibly a blackfish with its high dorsal fin, at the high tide line on sandstone bedrock which slopes into Degnen Bay. Behind the petroglyph rises a steep bank which appears to be entirely composed of midden deposit. To the north a small freshwater stream pours into the bay. Degnen Bay opens off Gabriola Pass separating Gabriola Island from Valdes Island, an excellent fishing area.

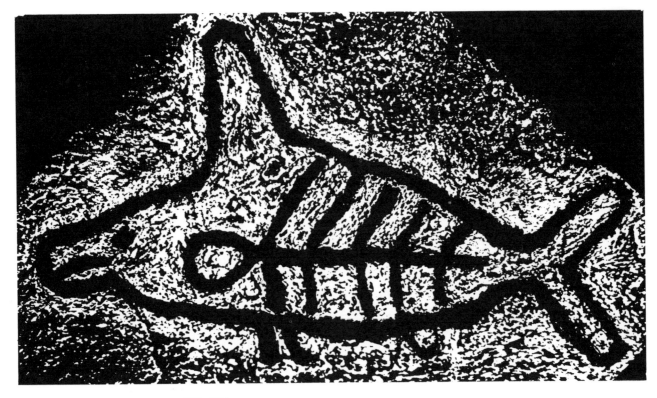

4'0" x 2'6"

Kulleet Bay "Shamans Pool"

DgRw 36

This site is on Indian Reserve 13, near Ladysmith. About a mile from Kulleet Bay village a small winter stream flows into the north side of Kulleet Bay. Just before it reaches the sea the stream runs through a natural oval sandstone bowl about five feet wide and fifteen feet long. Around the upper edge of this basin is a frieze of petroglyph figures. In the spring when the stream runs high, water fills the basin and completely covers the figures. Below the carvings a faint band marks the winter water level. In the summer no water at all is in the stream bed and the basin is dry. It is interesting to consider at what time of year the petroglyphs were made. Certainly they were not carved in the Spring. If they had been made in the summer or autumn, one would expect the entire surface of the sandstone bowl to be used. As the petroglyphs are all above the winter water level, it would seem that they had been made when the basin was full of icy water in winter, and unless they were carved upside-down, they were done by a person waist-deep in the water.

5'10" x 2'2"

At the time that this site was first investigated by C.E. Newcombe in 1931, the petroglyphs were almost completely covered with moss and earth. Newcombe reported that:

"the old Chief of the Kulleet Band had no knowledge of their existence but thought they had probably been executed by ancient Shamans during their initiation, part of which consisted of a prolonged fasting in the wood; the carved figures represented those seen in dreams."

The pool has ritual significance for the present inhabitants of the village. We were told that the young Indian dancers being initiated into the secret societies at the winter ceremonials, must come and bathe in the icy waters of the "Shaman's Pool".[18]

13'0" x 3'0"

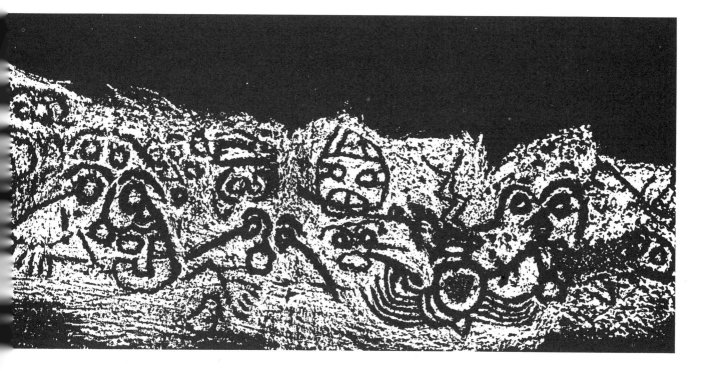

Kulleet Bay "Rain God"

About two miles from Kulleet Bay village along the south shore of the bay, which can be traversed at low tides, there is a large boulder about six feet wide and four feet high. In its original location, below the low tide line at the same place, the boulder snagged booms of logs and was such a nuisance that the loggers moved it to the top of the beach. They were surprised to discover the petroglyph, a deeply-cut carving of a mythical beast which the Indians promptly named the "Rain-god".

This is the most complex and carefully made petroglyph of Vancouver Island. The channels are about an inch deep and one and a half inches wide, and within the channels are ridges cut so delicately that the sharp edge comes out as a fine line in the rubbing. At the right end of the sandstone boulder, cleverly utilizing the eroded strata, a non-outlined face peers from the rock.

It is interesting that this petroglyph should have been given the name "Rain-God" by the Indians who knew nothing of its origin and one would wonder why any part of the west coast would require a rain-maker. A possible clue is in an account by E.L. Keithahn[19] in the Alaska Sportsman of March 1939 in which a Haida Indian states that the old people had told him that petroglyphs were made to cause rain. Keithahn says that the salmon, returning from the sea to spawn in the streams, often school up in salt water and wait for a heavy rain before ascending the streams. The Indians believed that the salmon were people who lived in their own country under the sea, and whose chief sent them each year in their salmon guise to be food for men. Salmon was the basic and essential food resource but the annual run was an uncertain and unpredictable event, dependent on the willingness of the salmon to be food for men. In the tense time of waiting, their fishing traps ready, one would expect the Indians to take all possible steps to influence the salmon chief and it is possible that the "Rain-God" was carved to invoke supernatural powers to assure the annual return of the salmon.

6'7" x 4'0"

Holden Lake

On private property, on smooth bedrock sandstone at the edge of Holden Lake, there is a dancing petroglyph figure with a grinning face above. At its south-east end the shallow lake becomes a low swampy area and a local informant suggested that this lake was once an inlet of the sea, connected to Boat Harbour. We were also told that there once was an Indian burial place near the petroglyph site and oldtimers could remember burial boxes in the trees.

2'8" x 4'10"

Cedar-By-The-Sea

DgRw 41

The site is an exposed area of flat bedrock sandstone so close to the road that the asphalt surface just misses the "running dragon" figure. On dry days the petroglyphs are so faint that they are almost impossible to see. They were discovered only a few years ago when Mr. McLean, who still lives at the site, cleared the soil down to bedrock to build a garage. He failed to see the designs at that time, but school children happened to notice them

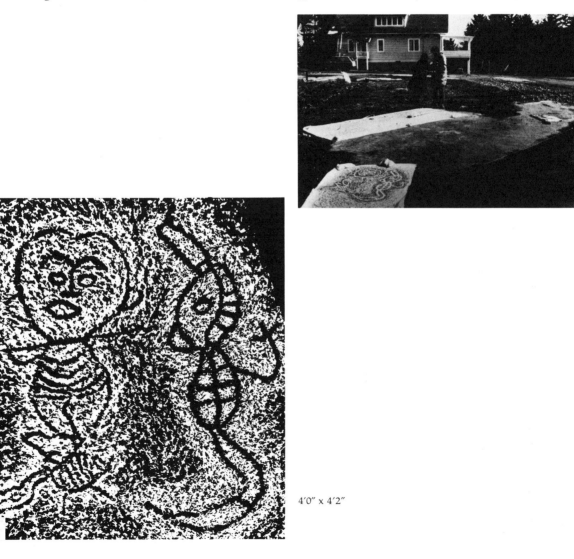

4'0" x 4'2"

when the rock was wet with rain, some weeks later. Mr. McLean does not think that they have been eroded by exposure but certainly the fragile sandstone has been damaged by the heavy vehicles which have used the rock for parking and turning. The crews of the B.C. Hydro and Power Authority blasted a hole for a power pole only inches from the petroglyph figures.

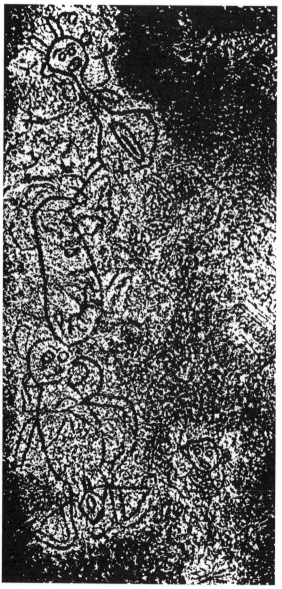

5′0″ x 11′6″

4′0″ x 8′6″

Petroglyph Park, Nanaimo

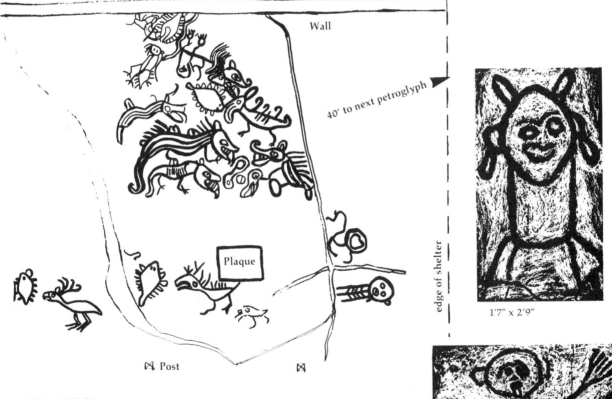

The site is a mile south of the city of Nanaimo along the Island Highway and is near the place where one arm of the Nanaimo River enters the harbour. As this is the petroglyph site most easily and frequently visited, it has also suffered the worst vandalism and has been disgracefully disfigured by ignorant and thoughtless visitors. It has also been damaged by Parks Department workers who constructed a shelter over part of the site in such a way that some petroglyphs were actually covered by cement. Moveover, the bronze plaque

Wall

40' to next petroglyph

edge of shelter

Plaque

Post

AREA APPROX.
14'6" x 10'6"

1'7" x 2'9"

2'5" x 2'0"

which marks this historic site has destroyed part of one petroglyph. The site is a ridge of smooth sandstone divided into five panels by long vertical cracks in the rock. The first three panels, at the west side of the site, are under the roof erected by the parks board. Below the exposed panels on the east side is a large natural bowl in the rock, too shallow and sloped to hold a liquid.

7'10" x 7"

Ten feet above this same area, at the highest point of the ridge, is a large sandstone boulder with a shallowly depressed smooth surface. It is not known whether these features have any significance at the petroglyph site.

Discussing the Nanaimo petroglyphs in an article in the Canadian Geographic Journal, Douglas Leechman[20] suggests that some petroglyphs may have been made by boys or medicine men seeking visions induced by fasting and privation, in which their guardian spirits might appear, the petroglyphs representing the powerful spirits they see in their vision. The local Indians have said that the petroglyphs were made by Thochwan who lived there "at the beginnings of time". Thochwan too is among the figures, put there by a supernatural visitor who changed him to stone, just as the shaman from the Jack Point site nearby was supposed to have been changed to stone by a traveller named Xaelt. [21]

AREA APPROX
11'0" x 10'0"

1'10" x 2'3"

1'2" x 1'9"

5'4" x 7'6"

8'6" x 2'6"

4'0" x 6'4"

4'0" x 3'0"

This photograph of the main petroglyph panel at Petroglyph Park is included because it shows the uppermost petroglyph figure complete. This figure has been partly destroyed by the inept construction of a shelter ostensibly designed to protect the carvings.

2'9" x 1'4"

LILO BERLINER Rubbing

1'6" x 1'6"

B.C. Provincial Archives photo

Nanaimo River

Until 1969 this site, on the west bank of the Nanaimo River near Cedar, was unknown, hidden beneath the forest floor. In the construction of a driveway the present owner had a bulldozer clear the earth down to the sandstone bedrock. Much to his surprise he discovered pecked pictures on his new road. Some of the petroglyphs have been damaged either by the

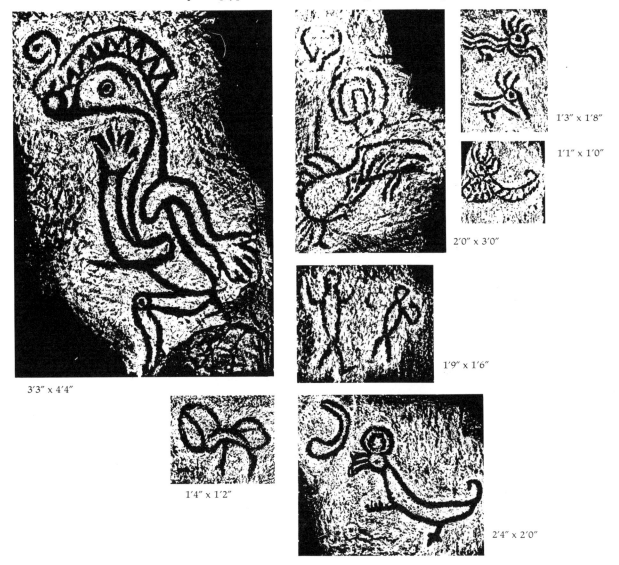

3'3" x 4'4"

1'3" x 1'8"

1'1" x 1'0"

2'0" x 3'0"

1'9" x 1'6"

1'4" x 1'2"

2'4" x 2'0"

5'0" x 9'4"

heavily wooded

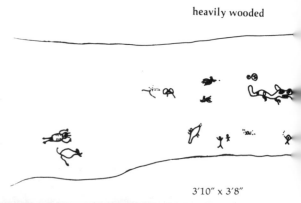

3'10" x 3'8"

Nanaimo River

heavily wooded

FIR

Stone Wall

House

bulldozer, or by the heavy logging equipment previously used in this area, or .by the vehicles moving building materials for the construction of the house. The drive has now been closed by a rope to stop casual vehicle traffic. Tapping the sandstone at certain spots produces a hollow sound, as if there were air spaces beneath a sandstone layer, and it is possible that frost action may cause further damage at this site.

6′0″ x 10′ 9″

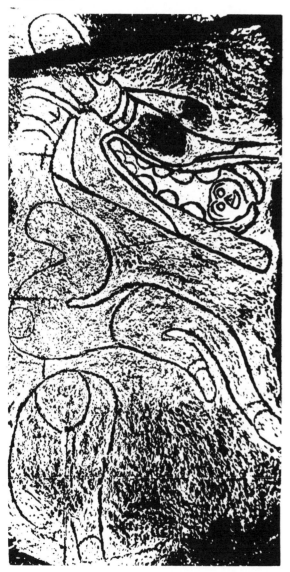

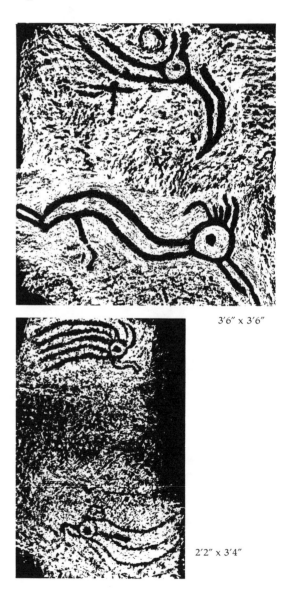

3′6″ x 3′6″

2′2″ x 3′4″

Nanaimo River

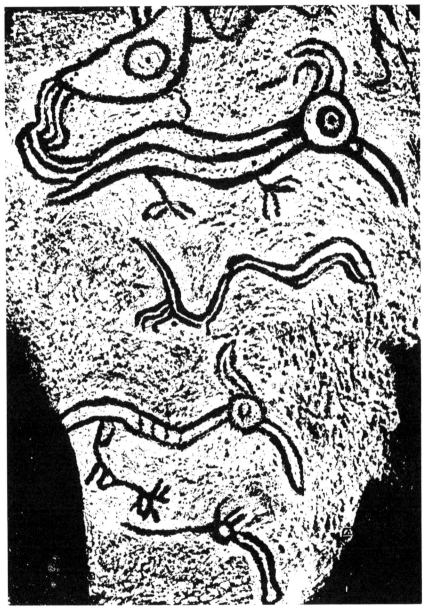

5'6" x 7'0"

2'6" x 5'10"

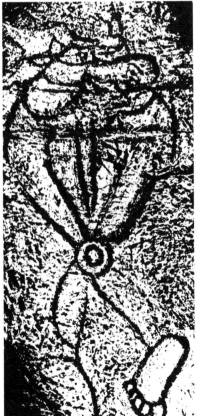

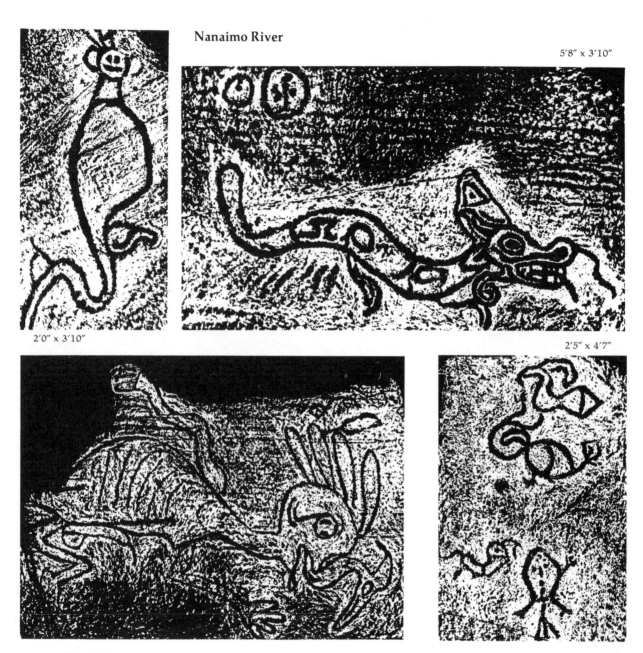

Nanaimo River

5'8" x 3'10"

2'0" x 3'10"

2'5" x 4'7"

6'0" x 4'2"

As the area has not been extensively cleared, it is not known whether more petroglyphs may be found. Neither has a careful study been made of the age of the soil cover, which has been roughly estimated at a thousand years.

Jack Point

Jack Point, long and narrow, juts into Nanaimo Harbour. At the end of the
point, like a sign to welcome the salmon, there once stood a large boulder,
five feet high and seven feet wide, one side covered with petroglyph figures.
This stone has now been placed in front of the Nanaimo City Museum. The
petroglyphs are stylized representations of fish. Birds' heads are also part of
the scene and parallel horizontal lines may be the ripples on the surface of
the sea.

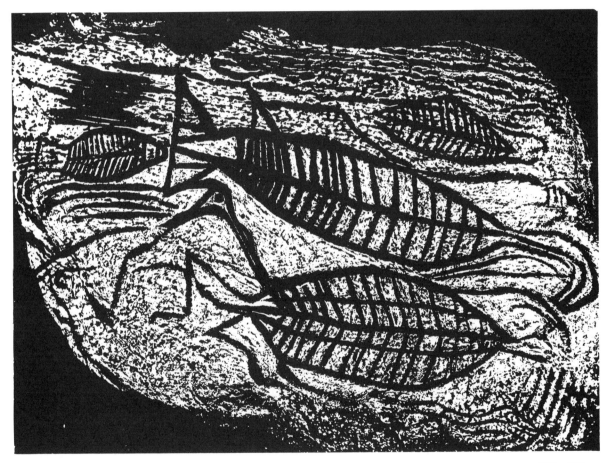

6'8" x 5'0"

An Indian informant, Mary Jane Peters,[22] told a tale of a contest of power
between a shaman who lived at Jack Point and a traveller named Xaelt. At
the end of the story, Xaelt changed the shaman to stone :

"It's a real image like. But the old people used to know where it was. But the younger generation never found it. Everything has changed."

She added that the petroglyphs are pictures of what died there, including the animals the old man had killed for food. When it rains the hill bleeds with the blood of the animals that died there:

"And the old people never went near that place. When it rains it is blood. But you can't see it now."

In an article in the Canadian Geographical Journal F. Barrow[23] relates another legend about the Jack Point petroglyph, a story he heard from an old Indian living in 1942 on No. 2 Reserve, Nanaimo. He tells of a strange fish which turned into a young man who married a local Indian girl. They disappeared into the sea but returned in the guise of a dog-salmon, bringing with them many of their friends. That was the first time the dog-salmon came into the Nanaimo River and though the Indians caught many fish they did not touch the two who leaped from the water side by side, for these were the young man and his bride. It was thought that the girl's father, who was a shaman, had carved the petroglyphs on the boulder at Jack Point.

Harewood Plain, Nanaimo   DgRx 9

Although this site seems remote, it is in fact only about two miles south-west of the Petroglyph Park site, at an altitude of five hundred feet, on a lonely stretch of sandstone covered with a thick mat of moss. As the three petroglyph figures known from this site were accidentally uncovered during the construction of the power line which crosses the plain, one wonders whether there may be more petroglyphs under the moss cover. There is a lake about a quarter mile from the petroglyphs.

One anthropomorphic figure at this site has been called a hermaphrodite because it appears to have three hairs on one side of the head only, and on the same side of the body, there seems to be a single breast. However, the three hairs may represent feathers and it is possible that the hand, which is in an unusual position for a petroglyph figure, holds some object mistaken for the breast. The so-called "snake and dancing-man" petroglyph has also been interpreted as a map. It has many small round smooth holes which also occur away from the petroglyph across the sandstone surface. Again, one is tempted to peel back the moss to discover how far they extend.

2′8″ x 5′3″

5′0″ x 4′0″

2′0″ x 3′3″

Brechin Mine Site, Nanaimo

Harlan I. Smith photographed this petroglyph in 1915 and stated at that time that it was visible at low tide on the Old Brechin Mine Point, which separates Newcastle Island Passage from Departure Bay. He listed the petroglyph in several of his unpublished documents written between 1923 and 1930, and the description given is:

"the petroglyph is on the point extending south into the bay towards the south from Brechin Mine. Human head and chest. Head north, face south. It is not detached."[24]

The petroglyph can no longer be found. As it was cut into the bedrock sandstone, it is probably now buried by the extensive oil company construction on the site.

National Museum of Canada photo

Millstone River, Nanaimo

Mr. Ken Kendall, a long-time resident of the Nanaimo area, stated that at the time of the construction of the Millstone River bridge in Nanaimo, workmen clearing to bedrock for the bridge footings discovered petroglyphs, but they were almost immediately recovered by fill.

Boat Harbour

DgRw 42

Unfortunately this site has been destroyed by bulldozing and the surviving photographs fail to show clearly the petroglyph figures.

Hepburn Stone

DgRx 15

This granite boulder with petroglyph face is now displayed in the Old Bastion in Nanaimo. It was found in 1923 by Mr. F. Hepburn, who occupied the old Trawford Ranch on the Yorke Estate on the Nanaimo River. He was digging a well in an old water course of the river, a few hundred yards up-stream from the traffic bridge on the old Island Highway and opposite Harrison Island, and he found the stone at a depth of twenty-eight feet.[25]

Englishman River

The old bridge across the Englishman River is gone now but the cement footings remain, and only narrowly did one petroglyph figure miss being under the cement. The site is dramatic. After making a last leisurely back eddy before plunging into the narrow gorge, the river has undercut the sandstone so that a wide ledge overhangs the river. It is on this ledge that the petroglyphs have been pecked.

An issue of the Colonist in February 1960 gave this account of the discovery of the carvings:

"About twelve years ago Harry Butler, a native son who knows the country around Parksville as few others do, was fishing at the river with his son. He happened to lean on the rocky ledge and noticed that the moss was growing in strange grooves. Curious, he pulled off the moss and saw the regular indentations underneath. He immediately forgot about his fishing and set to work to clear all the moss away. Thus he discovered the first of the carvings. He subsequently uncovered the other two and now they can be clearly seen."

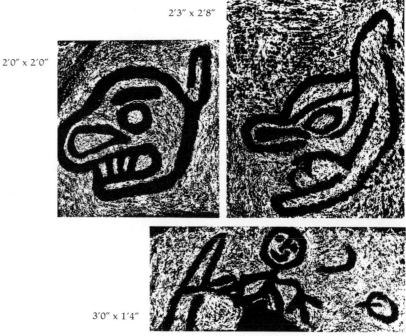

2'3" x 2'8"

2'0" x 2'0"

3'0" x 1'4"

However, there was a time when the petroglyphs were not overgrown with moss. We were fortunate to meet in Parksville an elderly gentleman of eighty one years, Mr. George Tranfield, whose father, Mr. Allvan Tranfield, worked on the construction of the old bridge. In 1886, Mr. Allvan Tranfield questioned the Indians fishing at the bridge and they pointed to a deaf-mute Indian fisherman, who, they said, was the carver of the pictures. Mr. George Tranfield thought the carvings represented the bear, the woman and two seals.

3'4" x 5'5"

Sproat Lake

The mythical sea creatures of Sproat Lake are carved on a vertical rock face and must be viewed in the summer and autumn from a platform floating on the lake. In the winter the water level rises to submerge the petroglyphs. It has been suggested that the deep smooth grooves of these petroglyphs were made not by pecking but with a sharpened stick using wet sand as the abrasive. The sea monster appears frequently in Pacific Coast art and mythology. C.F. Newcombe writes that possibly some of the Sproat Lake [26] petroglyphs depict the mythical snake Haietlik, or Hahektoak. He discusses an entry from the journal of the clerk of the ship Columbia in winter quarters at Clayoquot in 1791:

"Going on a hunting expedition in a canoe, his man suddenly saw 'a frightful monster near the shore shaped like an alligator'. The Indians

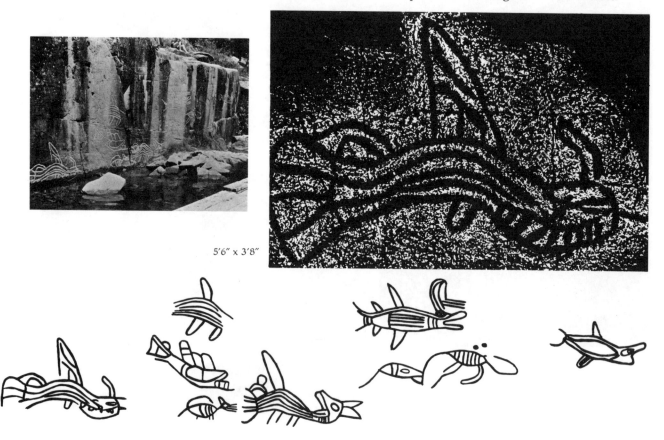

5'6" x 3'8"

120

knew all about it and described it as a long creature with huge mouth and teeth; in every other respect like a serpent. They called it Haietlik and said it was very scarce. They offered twenty sea-otter skins for a specimen for 'if they should have but the least piece of this animal in their boat they were sure to kill a whale, which among them is deemed one of the greatest honors. Indeed, a piece of this magic animal insures success at all times and on all occasions'."

10'6" x 6'2"

7'6" x 6'2"

4'8" x 2'2"

Great Central Lake

Five miles north of Sproat Lake and parallel to it lies another long, narrow body of water, Great Central Lake, fifteen miles long. At the water's edge on the point at Lot 749 at the western end a petroglyph was recorded in 1910 by R.H. Chapman, a geological surveyor for the Canadian government. The petroglyph was called the "Fish Devil" and one story claimed that it was carved to warn Indians of the presence of a supernatural fish.

In 1974 a careful search failed to find the "Fish Devil", but half-drowned trees along the edge of the lake and submerged pilings at an old mine railway dock at the north end give evidence of a substantial rise in lake level. Possibly divers could locate this petroglyph.

B.C. Provincial Archives Photo

B.C. Provincial Archives Photo

Chrome Island

Few sites can match this dramatic location. Chrome Island is a high flat rock rising sheer from the sea a few hundred yards from the south tip of Denman Island. As there is no dock or beach, supplies for the lighthouse must be taken off the supply ship by crane, and small boats have to be lifted out of the seas that surge against the islet. There is room on the top of the rock for the light, two houses for the lighthouse keepers, a helicopter pad and a workshop. The light tower was built precisely over the main petroglyph site, one of the cement footings partially destroying some figures, and the site is flecked with the red paint used on the tower overhead. There are many figures pecked into the granite bedrock and other petroglyphs on a vertical rock panel nearby. Upon peeling back the mat of grass adjacent of the main group of petroglyphs, more figures yet were discovered, and only further work with the shovel can determine their full extent. There are six other small groups of petroglyphs on other parts of Chrome Island.

Chrome Island

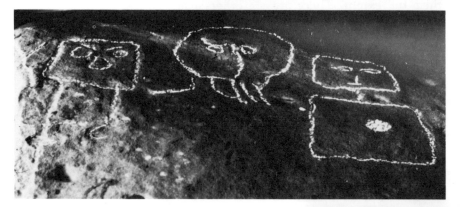

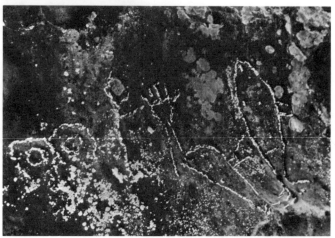

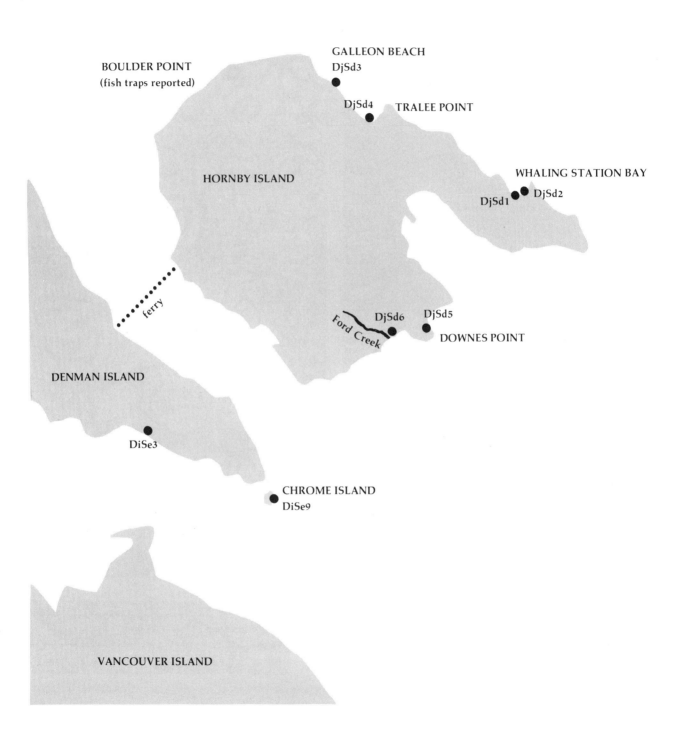

BOULDER POINT
(fish traps reported)

GALLEON BEACH
DjSd3

DjSd4

TRALEE POINT

HORNBY ISLAND

WHALING STATION BAY

DjSd1   DjSd2

Ford Creek   DjSd6   DjSd5

DOWNES POINT

ferry

DENMAN ISLAND

DiSe3

CHROME ISLAND
DiSe9

VANCOUVER ISLAND

125

Chrome Island

4'5" x 5'4"

4'0" x 6'6"

3'9" x 1'6"

3'4" x 1'0"

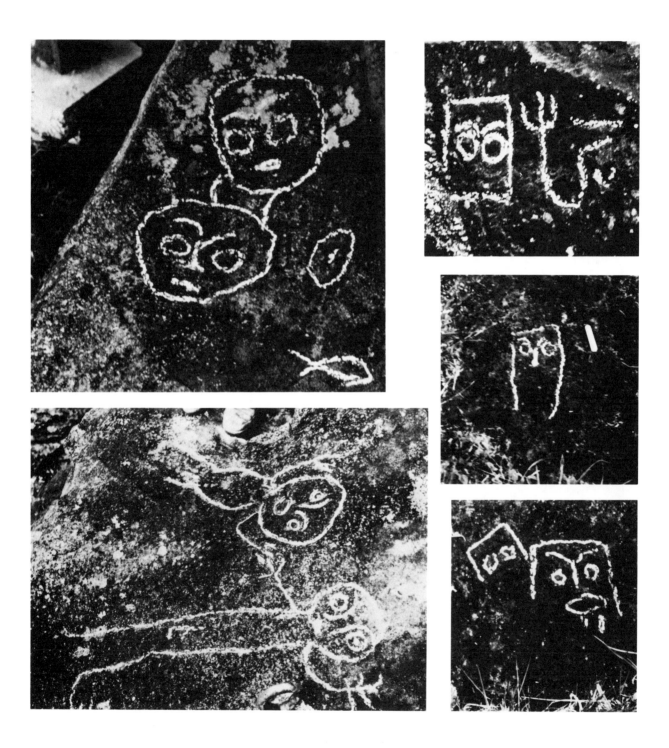

Chrome Island

6'6" x 9'6"

6'6" x 2'0"

6'8" x 11'0"

Denman Island

On the southwest shore of Denman Island on the Lacon Farm near Repulse Point, low sandstone bluffs come within fifty yards of the shore. Here, sheltered under an overhanging ridge of sandstone in a rocky grotto, there is a small petroglyph head with an ornate headdress. Midden deposits extend all along this part of the shore and there is an all-year stream.

1'0" x 1'0"

Tralee Point, Hornby Island

The eroded condition of the petroglyphs made the Tralee Point Site one of the most difficult sites to record. It is almost a thousand feet in length, the petroglyphs scattered on irregular areas of uneven sandstone on a rocky shore, below a steep wooded bank about fifty feet in height. The petroglyphs seem to be located in relation to the all-year stream, for there are much smoother areas of sandstone to the north of the site which the carvers have not touched. According to the local residents, the designs are being rubbed out by the waves and are much fainter than they were some years ago. It is impossible to be precise about these changes, but certainly most of these carvings are washed by daily high tides.

1'5" x 2'0"

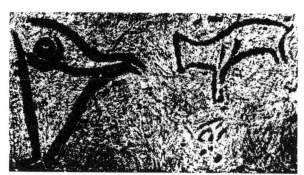

4'4" x 2'4"

3'4" x 3'7"

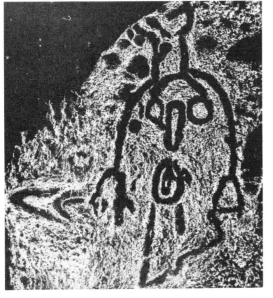

Tralee Point

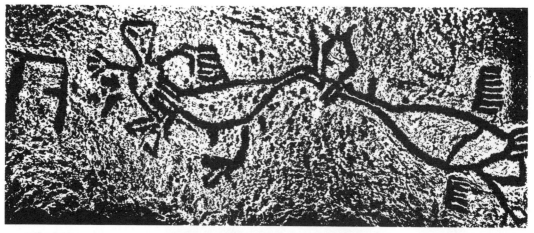

6'8" x 2'8"

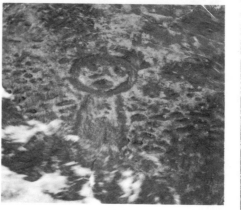

1'9" x 4'0"

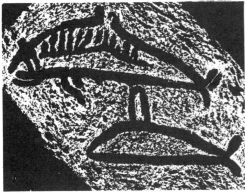

3'3" x 2'5"

5'5" x 2'0"

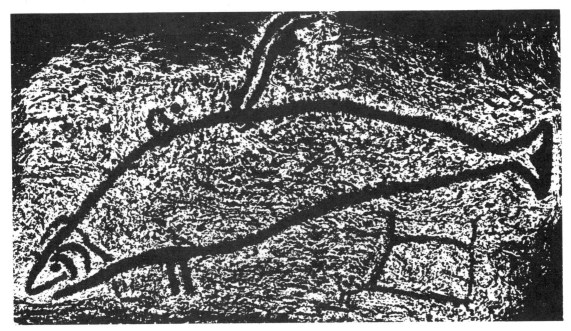

7' 0" x 3'9"

Tralee Point

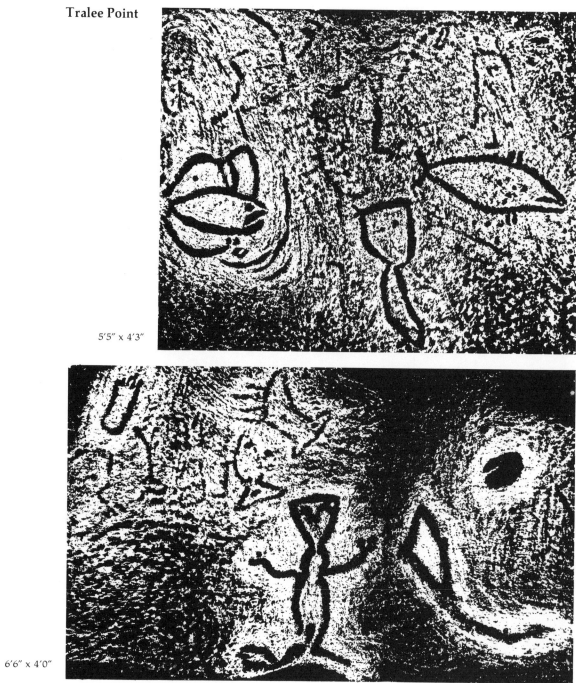

5′5″ x 4′3″

6′6″ x 4′0″

Downes Point, Hornby Island

DjSd 5

A single anthropomorphic figure may be found on the southern shoreline of Hornby Island near Tribune Bay. From the Ford Cove Road a subdivision road leads south to the sea and an open grassy parking area above spectacularly eroded conglomerate rock. The petroglyph is nearby, on flat sandstone bedrock below the high tide line. It appears to be eroding rapidly.

3'8" x 2'9"

Whaling Station Bay, Hornby Island

Each of these sites consists of a single petroglyph figure pecked and abraded into the bedrock sandstone exposed at the high tide line of this white sand

DjSd 1

3'10" x 3'10"

beach. At the east side of the bay (DjSd 2) the distinctive high heel of the gay dancing figure has caused considerable speculation. It has been suggested that it is an imitation of the heeled boots of the early explorers of the coast.

DjSd 2

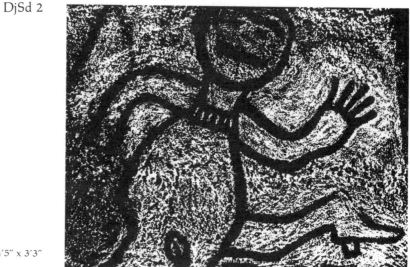

4′5″ x 3′3″

Ford Creek, Hornby Island

DjSd 6

West of Downes Point along the south shore of Hornby Island, Ford Creek slides and falls over wind-sculptured sandstone cliffs. Near the top of the fall a split-rail cedar fence zig-zags across the stream. About ten feet below the fence the anthropomorphic petroglyph is hidden until late summer. For

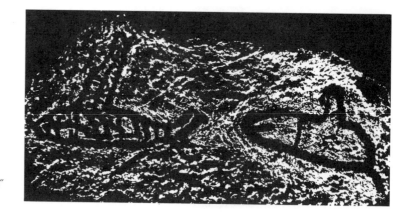

2′8″ x 1′4″

most of the year it is covered by mud and a green growth and the flow of the stream. Even after the stream dries in summer, one must wait while the sun bakes the green weed. In August when the dried growth has blown away, the petroglyph is finally revealed.

Near the bottom of the waterfall on the north side, some fish petroglyphs are carved but they may be hidden under logs thrown up by the winter high tides. At the top of the cliff the stream is caught in two pools, deep and clear and fringed with grass and flowers.

3'3" x 4'0"

Galleon Beach, Hornby Island   DjSd 3

On the north-east side of Hornby Island signs direct the visitor to the Galleon Beach subdivision. Beside waterfront Lot 7, a beach access road leads to a grassy park area above the sea. A huge white boulder is conspicuous at the high tide line a short distance to the south. The petroglyph figure is on flat sandstone bedrock appearing near conglomerate rock adjacent to the grassy park area. The petroglyph appears to be an anthropomorphic figure but is too eroded to be reproduced by rubbing.

Royston

This petroglyph boulder may now be seen in the Courtenay Museum. For many years it lay in the garden of Mr. J.R. Ulrich, several miles south of Royston. It had been dragged up from the beach by a previous owner of the Ulrich property.

1'6" x 9"

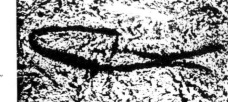

Comox

According to a descendant of the Carthew family, this black diorite boulder stood originally on the beach below the old Carthew farm, now the site of the Comox hospital. About forty years ago it was built into the stone fireplace of a Comox resident.

National Museums of Canada, photo

Courtenay

[27]Harlan I. Smith in 1929 reported this petroglyph on the west bank of the Courtenay River. His description is quite specific: it lay below high tide line on the west bank and was a detached and waterworn rectangular piece of sandstone about five feet long and three feet wide, the largest rock on that particular shore. He described an outlined head, with eyebrows, triangular nose, dot eyes and a neck. Nothing of the original shore line of the west bank of the river survives, as it has been dyked and filled for the construction of buildings, a small boat basin and an extensive sewage aeriation tank. Though it is possible that the petroglyph still lies somewhere beneath the fill, it cannot be easily located.

Campbell River

This stone was found on the beach at Campbell River just below the Pine Grove Motel by Mr. N. Richardson who gave it to the Campbell River Museum. The widest side of the stone has a large pecked face with one eye a plain depressed disk while the other eye has a raised pupil and one concentric circle. On the other four faces of the stone are four non-outlined faces in two of which the eye treatment is the same as on the front of the stone. On one of the side faces, however, the eye treatment appears to be reversed. The faces on the back and sides are very faint and can only be seen if the rock is carefully examined.

11" x 3"

Cape Mudge, Quadra Island

From the cliffs above this boulder-strewn shore on the south coast of Quadra Island, the Strait of Georgia fades away to the south-eastern horizon. When Captain Vancouver stood here in 1792 he was the guest of the Salish Indians then occupying the village on the white cliffs. About 1845 the Kwakiutl Indians pushed down from the north and occupied this strategic site at the entrance to the maze of northern channels and adjacent to the fishing ground of the Wilby Shoals. Captain Vancouver's diary does not mention the twenty-six carved beach boulders, although he strolled past them on a summer evening:

"Having gratified our curiosity, and in return for the cordial attention of these friendly people, made our acknowledgments by presents of such trivial articles as we had about us, we took our leave of the village for the purpose of indulging ourselves before dark, with a refreshing walk on the low margin of land extending from the more elevated woodland country, some distance along the water-side to the northward ..."

2'0" x 3'0"

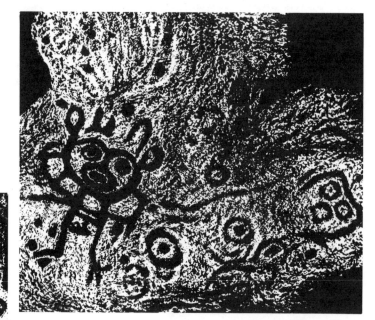

3'8" x 2'3"

3'8" x 4'6"

As the boulders are all below high tide line, they may have been hidden beneath the waves at the time of Captain Vancouver's visit. Or perhaps, since they face out to sea, he just didn't notice them.

The present Indian residents of Indian Reserve No. 10, deciding to protect the petroglyphs from erosion and vandalism, have begun transporting the boulders to a proposed park site in Yaculta village.

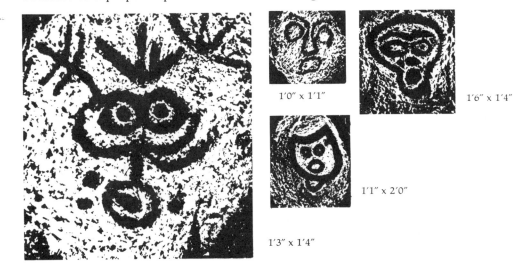

1'0" x 1'1"

1'6" x 1'4"

1'1" x 2'0"

1'3" x 1'4"

Cape Mudge

5′8″ x 4′0″

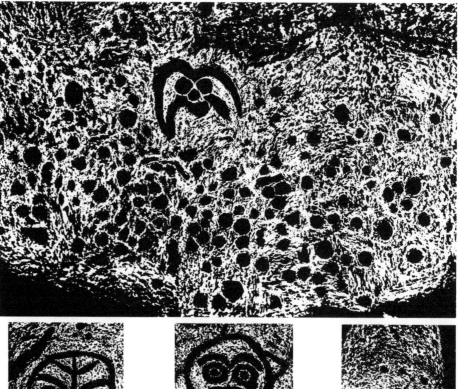

1′5″ x 1′0″

1′8″ x 1′7″

1′7″ x 2′0″

1′9″ x 1′10″

1′6″ x 2′0″

5′0″ x 2′4″

142

Chas F. Smith[28] of Gibson's Landing visited Cape Mudge in 1929 and then sent pictures of the petroglyphs to Harlan I. Smith as well as this information:

"One carving is on a large flat rock laying like a bed and at the top end is a rude carving of a man's head. This rock I was told by one of the old Indians from the New Village was used to lay prisoners on, and their heads were smashed with a club. This rock is covered at high tide."

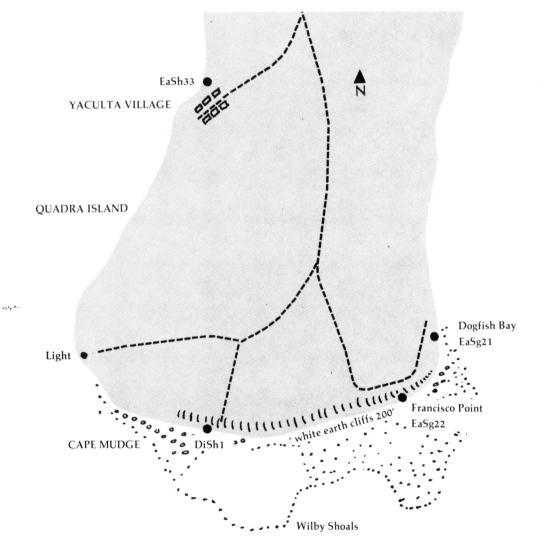

Francisco Point, Quadra Island

Of the four granite beach boulders with petroglyphs at this site, the one with the mask faces is not facing the sea. Local informants stated that the winter storm action is extremely violent here and as the boulders are below the high tide line, this one may have been shifted into its unusual orientation by the force of the sea.

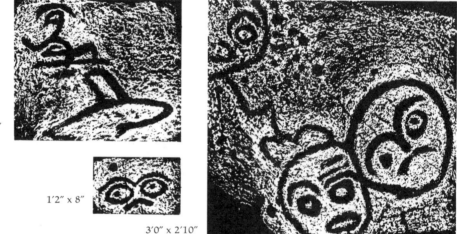

1'2" x 1'10"

1'2" x 8"

3'0" x 2'10"

Dogfish Bay, Quadra Island
EaSg 21

(near Francisco Point)
The wash of the sea has completely eroded the bottom of this petroglyph.

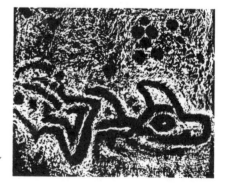

2'6" x 2'2"

There are many pecked holes on the boulder, and what may have been a face. Near the petroglyph is a freshwater spring. Mr. F.J. Barrow, an early observer of[29] petroglyphs, noted a Quadra Island resident's statement that according to Indian legends the petroglyph was for the purpose of indicating the spring.

Emmons, writing about the petroglyphs of Alaska, noted[30] that Kun-nook the guardian spirit of fresh water sometimes wore the guise of a wolf. The Dogfish Bay petroglyph is locally known as "the sea-wolf."

Theodosia River EaSd 4

This four hundred and eighty pound granite boulder was discovered in shallow water at the mouth of the Theodosia River where it enters the tide flats of Theodosia Arm. This bay is an eastern extension of Malaspina Inlet, which penetrates the mainland of British Columbia at the north eastern end of the Gulf of Georgia, south of Desolation Sound. Found in the 1950's by Dr. G.W. Bissett, the stone is now in a private garden near Victoria.

British Columbia Provincial Museum Photo

British Columbia Provincial Museum Rubbing

2'6" ACROSS

145

Yaculta Village, Quadra Island

EaSh 33

Originally located two hundred yards north of the present dock at Yaculta village, this boulder with petroglyph design has now been moved to the proposed park site in the centre of the village.

1'8" x 2'0"

McMullen Point, Discovery Passage

EbSi 10

This site may be found on the Vancouver Island side of Discovery Passage about six miles north of Seymour Narrows. It is most easily accessible by boat as the logging road to the site is open during the summer months only. The petroglyph is pecked into a large boulder originally on the beach at the low tide line and now moved to a spot next to one of the logging camp buildings. There is a large stream near the site and extensive midden deposit.

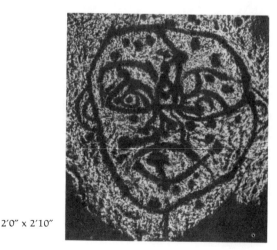

2'0" x 2'10"

Cortes Island EaSf 10

South of Manson's Landing and north of the old Indian village of Paukeanum, the outline of a fish is pecked on a huge granite boulder at high tide line on the beach. Unfortunately part of the outline has been filled with cement and a vandal has also carved his name on the rock.

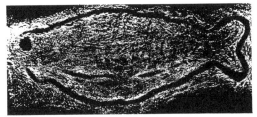

9'4" x 4'0"

Grey Creek EdSj 8

The photograph of the Grey Creek (Loughborough Inlet) petroglyph was taken by F.J. Barrow in 1934. At that time a Mr. Myers,[31] a resident in the area, stated that the petroglyph was much plainer in 1924. Ed Meade was unable to find it in the 1960's. A site description from 1934 places the carvings close to an old saw mill on the east side of Loughborough Inlet and on the north-east side of Grey Creek, twenty feet down the beach below high tide line and covered three feet deep at high tide. The carvings cover an area 33 inches by twenty three inches. The boulder is described as a "much eroded schist". It is possible that the further erosion of the rock since 1934 has made the petroglyphs too faint to see, or perhaps gravel has washed over the carvings.

National Museum photo

147

Forward Harbour

The petroglyphs are on three granite beach boulders at medium tide line, near the head of the harbour and close to the logging camp buildings. The largest boulder has faces, an anthropomorphic figure and a fish with x-ray skeleton. A second boulder, to the west a few feet, has three faces, one outlined and two non-outlined. Further west again is a third boulder with a very crudely pecked figure, so battered that the design cannot be determined. A creek runs near the site and extensive clam beds fill the head of the harbour. At the west end of Forward Harbour is the only safe anchorage, just off an midden with a freshwater stream at the end of the white shell beach.

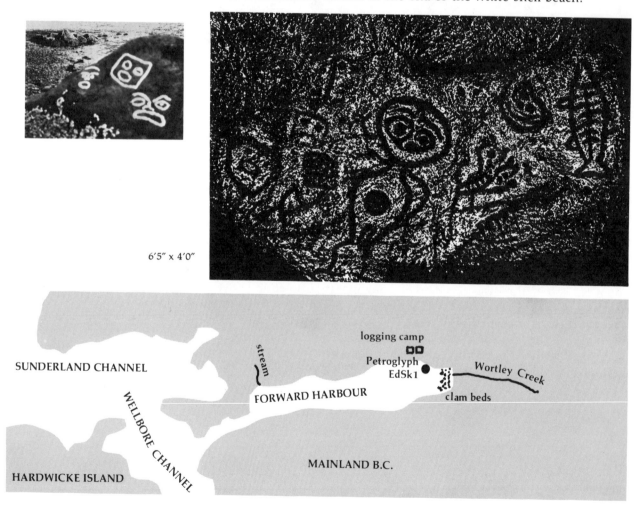

6'5" x 4'0"

148

Port Neville, Robber's Knob

This inlet opens off Johnstone Strait and offers welcome shelter when the westerlies blow down the strait. All boat traffic north and south must pass the mouth of the inlet so it is not surprising to find a midden just inside the entrance, where gas, food and a post office are available to serve today's traveller. Further east, on a point named Robber's Knob which juts into the inlet, are a deep midden deposit and a freshwater stream. Here also, on the west side of the "knob", are petroglyphs, pecked into the flat sandstone bedrock at about medium tide level.

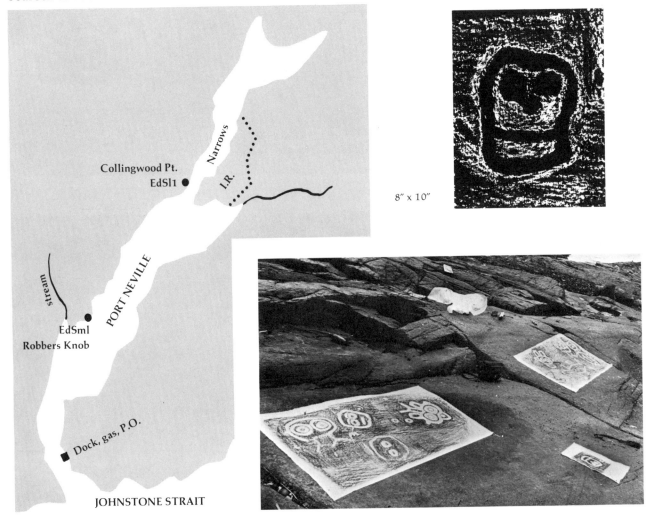

Collingwood Pt.
EdSl1

Narrows

I.R.

stream

PORT NEVILLE

EdSml
Robbers Knob

Dock, gas, P.O.

JOHNSTONE STRAIT

8" x 10"

149

At this site it is possible to distinguish between the wide deep smooth line of the stylized "deer's head" and the roughly pecked, crude line of the pair of figures (one with round head and the other square), but there is no way of determining whether they were made at different dates or by different artists at the same period of time.

4'4" x 2'3"

4'0" x 4'4"

Port Neville Narrows

EdSl 1

To the east of Robber's Knob, on the Collingwood Point side of Port Neville Narrows, there are a number of petroglyphs pecked into the sandstone bedrock at about the medium tide level.

1'4" x 1'2"

1'8" x 1'10"

2'8" x 2'4"

Lizard Point, Malcolm Island

EdSr 1

On the northeast coast of Malcolm Island there is a single petroglyph, a partially eroded non-outlined face, pecked on a large granite boulder whose flat surface is just above the present level of beach gravel and below the high tide line. The lower part of the carving has been completely worn away. The beach curves around to Lizard Point and encloses an exposed bay which has very large clams, famous in the area. Above the beach in a midden much disturbed by logging operations are huge clamshells and very large barnacles.

Thinking that the fine beach gravel was probably a recent deposit possibly hiding further petroglyph figures, we dug at one side of the boulder. We found no further petroglyphs but we did discover that a freshwater spring flowed from under the stone.

2'4" x 3'5"

Hardwicke Island

EeSl 1

Offshore the Johnstone Strait current forms heavy tide rips and swirls over Earl Ledge, Hardwicke Island, but on the land there is a small white shell beach with fresh water springs and a midden cut by a small stream. Today logging camp buildings stand where once the long houses faced the strait,

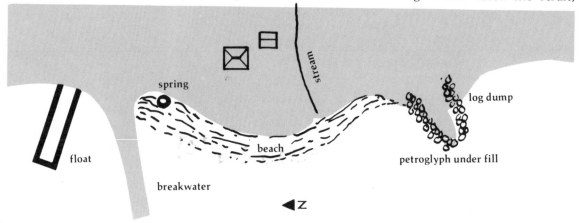

spring

stream

float

breakwater

beach

log dump

petroglyph under fill

N

and a breakwater has been built to protect a log booming ground and a float. On the point at the south end of the beach the rock fill, bulldozed to build a log dump, has buried the petroglyph boulder. No photographs or sketches were made before the petroglyph was covered.

Fort Rupert
EeSu 1

Although Boas[32] records an historical account of the pecking of a petroglyph at Fort Rupert, we do not know precisely which of the carvings was made in connection with the ceremonial killing of a slave described. Boas says that Mr. George Hunt told him this story as reported to him by his father, who had been an eyewitness.

"In olden times, when the hamatsa was in a state of ecstacy, slaves were killed for him, whom he devoured. The following facts were observed by Mr. Hunt and Mr. Moffat in the early days of Fort Rupert: When a hamatsa had returned from the woods, a slave, a man of the Nanaimo tribe, named Xuntem, was shot. They saw him running down to the beach, where he dropped. Then all the nulmal of the Kuexa tribe went down to the beach carrying knives and lances. The bear dancers and the hamatsas followed them. The nulmal cut the body with their knives and lances and the hamatsas

squatted down dancing and crying 'hap,hap.' then the bear dancers took up the flesh and, holding it like bears and growling at the same time, they gave it to the highest hamatsa first and then to the others. In memory of this event a face representing BaxbakualanuXsiwae was carved in the rock on the beach at the place where the slave had been eaten. The carving is done in sandstone, which was battered down with stone hammers. Near this rock carving there are a number of others and much older ones. The Indians have no recollection of the incidents which they are to commemorate. They say that they were made at the time before animals were transformed into men."

2   3'0" x 4'0"

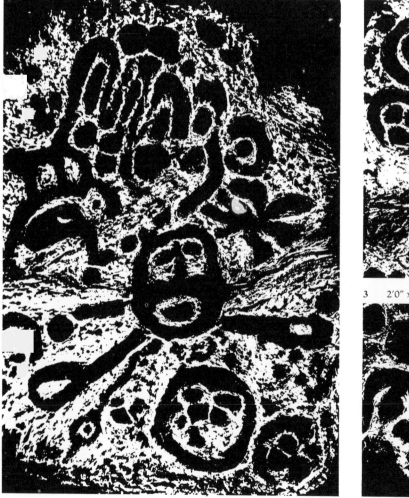

1   2'3" x 2'5"

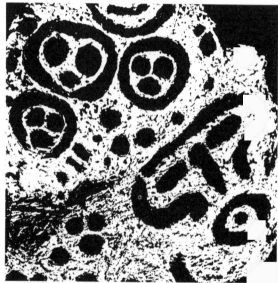

3   2'0" x 1'6"

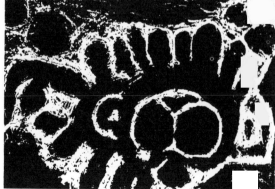

154

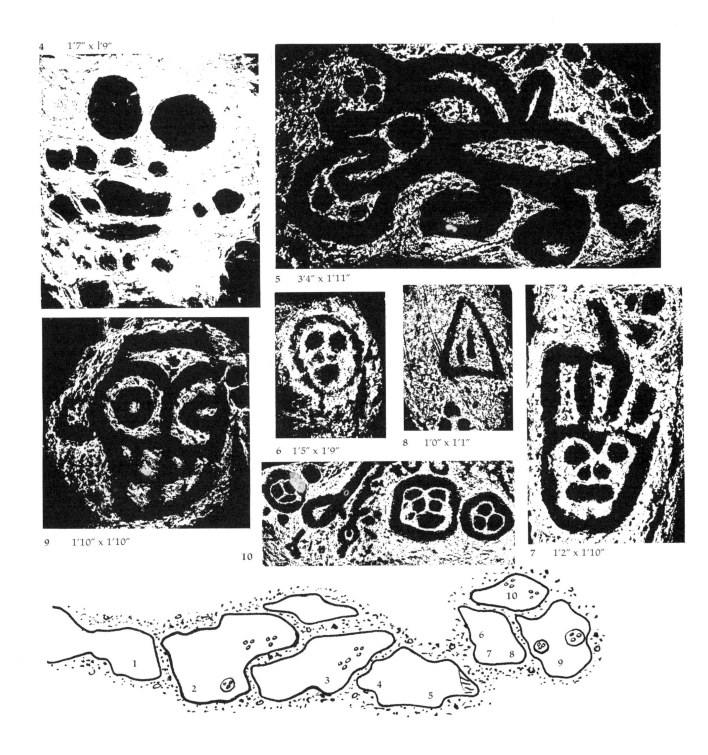

4   1′7″ x 1′9″

5   3′4″ x 1′11″

6   1′5″ x 1′9″

8   1′0″ x 1′1″

9   1′10″ x 1′10″

10

7   1′2″ x 1′10″

Cape Sutil

Alfred B. Williams of Sointula has made the rubbings of the Cape Sutil petroglyphs. In a Report of the B.C. Provincial Museum of Natural History for the year 1928, W.A. Newcombe[33] reported

"Photographs of petroglyphs were also sent us by Wm. Cox of Nanaimo, B.C. They were taken at Cape Commerell, near the old Nahwitte village and consist of four faces and some indistinct markings on a rock uncovered at half-tide".

We assumed that Cape Commerell was the present Commerell Point on the north-west tip of Vancouver Island until Mr. Williams informed us that Cape Sutil was once called Commerell, a fact confirmed by the 18th Report of the Geographic Board of Canada, 1924. There was once a Nahwitti village near Cape Sutil, at the mouth of the Nahwitti River. There remains the discrepancy that Mr. Williams found two faces instead of the four photographed by Mr. Cox. It is unfortunate that the Cox photographs cannot be found, but it seems probable that the reported site at Commerell is the same as the site recorded by Mr. Williams on the south-west side of Cape Sutil.

12" ACROSS

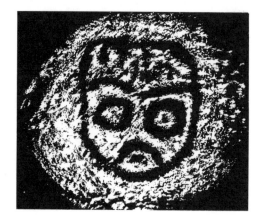

Alfred B. Williams Rubbing

10" ACROSS

Noeick River

Harlan Smith's[34] account of his visit to the Noeick River site in 1925 presents many contrasts with our visit in 1973, almost fifty years later. The two rivers still flow into the southern end of South Bentick arm about five miles from its head, but little remains of the Indian village of Talio. Smith described the location of the petroglyph site in relation to a small Indian reservation with fence lines, a garden and a plum orchard. He is accompanied by Captain Schooner, a member of the renowned Bella Coola family, who discusses the meanings of the petroglyph figures. Smith tells us that the slope of the petroglyph site for a space of about twenty feet in length and width is a slide used by mean, women and children "who slid for fun, seated on boughs of hemlock or other trees or on skins." One cannot think that the carvings had religious significance for the Indians of fifty years ago. How different is the place nowadays. A logging camp with a single inhabitant, the caretaker, occupies the delta of the two rivers. The big trees are gone and the land has been torn by logging operations. We groped in the scrubby underbrush for the long vanished trails which Smith walked. Then, happily, we found one straggling ancient plum tree and knew that we must be near the site. Back and forth we traversed the rocky land above the delta flats and slowly we realized that young trees and moss had completely overgrown the rock, hiding the site. The clues that enabled us to rediscover the petroglyphs were in Smith's description: "a slope perhaps forty five degrees towards the north ... about one hundred feet, estimating five feet to a double pace, east of the western edge of the foot of the rocky bluffs at this point, which in turn is about thirty five feet east of ... the plum orchard." From the ancient surviving plum tree we estimated our paces, searched for a forty-five degree slope, felled some trees, scraped off moss and earth and found the petroglyphs.

The designs are difficult to see and possibly the polishing of the granite slope by the sliders has something to do with the faintness of the carvings. There is a face at the top, and below this are two non-outlined faces, one inverted. The beaked figure on the lower left may be the Haohao referred to by Captain Schooner. McIlwraith's description tells us that the Haohao was a mythical bird of the Bella Coola with a long beak and teeth. Captain Schooner told Smith that another figure is the sniniq, but we can't be certain which of the figures he means. The sniniq is also part of the Bella Coola mythology and is an animal about the size of a large grizzly bear, with short front legs and long hind legs; it has long blue-grey hair and the front legs have eagle's talons in place of paws. Smith compares the figure on the lower right to the bear paw prints of Interior petroglyphs. The three circles and the seven lines would make his second suggestion a more likely interpretation: that the figure is an inverted face. Captain Schooner did not tell us when or why the petroglyphs were carved, and the evidence of the happy sliders suggests that the carvings had no great significance for his generation. Fifty years later they were overgrown and we found only the loneliness of a deserted place. As we left, with a rising night wind and the darkness driving us back to the boat, I turned to take a last look at the stone, stripped of its cover, and wondered if anyone would come fifty years hence to search again for this deserted petroglyph.

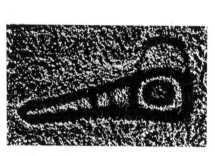

2'0" x 1'2"

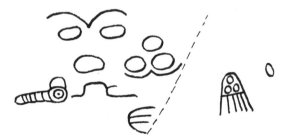

Benn Point

The faces are cut into a granite outcrop on the north side of a small beach south of Benn Point. There is a summer cabin about fifty feet from the petroglyph.

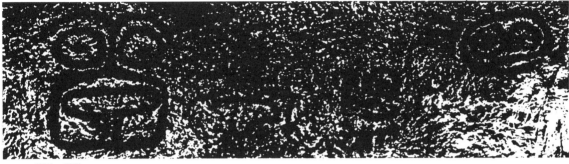

6'0" x 1'8"

Wallace Bay

FbSw 7

The original location of this petroglyph boulder is not known for certain, but it was probably found near its present position. It is now part of a low wall in front of a summer cottage near the north end of the beach at Wallace Bay.

1'8" x 2'9"

Small Island Near Beaumont Island

Flat rocks at the south end of this island have a number of petroglyph figures. The petroglyphs are very faint and difficult to find and are undoubtably being eroded by tidal action. In 1936 the remains of log defensive structures were observed and the small islet with steep and overhanging sides except at the southern end (where the rotting log walls may still be seen) may have been a fortified island.

2'0" x 1'6"

1'9" x 2'10"

6'7" x 3'0"

1'0" x 1'0"

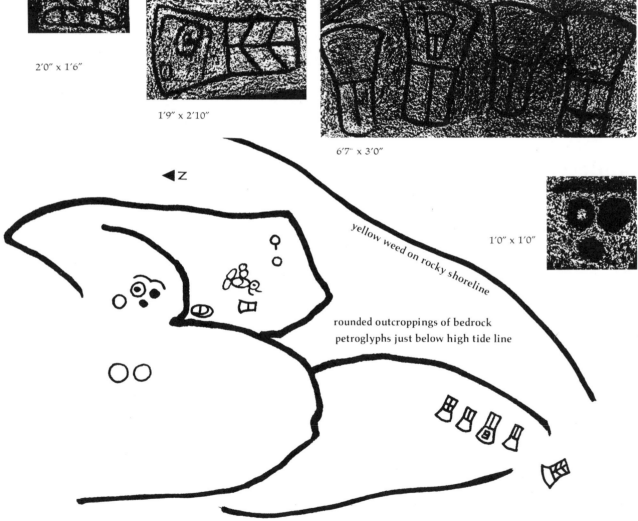

◄ z

yellow weed on rocky shoreline

rounded outcroppings of bedrock
petroglyphs just below high tide line

Return Channel

The petroglyphs are on a sloping area of bedrock at the water's edge, and the figures are submerged by the high tides. The only design which could be rubbed was the pentagonal face. As this design is lower than the others and therefore subject to a greater degree of water erosion, it is probably more recently carved. The other figures, too faint to rub, were chalked and drawn. This involved a certain amount of guesswork but we had no doubts about the top hat on one of the figures.

This site is associated with a deep midden deposit and the rotting remains of adzed beams show that this village was occupied until recent times.

2'0" x 1'4"

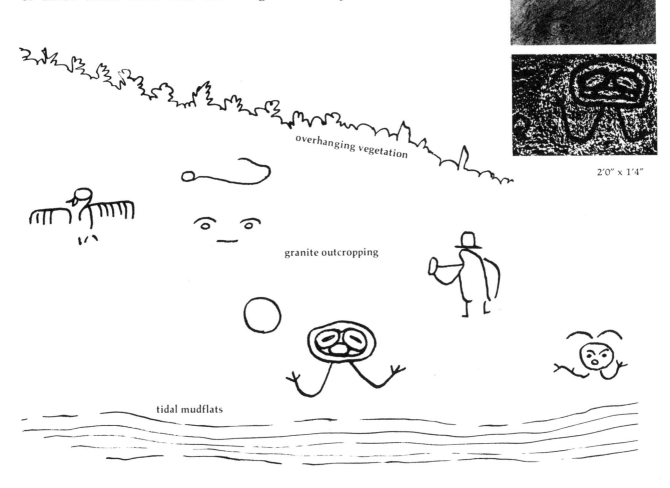

overhanging vegetation

granite outcropping

tidal mudflats

Meadow Island

On Meadow Island is the Bella Bella cemetery, a holy place where the forest floor is bright with the plastic flowers marking the graves. The petroglyphs are a short distance to the east, on the ridge of a high rocky point. Drucker in 1943 reported the discovery of the site "when a large tree (with seventy-five ascertainable annual rings) blew over". Drucker[35] found three styles represented, distinguished by technique: relief carving, intricate line incising and rather simple crude line incising. The three styles can best be compared in the large panel, where the square bowl with raised edge is cut deeply into the bedrock boulder and was filled with sky-reflecting water when we first visited the site. This feature occupies the dominant position at the site, in the middle of the ridge of the highest boulder. The face on the right of the bowl is done in the same low-relief technique and these two carvings were probably the earliest at the site. The low relief face and figure at the lower left corner of the first panel are sharply contrasted in style with the very faintly and crudely incised double cross and the carefully pecked copper to the right.

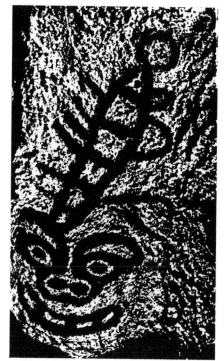

DETAIL A

1'6" x 2'0"

1'5" x 2'4"

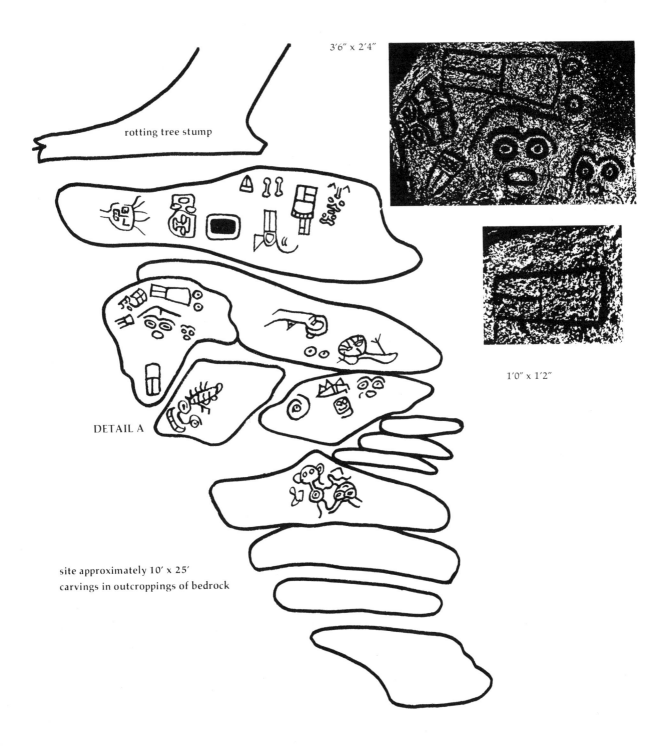

3'6" x 2'4"

rotting tree stump

1'0" x 1'2"

DETAIL A

site approximately 10' x 25'
carvings in outcroppings of bedrock

163

Associated with the potlatch and appearing among the petroglyphs are the copper plaques simply called "coppers". The origin of the copper and the reason for their distinctive shape is not known, but they apparently came originally from the Copper River district of the Alaskan coast and were traded southwards. In the earliest, made of placer copper, the T-shaped ridge was of solid metal but in more recent coppers, made of the traders' sheet copper, the ridge is repousse. The copper was a wealth symbol. In the northern area they were originally displayed then broken as a prestige and wealth demonstration during the potlatch for a dead chief, and the pieces given to important guests. In recent times at the rivalry potlatches they were frequently broken to demonstrate a claimant's wealth, thus compelling the rival to destroy a copper of equal or greater value. A list of coppers made at Fort Rupert in 1893 included the copper called Maxtsolem (translated 'All other coppers are ashamed to look at it') worth 7,500 blankets. Coppers appear to be chiefly associated with the Kwakiutl, Tlingit and Tsimshian, and the petroglyph coppers appear on the northern part of the coast.

3'3" x 2'3"

11'0" x 4'0"

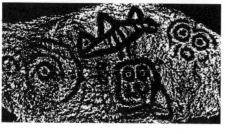

4'0" x 2'0"

7'0" x 2'6"

164

Return Channel

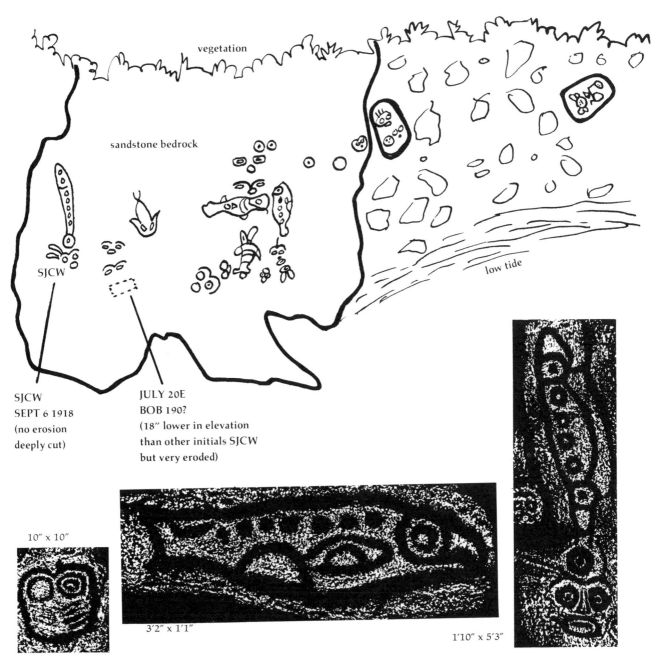

vegetation

sandstone bedrock

low tide

SJCW

SJCW
SEPT 6 1918
(no erosion
deeply cut)

JULY 20E
BOB 190?
(18" lower in elevation
than other initials SJCW
but very eroded)

10" x 10"

3'2" x 1'1"

1'10" x 5'3"

Return Channel

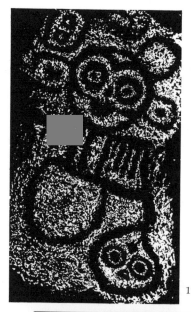

1'4" x 2'0"

1'9" x 2'9"

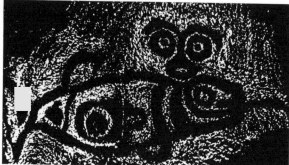

3'11" x 2'2"

2'0" x 3'4"

2'0" x 3'3"

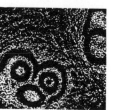

2'0" x 1'5"

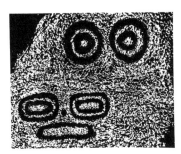

2'10" x 2'4"

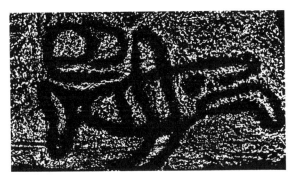

3'0" x 1'0"

Yeo Island

FbTb 15

The petroglyphs are cut into a boulder on the beach below Kilkitei village. Little remains of "Chief Kyet's village"[36] for the loggers have churned the midden area. Four coppers are pecked, one on each side of the large granite boulder, standing at the high tide line of the beach:

1. South face: copper with circle (9" diameter) Copper 20" x 34"
2. East face: copper 18" x 29"
3. North face: copper 23" x 36"
4. West face: copper 19" x 32"

The petroglyphs were very crudely pecked in a coarse irregular granite surface and could not be rubbed. They were chalked for photography as they are difficult to see. The boulder is about five feet high and about six feet in diameter.

Noosatsum Creek

Although this site is named Noosatsum Creek, the petroglyphs lie on the north bank of the Bella Coola River, opposite the **mouth** of the tributary stream. Harlan Smith [37] examined the site in 1923 and **made** the drawing which we use here. In 1973 we were unable to re-discover the site, although we cleared moss from a considerable area of rock.

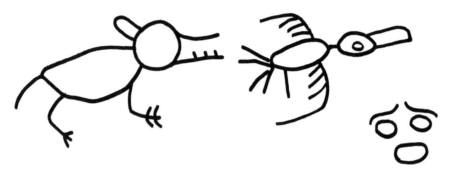

Thorsen Creek

1'0" x 9"

The Bella Coola Valley is like Shangri-la. The long fiord of North Bentinck Arm pokes far into the coast range. The very end of the long arm becomes the Bella Coola Valley, a flat green plain between sheer high mountain walls. The valley is watered by the Bella Coola River and sometimes ravaged by her floods. Until a few years ago visitors to the valley came either by sea or descended by foot from the Chilcotin Plain. The intrepid explorer Alexander McKenzie found his way into the Bella Coola Valley on the first crossing of the continent by a European. The Bella Coola people, a Salish-speaking group, welcomed him with feast and ceremony at a place he called Friendly Village, and then provided men and canoes to carry him down North Bentinck Arm and into Dean Channel.

His journey gives us a vivid picture of the Bella Coolas but there is no mention of the three known petroglyph sites of the valley, at Thorsen Creek, at Tastsquam Creek and on the edge of the Bella Coola River opposite the mouth of the Noosatsum River. This is not surprising for the sites seem to have been used for secret meetings and religious ceremonies. Though the Tastsquam Creek site has been destroyed and we were unable to find the Noosatsum mouth site, we found the Thorsen Creek petroglyphs easily, for the site has become a tourist attraction and an easy path climbs up from the valley floor along the western side of the creek.

1'0" x 8"

4'0" x 6'2"

7'0" x 2'2"

1'3" x 10"

1'0" x 10"

1'0" x 1'4"

Where Thorsen Creek comes out of the mountains on the south side of the Bella Coola valley it has cut a canyon about seventy feet deep, with steep sides overgrown with moss and trees. The petroglyphs are on sandstone rocks and outcroppings. The sandstone blocks are being pried out of the canyon wall by the twisting roots of trees, and the rubbings show the fragmented edges of the stones. As the path leads right across the face of some of the carved rocks, the designs are being worn off by foot traffic, as the sandstone is fairly soft.

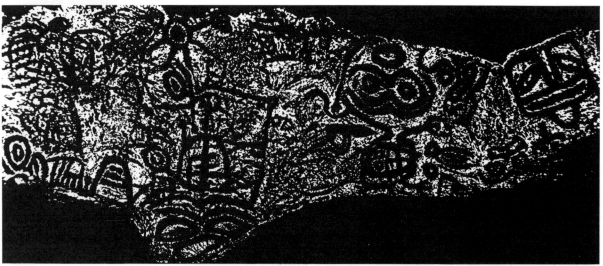

8'6" x 3'6"

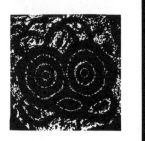

1'7" x 1'6"

1'5" x 2'2"

1'3" x 2'0"

1'6" x 1'0"

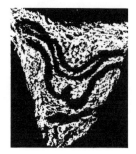

When Harlan Smith[38] passed this way he was told that the pictures at this site were made by a family while secretly singing its sacred songs. Smith states that the Tastsquam creek site nearby was "a secret meeting place for a certain organization of the Indians", and the Thorsen Creek site may have had a similar use.

1'0" x 2'0"

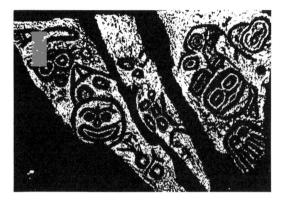

4'6" x 3'0"

2'4" x 2'6"

2'4" x 1'3"

3'2" x 2'0"

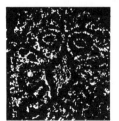

1'1" x 1'2"

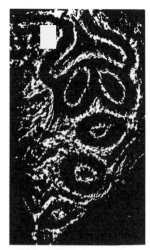

1'2" x 1'10"

It is possible that McIlwraith[39] is describing the Thorsen Creek site in his account of the ritual of a Dog-eating Cannibal, Olxan-i, at the village of Sinxl:

"Long, long ago one of the ancestors of this man saw a pack of wolves devouring some dogs. In some mysterious way, which even the Bella Coola do not profess to be able to understand, the power of a wolf entered the beholder so that he was impelled to eat dogs. He was then carried away to the mysterious land above where he saw and was assisted by several supernatural beings. The first Olxan-i was able to transmit to one of his relatives his ability to eat dogs, and the prerogative has since been carried out by his descendants ... The repository of the name Olxan-i is beneath a huge boulder not far from some carved rocks behind the village of Sinxl. It is said that many years ago some reckless uninitiated placed poles as levers beneath the rock and endeavoured to pry it over, but were driven away in fear by the sound of the snarling of wolves which came forth from beneath."

1'7" x 2'7"

2'3" x 1'6"

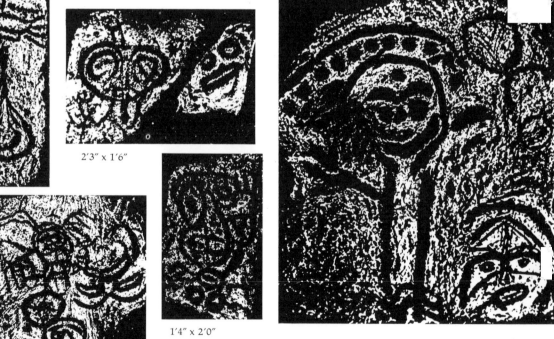

1'4" x 2'0"

2'6" x 2'10"

172

Tastsquam Creek

Harlan I. Smith described this site in 1924:

"About two miles south of the townsite (of Bella Coola) where the flat bottomlands of the valley reach the base of the very steep mountains, a small stream comes out of the mountains from the south, and here is a waterfall of considerable charm. On the west side of this fall, bathed by its spray at certain times, is a shelf in the rock wall of the canyon. This is three or four feet wide by something over twenty feet long. On the back of it, and on its floor, are petroglyphs bruised into the rocks by the Bellacoola Indians of long ago. Plaster of Paris moulds of these petroglyphs have been made and deposited in the National Museum of Canada. This was a secret meeting place for a certain organization of the Indians. It is of such romantic interest and there are such weird stories about it, that, taken together with its natural beauty and the petro-glyphs, it would seem to be well worth setting aside as an historic landmark of interest to tourists." [40]

Unfortunately Smith's moulds crumbled and were destroyed and his advice was ignored. In recent years the strange and beautiful ledge and the petroglyphs were simply dynamited out of existence to provide electric power for the valley. Although there were other streams flowing precipitously into the valley, the Tastsquam falls was closest to the townsite. It is small comfort that such a tragic loss could not occur today, under the Archaeological Sites Protection Act. McIlwraith,[41] writing in 1948, has recorded further details about this secret meeting place:

"Near every village is a place where the chiefs hold such meetings. All the inhabitants know the general locality, but there is such dread of the supernatural powers possessed by members of the Kusiut society that none would dare go there. If an uninitiated person should do so, he would formerly have been either killed or initiated into the society. The meeting place of the Qomqots chiefs is on a ledge of rock jutting out over a waterfall about a quarter of a mile from the village. The stream winds down a narrow cleft of the mountain side, screened by dense vegetation, and suddenly falls into a cauldron, so hemmed in by cliffs that no sunlight can enter. The ledge is immediately above the brink of the falls, one of the most aw-inspiring places imaginable. The meeting-places of other villages lack such natural settings, though all are at the bases of cliffs, or near some easily distinguished feature. Some of them are decorated with rude carvings, pecked into the stone. The meaning of the designs is not known to any of the present inhabitants. Some of them were made, long ago, by chiefs when they were composing tunes; they picked out the rock in time to the music forming in their minds. Others were mere memorials of certain events. If a chief gave an important ceremony, he or one of his friends carved a figure, perhaps that of a man, perhaps of some animal connected with the rite, to recall the occasion. No carvings have been made within the life-time of any Bella Coola, so it is probable that they had further significance, now unknown."

Elcho Harbour FcSu 2

Perhaps it is typically Canadian that we do not praise our famous men. Sir Alexander Mackenzie's intrepid journey to the Pacific, the first overland crossing of the continent, is honored only by an unimpressive monument on the lonely headland where he finally turned around and began the long trek back. In 1924 Harlan I. Smith proposed that a park of about 140 square miles be created to honour him, but the suggestion had little support. From Bella Coola, in canoes paddled by the friendly Bella Coola Indians, Mackenzie reached the promontory at the eastern side of the entrance to Elcho Harbour, and probably beached his canoes near the petroglyphs on that tiny beach. Harlan Smith[42] was told by the Bella Coola Indians that this promontry was once fortified with a high strong wall of logs and that there had been about four houses inside the log enclosure. They said that the point was held by the Bella Bella people. These were undoubtably the hostile Indians whose threats caused Mackenzie to decide to turn back.

1'2" x 2'6"

2'7" x 2'9"

174

There are petroglyphs on three large rocks imbedded in the beach. The two petroglyph coppers (one as a headdress) at this site suggest that these were made by the Kwakiutl Bella Bellas.

Jump Across Creek

FdSr 1

I wish this small corner of earth could remain forever secret. I wish no tourists' beer cans to desecrate this place. I thought of omitting this site and pretending that it didn't exist ... but it is already recorded by archaeologists and is well known to many people.

Searching along the shore for the site, chart in hand, we first noted the tiny sand beach where we would soon haul out the dinghy. Then we were aware of the stone sloping down into the sea, white and smooth, an unusual sandstone outcropping. Next we could see where a stream came sliding out of the stone. The stream has worn its convoluted passage through the body of the stone and then the top of the tunnel has collapsed; the gap is so narrow that you can jump across. When we walked on the stone we found it as smooth as marble, softly curved like flesh. We crawled up the rock and discovered that the almost tunnel led to a deep round white pool, perhaps fifty feet across. Later we forced the dinghy, motor-powered, through the jump-across tunnel and into the deep bowl, where we circled slowly on the milk-green water. The bowl is filled by a stream which issues from between the high walls of a narrow crevasses whose jagged edges fit like two pieces of a jigsaw puzzle. A tree trunk, wedged between, seems to hold the crevasse open, to allow the stream to escape. The sunlight poured into the bowl.

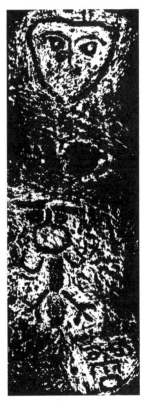

18" x 4'4"

1'0" x 1'4"

175

We returned to work at making rubbings of the petroglyph carvings and had finished one figure and were starting another, when something caused us to pause and look down Dean Channel. There were strange sinuous movements in the clouds there, and the water was changing colour. A storm was moving towards us. As our anchor was only holding tenuously at the very mouth of the stream and the fathoms falling away offered no safety for LIZA JANE, we worked feverishly to finish the rubbings. But the whitecaps were racing towards us and the wind was starting to sing high on the mountain slopes above. We scrambled the gear together and pushed the dinghy into the freshening sea, just in time. We spent the next few hours battered by wind and waves as we struggled to a safe place to wait out the storm.

1'6" x 1'0"

3'8" x 3'4"

3'8" x 4'4"

4'2" x 3'2"

176

The sudden storm blew itself out overnight and the morning sun shone on the petroglyphs when we returned. The carved faces at this site have an unusual style of nose, like a stirrup, which we observed at no other site on the entire coast. There are two canoe-like figures; although there are many pictograph canoes, there are no other petroglyph canoes. The details of the figures are also unique: the strange object like a handbag held by one figure; the designs on the bodies of the three main figures, ressembling the X-ray rib motif but each somewhat different; the unusual double pendants dangling from the ears of one figure and the band (like part of a set of ear-phones) which decorates the head of another figure. So many unusual style features, and the fresh sharp edges of the pecked lines, suggest that this site is comparatively recent.

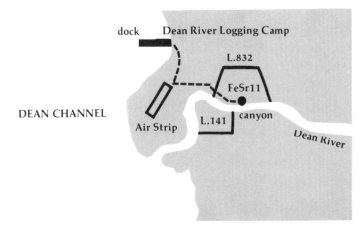

1'5" x 10"

Dean River   FeSr 11

We found the Dean River petroglyphs without too much trouble. We walked for about an hour along a road bulldozed by the logging company from the end of the airport-under-construction and then followed a fishermen's trail down to the river. From there we picked up traces of the old Indian Trail leading into the canyon. Where this trail narrows down to a mere ledge of rock overhanging the foaming gorge below, the petroglyphs are carved on the flat rock of the path. One gets the impression of great antiquity here, for the carvings are much fragmented and eroded, and there seem to be petroglyphs carved over petroglyphs, but none very clear. The carvings and the rock are so rough and uneven that rubbing was impossible. We tried one rubbing of the main panel and then chalked and photographed. Just below the site there are places where Indian fishermen could have stood at the water's edge for fishing. The petroglyphs are located where the river narrows at the beginning of the canyon.

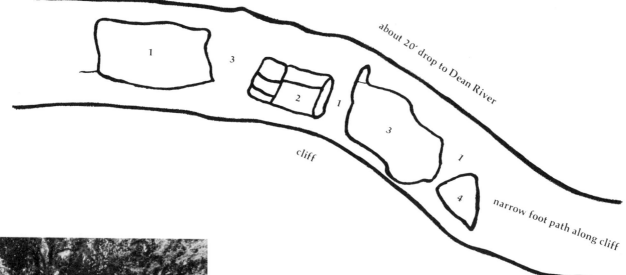

about 20' drop to Dean River

3

1

2

1

3

1

4

cliff

narrow foot path along cliff

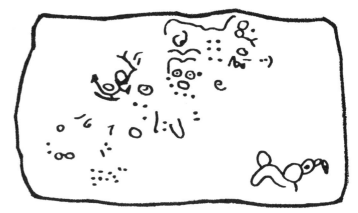

1
3'6" x 5'0"

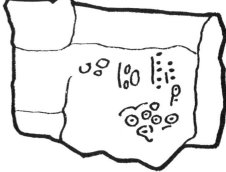

2
2'0" x 4'0"

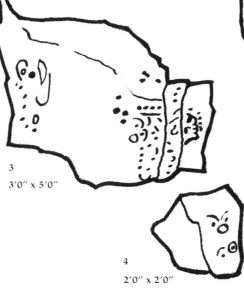

3
3'0" x 5'0"

4
2'0" x 2'0"

Price Island

FbTd 1

We have not been able to find this petroglyph. We did, however, find an informant who had actually seen it: Fisheries Inspector A. Aitchison wrote that it was impossible to direct anyone to the owl figure on Price Island. "One would have to be taken and shown as they are very hard to find". Mr. Aitchison was shown the petroglyph by an Indian friend.

Nowish Island

FdTc 8

The photograph of the petroglyph at Nowish Island was taken by Honor Mowinckel.

Honor Mowinckel photo

Myers Passage

FdTd 5

This site is located at the narrowest and shallowest part of Myers Passages Narrows, probably the best location for netting or spearing salmon. The petroglyphs are cut into dark sandstone bedrock between high and low tidelines.

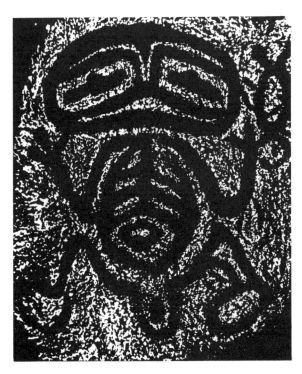

1′2″ x 1′6″

1′3″ x 1′9″

2′4″ x 2′8″

181

Moore Islands

After a rough pounding by heavy seas, we were thankful to come into the lea of the Moore Islands and then into the clam lagoon they enclose. Although we could hear the waves crashing on the west coast of the islands, inside we rested on quiet water. In this sheltered haven the petroglyphs are cut into rough sandstone bedrock and boulders below the high tide line. The carvings, consisting of eight faces, are very faint and only one could be rubbed. These islands are the site of a seasonal fishing camp, traditionally used by the people of Hartley Bay.

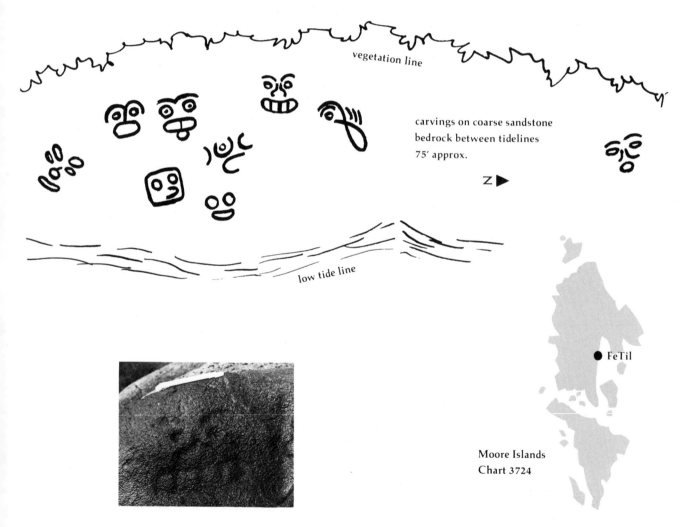

vegetation line

carvings on coarse sandstone bedrock between tidelines 75' approx.

Z ▶

low tide line

● FeTil

Moore Islands
Chart 3724

182

Keecha Point

FhTk 1

It would be easy to miss this small face cut into bedrock sandstone below the high tide line. In fact, the next visitor may not find it at all because the sea-washed sand may cover it.

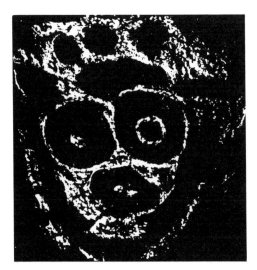

1'3" x 1'3"

Douglas Channel

In contrast to most sites where there are a few clear figures, at Douglas Channel we found a profusion of petroglyphs, with many birds, some frog-like figures, one "mermaid" and many faces and eyes and small round pits. Although we spent several days on this site, new petroglyph eyes would suddenly look up at us from rocks we had missed. Here for the first time we encountered the frustrating task of trying to record a proliferation of pits. A little further north, at the sites along the Venn Passage near Prince Rupert, we were to encounter sites where the dominant design is a series of three dots, representing two eyes and a mouth, with sometimes the eyebrows added and less frequently the outline of the head. At both Douglas Channel and the Venn Passage, the petroglyphs are cut into a schist rock which fragments easily. As both sites are covered by tide changes, one would assume that the petroglyphs have no great antiquity. We do not know what different function is indicated by the occurrence of many small petroglyphs and the uncountable pits.

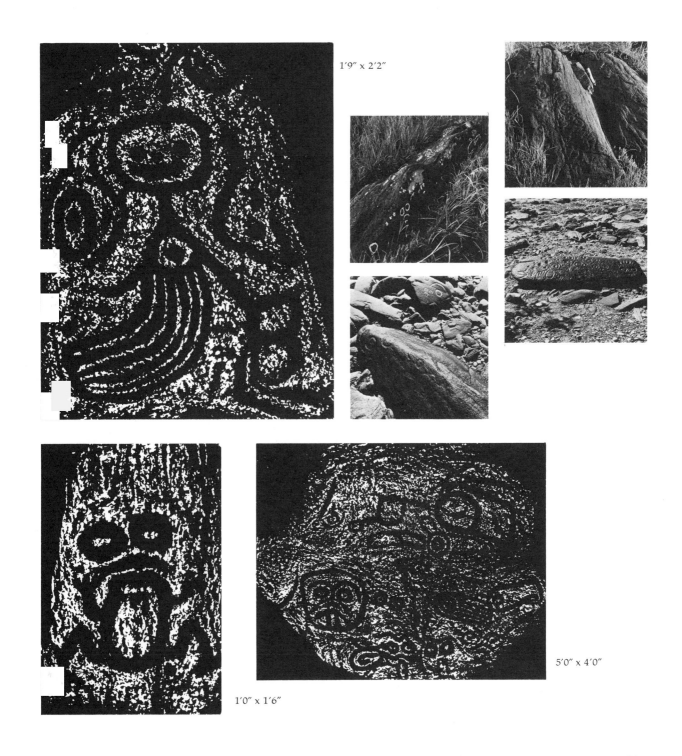

1'9" x 2'2"

1'0" x 1'6"

5'0" x 4'0"

Douglas Channel

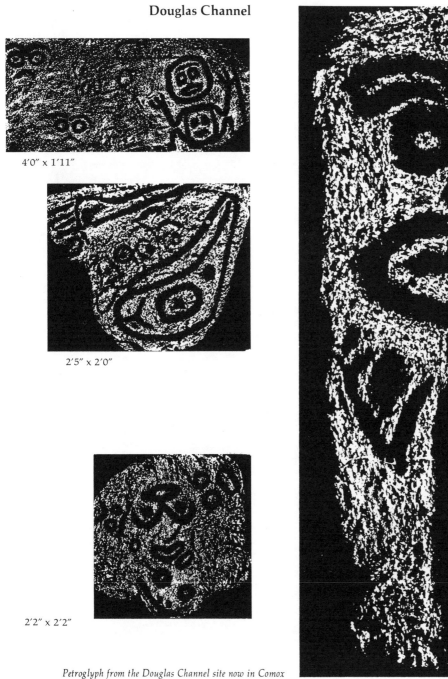

4'0" x 1'11"

2'5" x 2'0"

2'2" x 2'2"

Petroglyph from the Douglas Channel site now in Comox

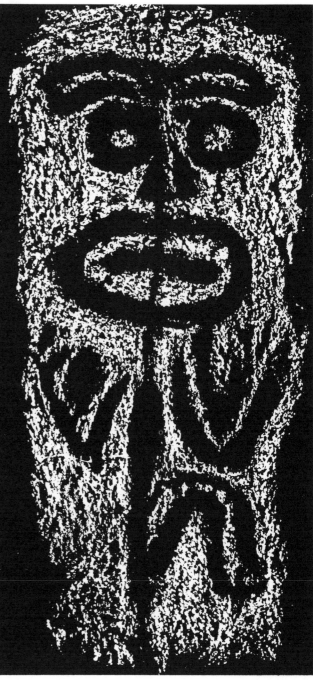

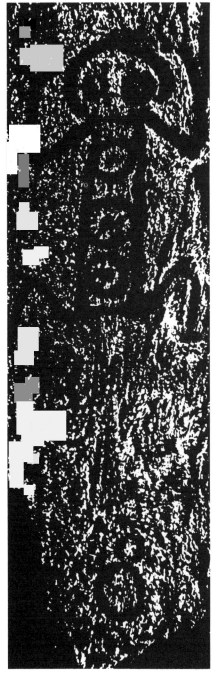

1′6″ x 5′0″

6′4″ x 3′4″

Venn Passage Area

The Venn Passage, separating Digby Island from the Tsimshian Peninsula, is an entrance to Prince Rupert Harbour. Along each side of the passage are old village sites marked by deep midden accumulations and occupied in the early historic period by the energetic Coast Tsimshian. As the Tsimshian have a tradition that they came from the interior via the Skeena to push out the Tlingit and occupy this area, the question arises as to whether the petroglyphs were made by Tlingit or Tsimshian. But the question of traditions is not so simple, for as well as the legends of interior origin there were traditions held by some Tsimshian of Tlingit origin, or Bella Bella or Haida. Moreover, the other two groups of the Tsimshian language family, the Niskae of the Nass River and the Gitksan of the Upper Skeena River, speak a variety of Tsimshian not intelligible to the Coast Tsimshian, which suggests that the Coastal people have been separate for a long period of time from their interior relatives.

Recent archaeological work[43] also suggests a long history for the Tsimshian in the Venn Passage. The work of MacDonald and Inglis has shown that there has been continuous occupation of the Prince Rupert harbour area for more than four thousand years. Although there are three distinguishable horizons, all artifacts relating to economic activities show continuity from lower through to upper and with the ethnographically known Tsimshian tools. And further, the artifact forms are very similar in comparable horizons between Haida, Tlingit and Coast Tsimshian. It would seem that the relations between these groups have very deep roots and it is unlikely that Tsimshian are recent arrivals on the coast. It is possible that the traditions of origin elsewhere may represent interior (or other) groups moving into the Tsimshian orbit, and adopting the traits of the more dynamic Tsimshian people.

For the Tsimshian were certainly a wealthy and powerful group. In the early spring the Tsimshian of the Venn Passage villages journeyed to the Nass to harvest the oily olachen, rendering the oil and then trading the grease to both coastal and interior people, a lucrative business. They stored large amounts of grease in the Venn Passage houses and then set out to catch salmon at their summer fishing sites. In the autumn they hunted, returning with the cold weather to a winter of feasts in their great plank houses in the villages of the Venn Passage. Drucker[44] describes these as "a concentration of riches almost beyond belief to neighbouring people, whose winter villages, consisting of similar houses, were scattered and remote from one another".

As the petroglyphs are near the Venn Passage villages, not in remote places nor associated with either the olachon industry nor the summer fishing sites, it

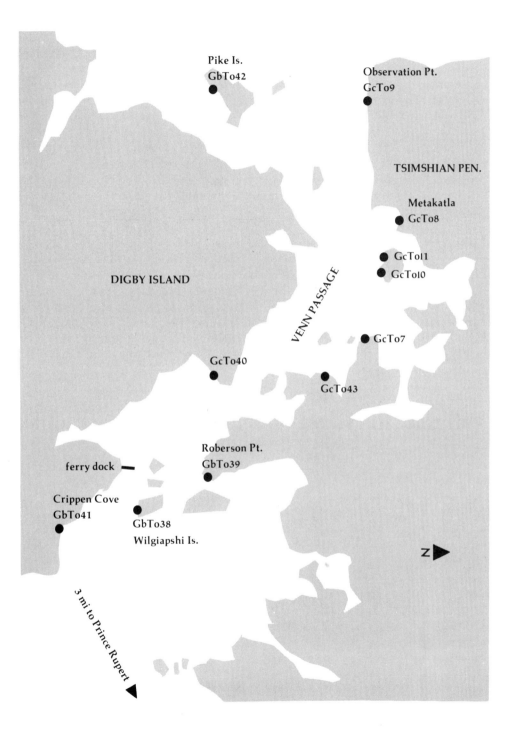

Pike Is.
GbTo42

Observation Pt.
GcTo9

TSIMSHIAN PEN.

Metakatla
GcTo8

GcTo11

GcTo10

DIGBY ISLAND

VENN PASSAGE

GcTo7

GcTo40

GcTo43

Roberson Pt.
GbTo39

ferry dock

Crippen Cove
GbTo41

GbTo38
Wilgiapshi Is.

N

3 mi to Prince Rupert

would seem that the carvings are associated with some winter activity of these wealthy and ceremonious people. That the carvings are fairly recent, one may judge from the rate of erosion of the fragile schist. Inglis[45] tentatively places them late in the prehistoric occupation, perhaps being not more than 300 to 500 years old. There are older, more eroded carvings, but what time depth is indicated by different degrees of erosion cannot be precisely determined. In 1834, when the Hudson's Bay Company built a trading post at Fort Simpson, the Tsimshian groups began to move to the Fort, leaving deserted villages behind them and forming a town of about four thousand people at Fort Simpson. They left petroglyph making behind them also, and the only carved stone from Fort Simpson is a white quartzite boulder found on the beach below the town.

Portland Art Museum photo

The petroglyphs of the Venn Passage are somewhat different from the carvings at other sites. The numerous small faces and pits, which we first noted at the Douglas Channel site are here the dominant form. There are uncountable numbers of groups of three small pecked holes, representing two eyes and a mouth, sometimes with eyebrows, sometimes with the mouth stretched into a curved line, and less frequently with head outline, or a round pecked circle for a body. The frequent occurrence of this simple design suggests that the petroglyphs had a different purpose in the Tsimshian area, but what that function was we do not know.

Wilgiapshi Island GbTo 38

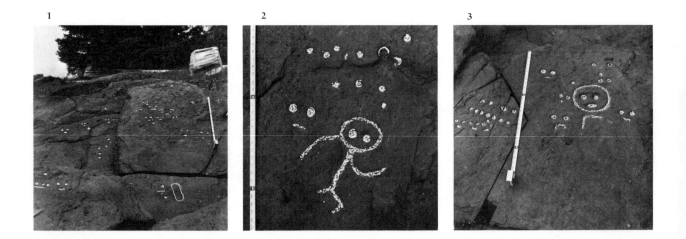

1   2   3

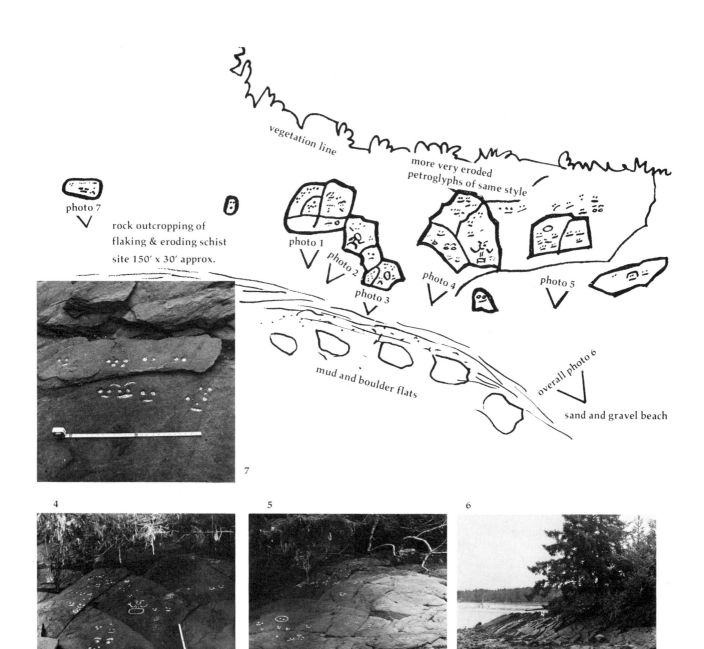

vegetation line

more very eroded
petroglyphs of same style

photo 7

rock outcropping of
flaking & eroding schist
site 150' x 30' approx.

photo 1

photo 2

photo 3

photo 4

photo 5

mud and boulder flats

overall photo 6

sand and gravel beach

7

4

5

6

191

Roberson Point

At this site is a unique carving: the hollowed-out form of a human, life-sized. The "man petroglyph", as Harlan I. Smith called it, lies a few feet from the water's edge, deeply cut into the dark schist, arms straight at each side and legs stretched straight with the feet out-turned. When Smith visited the site many years ago he made a Plaster of Paris mould for the National Museum of Canada. It would be interesting to compare the mould with the petroglyph as it is now, to determine the rate of erosion. The high tides wash into the carving and rain collects in its hollows, and the stone in which it is carved is a fragile schist which yields easily to the pressures of frost and ice.

Smith[46] records two stories from the local Tsimshian people, who call the figure "The man who fell from heaven". The Indians say that an important Indian told everyone that he was going up to heaven. He departed, but of course he was forced to return when he was hungry. To prove that he had actually been in the skies, he showed people the figure carved in the rock and said it was the dent he had made when he fell from heaven. However, the Indians say that he really made the figure himself while he was hiding. The second explanation given by the Tsimshians is that the figure was carved where the body of a drowned Indian was found.

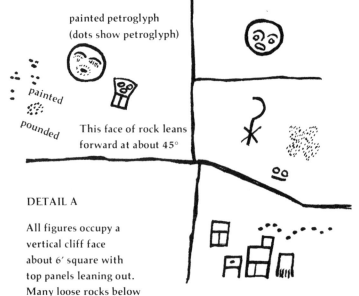

painted petroglyph
(dots show petroglyph)

Painted

Pounded

This face of rock leans forward at about 45°

DETAIL A

All figures occupy a
vertical cliff face
about 6' square with
top panels leaning out.
Many loose rocks below
pecked with 3 hole faces.

Near the figure there are other small petroglyph faces. About three hundred feet from the "Man who fell from heaven" on a low, overhanging cliff is a panel of pictographs with a very unusual feature: a painted petroglyph. Red paint has been added to the familiar small pecked face design. It is quite possible that the pecked face was already on the cliff face when the pictograph artist began his work and that he simply added the ochre to a design already cut into the rock. The only other painted petroglyph we observed was at Wishram near The Dalles on the Columbia River.

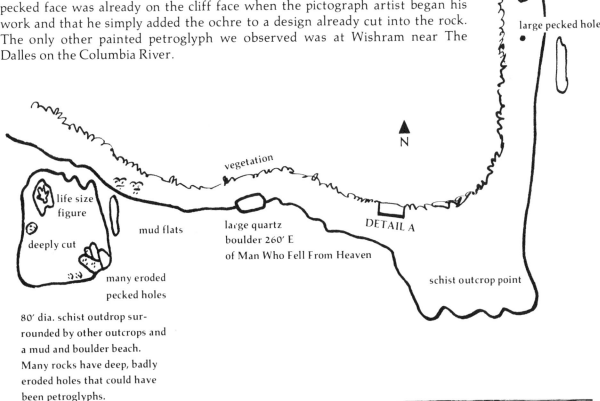

large pecked hole

N

vegetation

DETAIL A

life size figure

deeply cut

mud flats

large quartz boulder 260' E of Man Who Fell From Heaven

schist outcrop point

many eroded pecked holes

80' dia. schist outdrop sur-
rounded by other outcrops and
a mud and boulder beach.
Many rocks have deep, badly
eroded holes that could have
been petroglyphs.
Petroglyphs are generally 4'
to 6' below winter High Tides

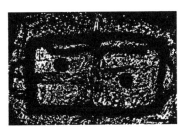

11" x 11"

193

Venn Passage

This petroglyph site is on a point of land on the south side of the Venn Passage, near Site GbTo 5. On a rock shore we observed about two dozen boulders with petroglyphs, although there may be more, some possibly hidden by the yellow rock weed. Rubbings were made of the three large face designs.

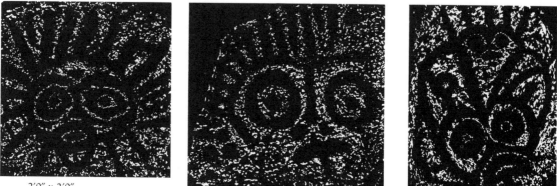

2'0" x 2'0"

1'3" x 1'9"

Crippen Cove

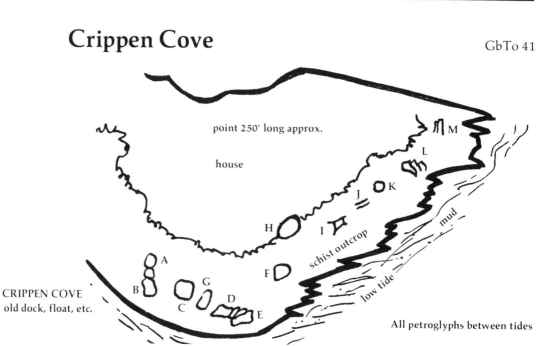

point 250' long approx.

house

M

L

J O K

H I

schist outcrop

mud

F

A

B G

C D

E

low tide

CRIPPEN COVE
old dock, float, etc.

All petroglyphs between tides

194

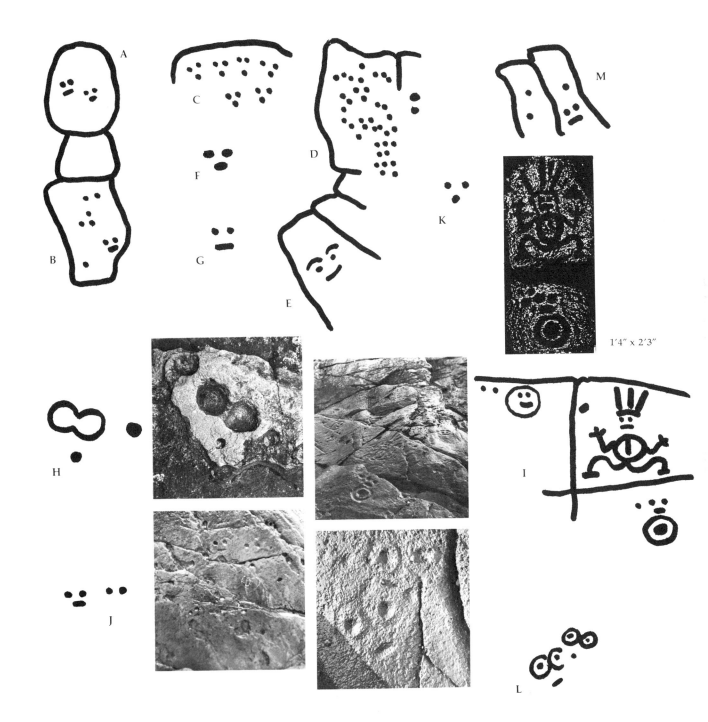

A

C

D

M

F

B

G

K

E

1'4" x 2'3"

H

I

J

L

195

Pike Island

A few schist boulders on the rocky shore of Pike Island have petroglyph figures and others are marked with eroded holes which may be earlier petroglyphs. In schist rock the action of water freezing in depressions tends to gradually enlarge and distort the holes until it is impossible to tell whether or not the process began with a petroglyph design. The most interesting stones at this site are shown here. Others were marked with the trio of pecked holes so familiar at the Venn Passage sites.

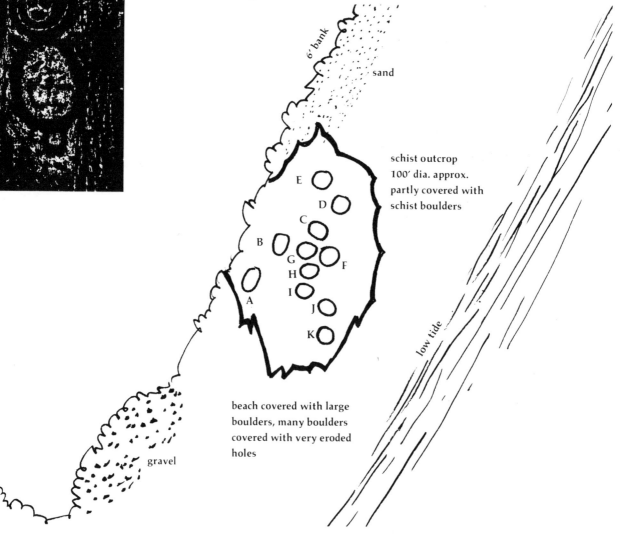

6' bank

sand

schist outcrop
100' dia. approx.
partly covered with
schist boulders

E
D
C
B
G
H
F
I
A
J
K

low tide

beach covered with large
boulders, many boulders
covered with very eroded
holes

gravel

A

B

C

D

E

F

G

Tsimshian Peninsula

approx. 250' across grassy point

B.C. Survey Marker
1968 — 1455

canoe skid area

boulder beach

2 large granite boulders

low tide

Bencke Point

The main feature of this site is a concentration of faces and eyes associated with abrader grooves for sharpening implements. There is also a large granite boulder with many pecked holes.

carved area
25' x 25' approx.

A composite photo from the Bencke Point site gives us a panoramic view of the western end of the Venn Passage facing west. In the foreground is the Bencke Point petroglyph site. In the distance the village of Metlakatla may be seen, another petroglyph site. Between the Bencke Point foreground and the village of Metlakatla lies Carolina Island, with two petroglyph areas. In the middle distance is Pike Island.

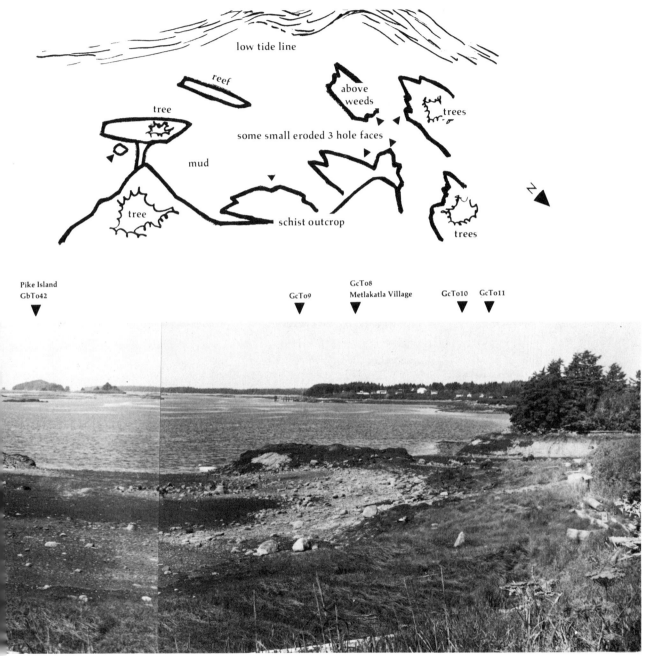

low tide line

reef

tree

above
weeds

trees

some small eroded 3 hole faces

mud

N

tree

schist outcrop

trees

Pike Island
GbTo42

GcTo9

GcTo8
Metlakatla Village

GcTo10   GcTo11

standing on Bencke Point site facing West   photo   about 300′
GcTo42

Metlakatla

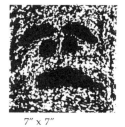

7″ x 7″

1′4″ x 2′1″

2′5″ x 3′0″

2′0″ x 4′0″

202

West of Metlakatla

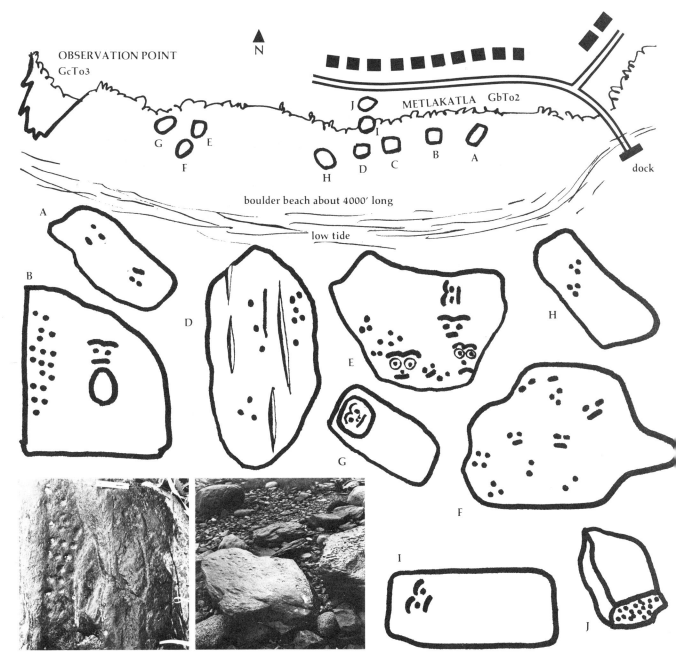

GcTo 9

OBSERVATION POINT
GcTo3

N

METLAKATLA GbTo2

J

I

G

E

F

H

D

C

B

A

dock

boulder beach about 4000′ long

low tide

A

B

D

E

G

H

F

I

J

East Carolina Island

1'0" x 1'0"

1'0" x 9"

West Carolina Island

The photograph of the petroglyph of West Carolina Island illustrates the problems of petroglyph recording in the Venn Passage, where older petroglyph have left strange patterns on schist boulders.

Ringbolt Island

GdTc 6

Unusually high summer water levels of the Skeena River covered the Ringbolt Island petroglyphs and we were unable to visit this site. We are therefore grateful to use pictures of the rubbings made in 1968 and 1969 by D.R. Walker and crew of Terrace in cooperation with members of the Kitselas and Kitsumkalam bands. The large panel is about forty feet above low water and is covered by the highwater rise of forty to fifty feet in the canyon in late May or early June.

The recording crew has had problems. In the winter the carvings are covered by snow. When the snow melts the early spring river rise makes rubbing impossible. A low water at the end of April is a good time to visit the site, before the high run off covers the petroglyphs again. Transportation to the site is by riverboat, with the permission of the Kitselas Band. The carvings are located on dangerous sloping rock faces above the swift river, and some are difficult to record without standing on the air. Ed Meade[47] has pointed out that such isolated and difficult petroglyph sites may be religious centres and that one reason so little is known of these sites was that the common people of the time probably had no knowledge of these secret and remote places.

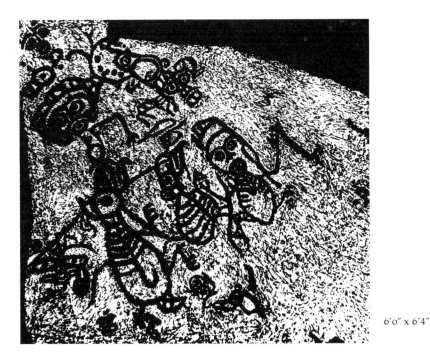

6'0" x 6'4"

Ringbolt Island

Walker[48] notes that "the one thing the people will say about these carvings is that the curliques on top of the man figure show he 'came from the sky', which also suggests shamanistic activities.

Two petroglyphs are not shown in these illustrations. One is a small fish carving (18" x 24") found in a panel of "vague figures and masks". The other is an eroded design, below water most of the year, which is a figure in the familiar west coast posture, a squatting position with arms raised.

A letter dated 1936 from Will Robinson[49] of Terrace records a frog carved on the rocks at the top end of Kitselas Canyon, on the east side, observed by Mrs. S.M. Dobbie of Copper River. A petroglyph has also been reported from Kleanza (Gold) Creek, but neither the frog nor the Kleanza petroglyph is now known.

Hagwilget Stone

A report in the Vancouver Sun[50] newspaper in 1919 reported that this sandstone slab, embedded in the gravel of a wagon road near Kispiox, had been unearthed by workmen from a depth of fifteen feet during road building operations. The stone is twenty eight inches high and has an even thickness of two and a half inches. The newspaper speculates that it came either from Nine Mile Mountain or from Kitseucla, twenty miles downstream from where it was unearthed. The Museum Notes[51] of 1927 give its provenience as Hagwilget, near Kispiox. Not only is the original site of this carved stone somewhat uncertain, but the present location is not known. Fortunately we have a photo of one of the casts made by Harlan I. Smith.

Two legends were told to "explain" the stone but doubts have been expressed about the authenicity of both. The first, attributed to an Indian named Mutiaimas, states that the heads in the corners represent two big hornets that followed a family for years, stinging them on every possible occasion, as a punishment for robbing caches. The crooked line is a trail the family would not use because of the hornets. The figure on the left is a bridge where the hornets met the eight members of the family and stung three of them to death. A second legend by Tuteige identifies the four heads as four big flies who poisoned the tail of a salmon, which then caused the death of the three Indians in one family who ate it. Tommy Jack is reported as saying that the stone was brought up from Kitseucla when the Eagles moved to Kispiox and that it belonged to the Chief and symbolized this chieftainship.[52]

National Museum photo

Kispiox

Originally reported as coming from a riverbank, near Kispiox, the stone was removed by Harlan I. Smith to the hospital grounds at Hazelton. It was subsequently taken from the Hospital and presented to the Old Hazelton Village "Treasure House", at the foot of Omineca Street in Old Hazelton. Unfortunately when the Treasure House was moved to the new 'Ksan village the stone was simply overlooked. Whether the petroglyph stone is buried under the library building now occupying the same site, or whether it rolled back into the river, no one knows.

Dr. Murphy photo

Prince Rupert

GbTo 8

A report in the National Museum files describes a petroglyph at the Government Wharf or at the C.N.R. Work Dock in Prince Rupert as being on a boulder the size of a table. No petroglyph can now be found along the Prince Rupert waterfront, but a petroglyph boulder stands outside the Museum in that city. The Museum has no information about the provenience of this boulder, but it seems smaller than table size. It has unfortunately been vandalized with the initials W. and J.

2'5" x 1'4"

Observatory Inlet

The petroglyph boulder now stands outside the Prince Rupert Museum. The plaque attached to it states: "Aboriginal pictograph presented to the City of Prince Rupert by Rev. Canon Rushbrook and Messrs. John and Albert Eyolfson." A booklet by F.W.M. Drew,[53] with information drawn from an article by Canon Rushbrook,[54] tells us that "This is really a totem in stone, and it marked the southern boundary of the hunting and fishing domain of the Nachklats family and was a deed to the land which stretched northward from An-ga-ish (where the boulder was carved) to Nishka-aks (Indian River) on Observatory Inlet. The figure in the left upper corner is identified as the Eagle crest of the Nachklats family, from whom the stone was purchased. Below is a halibut and a beaver face indicating "inter-crestal marriages". According to a record in the Department of Ethnology at the B.C. Provincial Museum, the boulder belonged to No-ak-laik, a chief of some two hundred years or more ago, who carved his crest sign first, to indicate his hunting and fishing rights in that vicinity, and his successors each added his sign or crest. This information apparently came from a descendant at Kincolith (a village on the Nass River) and was recorded by W.H. Collison.

6'0" x 2'9"

Canyon City

The private logging road into the Nass River valley crosses the desolate area of black lava. At Canyon City (Gitwunksithk, Place of Lizards) Mr. Peter Nice, eighty-five years old, showed us where the petroglyphs are carved by the old village landing, about six to eight feet above the swift flowing Nass River. The photo, in which the footbridge can be seen, shows how close the carvings are to the river and the village. Mr. Nice told us that the river had been pushed to its present location by the lava flow and that the present village had been built after the volcanic eruption by survivors of the destroyed village near the present Lava Lake. Barbeau[55] estimates the date of this catastrophe as about 1780. Mr. Nice said the petroglyphs were there before the village. In the old days, he explained, the women used to pick berries on the mountain slopes above and as it was a long distance to the old village, the men would come to help carry home the berries. As they waited for the women they amused themselves by carving the petroglyphs.

The petroglyphs appear to be carved in relation to both the present river level and the landing, which is the only suitable place for a landing for some distance, as the canyon walls are steep. Possibly future research will determine whether the present route of the Nass through the canyon is more recent than about 1780 or whether the petroglyphs mark an ancient landing.

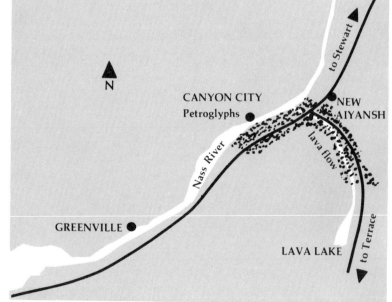

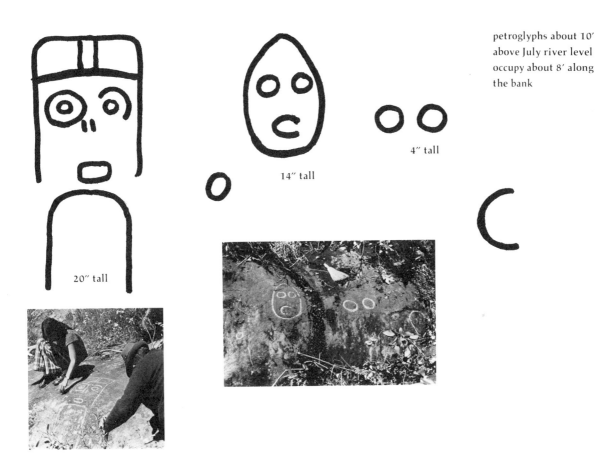

petroglyphs about 10'
above July river level
occupy about 8' along
the bank

20" tall

14" tall

4" tall

Parry Passage

GbUg 5

Petroglyphs at the north end of Graham Island have been reported by Gessler.[56] He found carvings on twenty small boulders (the largest had a circumference of three metres), the designs consisting of five faces and four motifs (a concavity, a circle, a circle and dot, and a dot).

All boulders along the beach were examined and frequently petroglyphs were found on the undersides. Although there were both sandstone and porphry boulders, only those of sandstone had petroglyphs. By experimenting, Gessler found that it would take no longer than an hour to carve the most complicated glyph. As there was no correlation between the condition of the carvings and their position (face up or down), Gessler concluded that the boulders are subject to continual movement by the surf during storms.

From a study of Gessler's precise drawings we note that the circles, and circle and dots, are usually paired as if they were meant to represent eyes.

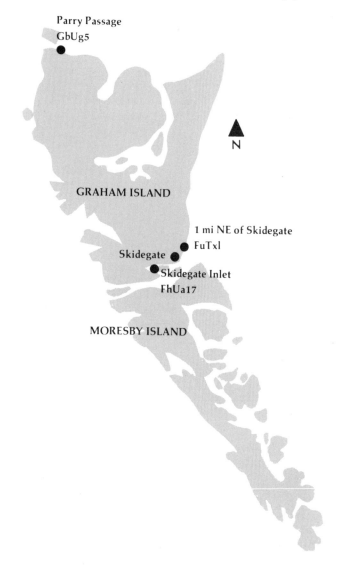

N. Gessler photo

Skidegate

C.F. Newcombe[57] took the photograph shown here of the petroglyph boulder found about a mile northeast of Skidegate on the site of a long-deserted village. He examined this stone in 1900 and noted that the Indians could give him no explanation of it. A year later he examined similar carvings near Copper Mountain Alaska but could find no interpreter for these either.

British Columbia Provincial Museum photo

Skidegate Inlet

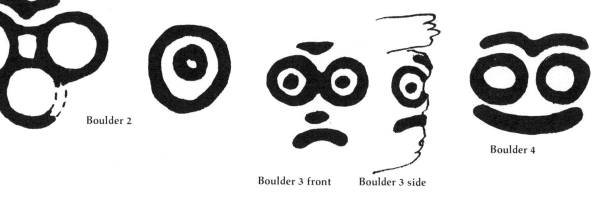

Boulder 1

Boulder 2

Boulder 3 front

Boulder 3 side

Boulder 4

Nick Gessler[58] has also reported the discovery of petroglyphs on an island in Skidegate Inlet in 1972 by the Queen Charlotte Islands Museum Society. They found petroglyphs on four boulders, each with an estimated weight of from three hundred to five hundred pounds, all within five metres of one another along the top edge of the tidal zone. The very faint designs consist of two faces and a number of circular motifs. The drawings are copied from sketches made by Gessler.

Shakes Creek

W.F. McCulloch reported this petroglyph boulder on the bank of the Stikine River across from the mouth of Shakes Creek some miles southwest of Telegraph Creek. We are also indebted to Mr. McCulloch for the photographs of the carvings.

W.F. McColloch photo

Stikine River

Approximate six miles downstream on the Stikine from Telegraph Creek between the road to Glenora and the riverbank, on a large boulder "the size of an oil drum" facing the river, is the carving of a face, approximately ten inches square. Mr. McDonald of Bobquin Lake who informed the Provincial Museum of this carving, reported that the stone had something to do with an agreement struck between Tahltan and Tlingit.

Warm Bay, Atlin Lake

Reporting a petroglyph face on a boulder on a beach at Atlin Lake, Leechman[59] stated that a local Indian claimed that the carving had been done by order of his grandfather: One of his slaves had built a long caribou fence which enabled him to get enough animals to save the tribe from starvation. The petroglyph was carved in memory of this event.

S. Connolly photo

Port Alice   *Alaska State Museum Photo*

216

5. Petroglyphs of Alaska: A Fascinating Enigma

by Michael Stephen Kennedy

An outstanding Alaskan explorer, Lt. Henry T. Allen wrote in 1886: "It is a very remarkable fact that a region under a civilized government for more than a century should remain so completely unknown as the vast territory drained by the Copper, Tanana, and Koyukuk Rivers". Allen had reason to wonder. The Copper River of Alaska was discovered in 1783, and various attempts were made thereafter to explore the stream. Topographic, climatic and natural barriers were formidable, but if, as the famed American West frontier explorer John Wesley Powell believed, "discovery breeds discovery", then almost two centuries does seem a long time. Physiographic barriers are of minor importance in explaining the lag between topographic discovery and ethnological and archaeological exploration.

Earliest known maps and even some done well into the 18th century depicted Alaska and her west coastal North Pacific and Arctic Ocean waters as *"Terra Incognito"*. Even today, nearing the end of the 20th Century, there are vast reaches of the Great Land that have not yet been surveyed, and some that are rarely traversed or seen by living man.

Historian Morgan B. Sherwood provides a fine word picture of its gargantuan scope: "Alaska is one-half larger than the thirteen original American colonies, nearly twice the size of California, Oregon, and Washington together, and as large as Great Britain, Denmark, Sweden, Norway, and the old German Empire combined. It sprawls over 16 degrees of latitude and, excluding most of the Aleutian Islands, about 36 degrees of longitude. The Yukon River drains an area in Alaska and Canada roughly equal to the combined area of California, Washington, Utah, Nevada, and Idaho — that is, most of the Far West".

As early as 1655 a Cossack named Deshnev had reported to the Imperial Russian government authorities at Yakutat that he had rounded the 'East Cape' of Asia and had sailed southwards from the 'Icy Sea' to the Pacific, thus proving that Asia and North America were separated. Again, in 1713, the Governor of Siberia sent out Henrich Busch who crossed from Kamchatka either to the Alaska mainland or the Aleutians. These reports, and other significant accounts, however, lay pigeonholed with the Siberian authorities. In order to ascertain the truth, Peter the Great designed, and his successors, the Empresses Catherine I and Anna, dispatched under the Dane, Vitus Bering, two famous expeditions. Aboard on the second expedition was the able George Wilhelm Steller, the first Naturalist to visit Alaska. It would, however, be many, many years later before any significant ethnographic studies would be made.

The pace and extent of Russian and earlier American exploration in Alaska were intimately related to the social and political atmosphere in the parent nations. During all of the Russian period (1741-1867) political attitudes in St. Petersburg were barely congenial to the promotion of inland exploration or science. In 1796 Gregory Shelikof, of the Russian American Company, however, instructed his chief manager to "note down where anything may be found in the entrails of the earth, and where beasts and birds and curious sea-shells, and other things may be found". Though Shelikof himself made reliable observations on natural history and some ethnology, his men displayed slight concern for "birds and curious sea-shells"; but they did pay attention to "beasts" that wore fur coats. When the sea otter retreated, the easy income disappeared, and with it Imperial interest in Alaska save as a pawn in the game of international politics.

The succession of naval officers to Russian company management after 1818 saw some sporadic but also some useful work by Ferdinand von Wrangell in geography, and Father Veniaminov and H.J. Holmberg in ethnology. But, in general, Russian science in Alaska for some 125 years was spotty, uncoordinated and weak. Russian inland exploration fared no better. A few probes were made along the lower Yukon, Kuskokwim, Susitna, and Copper rivers. The investigations hardly ever extended beyond the area immediately adjacent to the stream. Toward the end of the Russian period, P.N. Golovin reported officially: "The explorations that were undertaken at different times in the colonies were exceedingly superficial and wholly confined to the coast; the interior, not only of the continent but also of Sitka Island, is today still unexplored."

When the United States bought Alaska territory in 1867, it truly remained a vast *terra incognita*. Basic information was needed before anything like an intelligent understanding of the country could be entertained. In the years that followed, the Americans did a much more competent job of amassing general knowledge of Alaska; but as the Russians before them, they saw and learned very little about petroglyphs! (*Exploration of Alaska*, by Morgan B. Sherwood, Yale University Press, 1965).

The first published record of petroglyphs in Alaska, therefore, dates back only to 1890. It mentions the existence of rock carvings, and depicts two glyphs located at Wrangell. (Niblack 1890).

One of the earliest, yet most detailed descriptions of S.E. Alaska petroglyphs ever published appeared in the *American Anthropologist* in 1908. It was written by the eminent George T. Emmons. Because of its superb detail and analytic initiative it follows:

"Primitive man throughout all ages and in all regions has ever shown a desire to perpetuate the history of the past and to record the story of his life. Wanting in specific characters, he employes pictures, carvings and structures — the direct product of his surroundings — to illustrate and transmit his traditions, geneaology, and pursuits, and these are realistic or conventional according to his development.

The Tlingit of southeastern Alaska, living under most favorable conditions of climate and food supply, with abundant leisure to cultivate an innate sense of art, evolved a rich ceremonial tradition. This had for its purpose the glorification of the family in (1) the display of the totem, (2) the practice of shamanistic rites, which constituted the nearest approach to any form of religion or worship. Having at hand a variety of material, as rock, wood, grasses, the pelts of animals, and wool for weaving, besides mineral and vegetable coloring substances, Tlingit thoughts found expression in many forms of art, and they carved, painted, or wove realistic and conventional forms upon all belongings, which give a distinctive character and wealth of color to the life of this section of Southernmost Alaska.

Most permanent, but least intelligible of all the earlier works of the Tlingit are their petroglyphs. They are of frequent occurrence in the vicinity of old village sites on the islands of the Alexander archipelago and the adjacent littoral. Recent generations, even 19th century oldest natives, had no knowledge of their origin or of their raison d'etre. Some even denied that they were the product of their ancestors. Instead they attribute them to a stranger early people who, in traveling along this shore, before the Tlingits' existence, made such signs to guide them on their way in returning or in again going over the ground. But this explanation is not worthy of consideration, for the carvings are very often in secluded bays beyond the routes of travel. The glyphs mark old living sites that are still traditional with the Tlingit people, and aside from the circles, spirals, and a few indistinguishable figures, they generally agree quite literally with the characteristic art of the Tlingit for us to ascribe them to other non-Tlingit peoples.

While some are found on prominent ledges and cliffs overlooking the water, in most instances the petroglyphs ornament isolated boulders and beach rocks imbedded in the sand of the shore near the level of the tide. In the latter position they would seem to have served no useful purpose other than as a record of some tradition or legend, or as a means of displaying the emblem of the clan. In some instances they are simply the product of leisure moments and that love of the ornate that manifests itself throughout the life of this region.

In all the petroglyphs examined, the grooves, apparently made by pecking, are in width from one half to three quarters of an inch, ranging in depth from one eighth to one fourth of an ínch according to their state of preservation.

Some glyphs show considerable age, while in others the marks of the pecking implement are still clearly visible. From the corroborative evidence of contemporary events the one discovered on Baranof island was in situ at the beginning of the nineteenth century; but how much earlier is unknown, for the Kake-satter family of the Sitka tribe, whose country this was, say that their chief, Katlean, who led the attack and destroyed the first Russian fort at Old Sitka in 1802, had a house on the shore at this point and used this rock as a seat.

What appears to be the older carvings show less realism, are more severe in outline, and are wanting in detail; and more often the principal characters are joined by means of numerous lines, circles, and irregular forms that are meaningless in themselves, but serve the purpose of making one connected picture which represents a story. In those carvings that, from the roughly pecked fractures made by the hand-stone, can be identified absolutely as of more recent workmanship, the forms are very true to nature and are much more ornate; and in a majority of cases the figures occupy separate fields, or if together, are not connected and apparently bear no relation to one another.

In 1888, while hunting in one of the deep bays that indent the western coast of Baranof Island, I met a very old native who claimed the locality by hereditary right, and in consideration of some presents was induced to show me a carved rock that my native hunters knew existed but had never seen.

It was near the mouth of a stream, at the edge of the woods, a short distance above the high-tide mark. Hereabouts, at least a century back, was a small village of which nothing remains and even the exact site is uncertain. The boulder was irregular in shape but approaching a pyramidal form, some four feet high and of equal dimensions at the base. It was partly covered by a great decayed tree trunk, and wholly concealed by the branches and high salt water grass. We could remove the obstructions from but one of the three faces, which was completely covered with a single closely connected picture, made up apparently of five principal figures. The grooved lines were almost obliterated in places by weathering, giving evidence of considerable age. The two covered sides were, I believe, ornamented. Although I could not clear them more than to feel some grooves, my guide interpreted the design, not perhaps from his own ideas, but rather from what he had been told by those who had gone before. When I had finished my examination, with something akin to reverence he covered the markings over completely with branches and debris, and as he and the native hunters who accompanied me have long since gone to their fathers, it remains today a forgotten monument of the past.

The picture is a complex arrangement of distinct figures connected throughout. My guide, a very primitive old Tlingit, could identify only the individual forms. To any one familiar with the mythology of this people their context clearly tells the oldest story of mankind — the creation.

This legend, common to all the Northwest Coast tribes, is familiar. The world in the beginning was a chaotic mass of rock and ocean, enveloped in darkness and possessed by a few powerful spirits which jealously guarded the elements necessary to human life. A benign spirit, known as Yehlh, who assumed many

Baranof Is.

221

forms but more often appeared in the guise of a raven, came upon the scene, created man, and wrestling from the other spirits light, fresh water, and fire, he governed the winds, gave to his children all these benefits, and then disappeared.

In the glyph picture Yehlh is distinguished by the head and long bill attached to what appears to be a body with a leg and a foot in the double curved line depending from the head. To the rear the tail coming from the circle connects with *Una kgna hihk,* 'where the sunlight comes from'. In the bill of the raven is a half-obliterated line which might signify the piece of fire that Yehlh stole from the sun and gave to the earth, but his principal connection with the sun was its release from captivity to light the world. Joined with the raven above and to the right is a figure, made up of three concentric circles that represents the earth. Directly above this is a highly conventional form identified as *Hoon,* the north wind, that plays an important part in the life of this northern country. To the left, above and over the center is *Kun-nook,* the guardian of fresh water, shown often in painting and carving as a wolf form, from whom Yehlh stole a few drops in his bill and which, as he flew over the world, he let fall here and there, forming the rivers and the lakes.

Near the northwestern extremity of Etoline Island, included between two jutting rocky points, is a stretch of sand beach, and scattered along at and above the level of the tide are numerous smooth dark-gray rocks, seldom exceeding three feet in dimensions, irregular in shape, but generally presenting a flattened surface suitable for petroglyphs. Nearly all of these bear single

Etoline Is.

figures, pecked in shallow grooves, representing a variety of subjects, in most instances so realistic that the artist's meaning is unmistakable. Parts of several have been obliterated by the elements and the wash of the tide, or have never been finished, which make their identification uncertain, while two or three in which several indeterminate figures are grouped convey no intelligent meaning. The animal designs, which largely predominate, are all totemic in character, representing the principal emblems of the family divisions of the

Sitkine tribe that inhabits this locality. Within the limits of the choice of subjects it would appear that the shape of the rock surface to be ornamented determined the selection of the particular character to be employed, that it might cover the greater space.

These carvings are unquestionably of two distinct periods. In the older ones the grooves are worn smooth and in places are almost lost to view through weathering and the action of the higher tides. Others, of a comparatively more recent date, show the roughened indentations of the pecking implement. Explanation of this difference is that the old village site at this point was occupied at two different periods, which with the Tlingit was not an uncommon practice. The natives hereabouts can offer no explanation for the making of these pictures, nor as to their age; they simply say that they were there in the lives of their fathers, which means nothing," Emmons stated.

In 1917, a series of petroglyphs further north on Kodiak Island which, during the Russian period was Aleut sea otter hunting grounds, was reported by Captain C.A. Halvorsen of the Alaska Packer's Association (320-2). The designs on a cliff face of this large and historic island included several human faces (consisting of eyes, eyebrows, nose and mouth, and "minimal face" [Clark 1960:18]), animal figures (whales, porpoises), and geometric designs. Although these glyphs differ markedly from those in the panhandle of Southeastern Alaska, they have since been considered by both Heizer and Clark to have also derived their basic style from Northwest Coast petroglyphs (Heizer 1947:292-3; Clark 1971:14).

During the 1920's, many petroglyph sites in British Columbia and the northwestern states were reported, to shed further light. H.I. Smith of Canada contributed much of the new and valuable information; and any study of the meaning and artistic style of petroglyphs of the Northwest Coast Indians should refer to his work (Smith 1909; 1923; 1924; 1925; 1927a; 1927b). (See also de Laguna 1956:106-7). None were reported in the Aleutians.

In 1927, interest developed again in the southeastern Alaska petroglyphs. In the summer of that year, several new petroglyphs were discovered at Kalinin Bay near Sitka, (a site still rich in rock carvings). An agreement was made between the mayor of Sitka, W.R. Hanlon, and Father Andrew Kashevaroff, the first Curator of the Alaska Territorial Museum. The two men agreed to remove these petroglyphs from their original site and for better surveillance and preservation display them in the two towns. Two would be taken to Sitka (the two now at the base of the flag pole there are presumably the same), and two would go to the museum in Juneau. Unfortunately, the location of the petroglyphs slated for Juneau has not been discovered; apparently they never arrived, or were lost or stolen.

Following the discovery of these glyphs, Father Kashevaroff inquired further of the native community about such carvings. He received an explanation from Andrew Davis of Angoon in January of 1930 (private communication to Fr. Kashevaroff, January 11, 1930, in Alaska Historical Library files). Davis, a Tlingit Indian, explained that the petroglyphs might: (1) be ownership signs, designating that a certain area was owned by a particular clan; (2) signify the story or creature from which a certain place derived its name; or (3) commemorate a tragic death or battle.

Although Davis' explanations seemed plausible, one must remember that a generation before his letter was written, a more experienced seeker, Emmons, had been unable to find a single native who could explain the presence of petroglyphs. Davis' testimony, therefore, must be taken in light of this knowledge. It is possible that he was simply offering to Kashevaroff a personal conjecture, and had no more real knowledge of the meaning of the rocks than had Emmons' informants.

By the 1940's, an increasing number of petroglyphs as well as pictographs (paintings on rocks, usually in red ochre, or hematite) had been reported; not only in Southeastern Alaska and Kodiak, but in some widely scattered locations of the vast interior, from the Arctic Sea to the Bering Sea; but still excluding the Aleutians.

Second Curator of the Alaska Territorial Museum, Edward Keithahn's article in *American Antiquity* was the first attempt to integrate available information on known Alaskan petroglyphs into a coherent theory and story. He, like Emmons before him, found that most natives were understandably unknowledgeable; they as well as the scientists neither knew who carved them, nor why they were carved. The work predated any record or direct knowledge of how done, or by whom. Glyphs were carved to "cause rain" (Keithahn 1940:130). Keithahn believed this was plausible, since only with an ample rainfall would there be a good salmon run and because salmon had been the staple food for southeastern natives in precontact days and perhaps for centuries. Keithahn felt it logical that the people would be concerned about the amount of rain they received.

Keithahn also presented a theory, based on all the conjectures he had heard and on the data he collected. His theory could further explain the existence of the petroglyphs. Since petroglyphs are often found by a particularly abundant stream than by one with a smaller salmon run, Keithahn rationalized that the carvings may have been part of a supplication ritual designed to insure a good salmon harvest. The images that were carved were totemic or legendary figures. Therefore, Keithahn reasoned, they were either creatures in favor with the Salmon Chief (the supernatural being responsible for sending salmon to humans), or were the clan crests of the Indian owners of the salmon streams. Furthermore, Keithahn had established that the images are always situated with the carvings facing the sea, and are often at high tide level. This indicated to him that the "Tlingit glyphs" were meant to be submerged by high tide each day, thus dispatching their potential prayer at regular intervals (1940:132).

There have been no later theories advanced in explanation since Keithahn's article. de Laguna, in 1949, again was unable to find any Tlingit informant who could tell her anything about the rock carvings of Angoon. These are quite similar to the Wrangell and Etolin Island petroglyphs, and presumably were done by the same group of people for the same reasons. Beyond this, de Laguna does not conjecture.

Wrangell

Determining the age of any petroglyph in Alaska has always been a problem, one which has not yet been resolved. Keithahn did attempt to set up a relative dating scheme; postulating that the simplest designs (those which were the results of abrading the surfaces of the rock) were the oldest. These simple designs consist of circles and grooves, and are said to have preceded the more elaborate designs, done later, made by pecking the rock. This chronology is a shakey one at best, for it takes no account of several factors which might have determined the aspect of a particular rock carving. The following, for instance, should be considered as variables affecting the design of a petroglyph:

1) skill of the carver
2) time available for executing the carving
3) purpose of the carving: was it simply a doodle, design or indeed a meaningful totemic symbol?
4) Hardness of the rock being carved.

There are undoubtedly other variables which can only be explained when more becomes known of the true history of petroglyphs. At present, the only substantive information on the age of known carvings is Emmons' estimation of pre-nineteenth century as a date. That Alaskan petroglyphs were carved in pre-contact times has been hypothesized by Keithahn on the basis of the tools supposedly used in the carving. Substantial numbers of hammerstones and stone tools have been found in pre-contact archaeological sites, and it is quite possible, as Keithahn suggests, that these were used in pecking out the designs on the boulders (Keithahn 1962:71-2; see also Keithahn 1953). On the other hand, the fact that the designs on many petroglyphs are quite elaborate, points to a date perhaps not long before contact (Heizer 1947:293).

By now, and for the past 70 years, most Tlingit Indians in southeastern Alaska have been aware of the existence of petroglyphs; and most Indians feel that their ancestors carved them. More stories connected with certain petroglyphs are now coming to light (Berner's Bay petroglyphs, near Juneau, for example), although it has not been determined whether such recent stories are a fairly new development or have been handed down in family legend for generations. Some Alaskan pictographs have specific legends attached to them as well which later prove of value for glyphs. For instance, the faded pictograph at Hoonah, said to have been painted with the blood of Angoon warriors who once attacked the village of Hoonah. A version of the legend is recounted in Swanton's *Tlingit Myths and Tests* (1909:72-9). Similarly, a pictograph at Halleck Harbor in Saginaw Bay was supposedly painted after a battle between the Tlingit people of Kake and a group of Tsimshians; and is said to have been painted in Tsimshian blood, according to Henry Davis of Juneau.

The legends associated with some pictographs point out what may prove an interesting possibility regarding their relationship with the more abundant petroglyphs. If Keithahn's theory, which holds that some petroglyphs were carved as part of a supplication ceremony to the Salmon Chief, is correct, and if the legends about the pictographs are to be taken into account, then petroglyphs and pictographs may have been either unrelated or related phenomena in pre-contact Tlingit culture. If pictographs were, in fact, drawn to commemorate a battle or other catastrophic event, they were a special phenomena. If petroglyphs, on the other hand, were a frequently executed art form, and occurred at most salmon streams, they may have had attached to them the aura of the rarer pictographs. Their carving may not have been an unusual event, but one which was repeated fairly often. The fact that there are many more petroglyphs than pictographs in S.E. Alaska also suggests that the two were not comparable art forms (although this could be due to the better preservation of the petroglyphs; while pictographs could have been more easily washed away or buried by cave-ins and rock falls).

While Keithahn was studying locatable petroglyphs in southeast Alaska, other archaeologists, anthropologists and laymen were studying rock carvings and paintings farther north and west. Heizer in 1947 studied the petroglyphs which Halvorsen had found in 1917 at Cape Alitak on Kodiak Island. More about this later. Osgood (1937) and de Laguna (1934) reported various pictographs in Cook Inlet (Tuxedni Bay and Kachemak Bay) and de Laguna investigated five important pictograph locations, alone, in Prince William Sound (1956). These petroglyphs and pictographs all resemble each other closely, as do the petroglyphs later found on Afognak Island near Kodiak (Clark: 1971). Petroglyphs are generally situated (as are those in Southeastern Alaska) facing the sea and near high tide mark. Pictographs are found, almost entirely, in caves, on cliffs, or overhangs. Heizer (1947:292) suggests that the Kodiak area petroglyphs were derived from early Northwest Coast forms. In both Kodiak and Southeast Alaska, identical cup shapes, circles, spirals, and five-pointed stars have been found. Heizer and de Laguna also suggest that the rock paintings and carvings may have been done by hunters; perhaps members of the secret whale hunting societies which existed in pre-contact and early contact Koniag and Chugach cultures (de Laguna 1934:153-4).

Heizer postulates that the petroglyphs on Kodiak and Afognak Islands could be assigned to the Koniag archaeological phase; that, late pre-contact up to the early 19th century. He has made this judgment on two counts: first, assuming that the Kodiak petroglyphs are derived from early Northwest Coast petroglyphs, they must have developed after other Northwest Coast art forms. The rather elaborate totemic designs on many southeastern glyphs point to a fairly late date; hence, a late date is assigned to the Kodiak glyphs as well. Secondly, Heizer and Clark (1964) compared Alaskan petroglyphs with other Koniag art forms which have been found in situ in archaeological sites and can hence be dated with reasonable accuracy. Specifically compared were the many incised slate tablets and figurines found by Hrdlicka at the Uyak Bay site and by Clark (1960;1964) at various locations near Kodiak. These figurines, whose use is unknown, are incised to depict human facial features and clothing. Many of the elements in the tablets, such as the "minimal face", are identical with those in the Cape Alitak and Afognak Island petroglyphs.

The dating of these incised figures is by no means certain. In Clark's "Incised Figurine Tablets from Kodiak, Alaska", he suggests that the slate tablets might be older than had previously been suspected. The Koniag culture phase, of which they are believed to be a part, could extend back as far as 1000 to 1200 A.D. (Clark 1964:123). Presumably, then, the age of many petroglyphs would also be pushed back several centuries.

The remaining petroglyphs and pictographs in the interior and northern coast of Alaska have not, to this date, been established into any general or unified scheme. Although there are pictographs in the Aleutians, no petroglyphs have been found. Not only are Alaskan petroglyphs isolated geographically, but they

Afognak

also seem to be isolated in meaning from each other, as well as from the Kodiak-Chugach-Tlingit phenomena. Compared to southeastern, not too many are known at this time.

During the summer of 1972, the Alaska State Museum, under the sponsorship of the Alaska Department of Natural Resources, State Parks Division, undertook the first complete survey of petroglyphs and pictographs in Alaska, including the vast Aleutian chain. The purpose of the survey was to draw together all previously published, as well as unpublished, records of petroglyphs and pictographs in Alaska. Further, as many petroglyphs as possible were to be located, studied, and photographed, in situ; with a future possibility of nominating them to the U.S. National Register as significant antiquities.

Two people worked on the museum survey. Edward T. Stevens, a graduate student at the University of Alaska, traveled to as many of the reported sites as possible, photographed all known or locatable petroglyphs, and gathered pertinent related field data; Patricia Partnow, Anthropologist, and Exhibits Specialist at the Museum, researched written records, obtained oral information on all known locations or sites, and collated the significant source information. Much of this chapter is based on the work of Ms. Partnow and Mr. Stevens.

The 1972 survey was not intended to be limited to any particular area of Alaska. It was decided, however, as a practical matter based on funds available, that field research should be focused only on southeastern Alaska; there being more reported petroglyphs there than in any other area; none known to be in the Aleutians; and the time allotted being limited to only the warm summer months.

The survey was further limited by weather and logistical factors. Any field study of Alaskan petroglyphs must allow for full-time use of a boat. Searching the shore from a boat is the only feasible way of locating most glyphs. Through the generous loan by the Smithsonian Institution of a Boston Whaler, Stevens was able to work the entire month of August, the last month of the survey, at a minimal cost. Had the boat been available in June and July as well, many more site reports could have been researched, or at least visited and photographed.

The procedure used in locating previously reported petroglyph sites was this: all available published resources had been studied in advance, and a list of known locations compiled by Ms. Partnow. Community resources were also tapped. Museum correspondence and unpublished records from the State Historical Library were fully reviewed. Local residents, particularly Tlingit and Haida people, with special knowledge of southeastern Alaska's terrain; and others who had spent years on fishing vessels in the area, were also questioned.

The United States Forest Service multiple-use grid maps of Alaska proved useful for Museum perusal. With as much information as possible in hand, Ed Stevens then traveled to the villages seeking actual petroglyphs in each area. If no petroglyphs were immediately discernible from the boat, Stevens then walked along the beach, and sometimes inland; either until he found a glyph or until he determined that to spend more time in one area was ill-advised. At all times care had to be taken not to visit areas at high tide, for many petroglyphs are submerged during high tide.

In photographing petroglyphs, Stevens attempted first to obtain pictures without using chalk to outline the grooves in the rock. It was felt that a photograph of an untouched petroglyph would be far more valuable for scientific study than would a chalked one. Tracing the pecked grooves involves a selective and subjective determination of where, or if grooves actually exist. In most cases, this is a difficult determination for the rock may have eroded so much since it was originally carved, that grooves are not visible to the naked eye. Rubbings, made on webril with printers' ink, were found to be preferable in depicting an accurate image of the petroglyphs; and where time allowed, this was done.

In many cases, it was impossible due to adverse light or weather conditions, to obtain a clear image without some outlining. In these instances, Stevens first experimented by rubbing clam shell into the grooves. He preferred this to the more permanent chalk, since it easily washes away. The clam shell was not of a consistency to rub off and fill grooves evenly, however, so this was abandoned. In the end, the stone grooves generally were chalked before glyphs were photographed.

For petroglyph photography, aluminum powder and water in the grooves, rather than chalk, appears to have definite advantages. Aluminum powder is less permanent than chalk and hence does not leave evidence of petroglyphs to potential defacers; aluminum also has light-reflecting properties, which enable photographs to come out more clearly than if chalk were used. This latter advantage will prove to be very helpful in working with the petroglyphs in Alaska, hereafter, because the summer season is so short and many days are overcast and dark due to heavy rainfall, fog and overcast.

In 1917 a brief note on the remarkable petroglyphs at Cape Alitak on the southwest side of Kodiak Island appeared in the *American Anthropologist*; then there was a long gap until 1944 when Dr. Ales Hrdlicka described this locality in detail and took a number of excellent photographs. Three years later, Robert F. Heizer produced an able, illustrated paper on the subject which valiantly attempts to provide a fairly full set of illustrations of the inscriptions, interpretations of the significance and age of these petroglyphs. According to Heizer, Kodiak Island was for centuries the home of the Koniag people or

Kaniagmiut, an Eskimoan group, who occupied the whole island as well as portions of the adjacent Alaska Peninsula. Archaeological investigations show that at an earlier time another people, physically and to a certain extent culturally distinct, held the island. The petroglyphic inscriptions are attributed to Koniag authorship.

The locale of the Kodiak Island petroglyphs is Cape Alitak, a seaward point, the extension of Tanner Head which is separated from the mainland of the island by Alitak Lagoon and Rodman Reach. There are two separate petroglyph localities. The first is at the tip of the Cape on the granite cliffs and boulders. The second location is about one half mile northeast on a cliff near the beach. The first locality covers an area of about three acres, but there is less detailed record of the extent of the second rather extensive area based on the number of known inscriptions both on the beach and on the hill which rises from the shore. More may yet be found.

Size of individual inscribed figures varies from six to twenty-four inches overall. The glyphs, according to Heizer, were made by pecking with incisions ranging from one-quarter to three-quarters of an inch in depth, and about three-quarters to one inch wide. "In general, they appear decisive, sure, and clean cut. Although this feature may be only the result of careful craftsmanship, it may also be an indication that the additional use of colored pigments in the incisions was not an absolute necessity, since the engraved lines alone were effectively sharply defined. The full figures (of humans and cetaceans) are incised overall; that is, the whole design is depressed by pecking. The technique is comparable to a silhouette rather than an outlined representation. The two techniques are combined in a cetacean where the mouth is left elevated (i.e. outlined). Ancient native pigments would have long since disappeared through weathering. None of the designs are protected by overhanging walls, and indeed, many of the symbols occur at points where the highest tides and storm waves cover them", Heizer reported in 1947.

Cape Alitak, Kodiak Is.

230

Cape Alitak, Kodiak Is.

The petroglyphic designs of Cape Alitak were classified as follows:

I. Human figure:
a. Complete figure.
b. Figure part: Faces with facial outline, and
c. Figure part: Faces without outline, features only.

II. Animal figures:
a. Cetaceans.
b. Land animals.

III. Azoic designs (mostly geometric forms)
spiral, star, X-figure, lines of dots, miscellaneous single elements.

The cetaceans are more concentrated on certain rocks. They represent the sperm whale, killer whale and perhaps porpoise or beluga. There are several complete human figures, simple "stick figures" with a dot for a head and one figure with a rounded body and holding a hoop in a half raised arm. A circle with an attached line with short spurs may also represent a conventionalized human figure. The attempt to represent the upper part of the human figure with the head, bent arms, and fingers is quite distinctive and unique. Land animals are not identifiable with certainty, but some horned form is suggested. Among the designs which bear no obvious connection to life forms there are clockwise and counter-clockwise spirals, an X-figure, a five pointed star with ring center, a wing-like design, intersecting circles and varied curvilinear lines and combinations.

Dr. Hrdlicka, Mr. Hart, and Captain Halvorsen all made inquiries among the neighboring later-day Koniag about these petroglyphs and always received the standard answer, "from the old people". Thus these can hardly be placed within the last century or two. de Laguna received similar replies, and in her analysis of the Cook Inlet rock paintings (which include pictures of whales) she suggests that they were probably made by shamans or whale-hunters. The Koniag hunted whales extensively, and hunters formed a small, hereditary socio-economic group of rich men who jealously guarded their secrets, and resorted to caves where mummified bodies of dead whalers were kept. The south coast of Kodiak Island had special whaling villages. One of them was near Cape Alitak at Sitkalidak according to Hrdlicka. Among the fragmentary data on record regarding ceremonial observances connected with Kodiak whale hunting there is no specific reference to whalers making petroglyphs, but rock paintings were generally made by hunters, and among these undoubtedly were those specialists who pursued the whale.

Evidence in support of the hypothesis that the Cape Alitak petroglyphs were the handiwork of the Koniags appears in two unusual thin flat ovoid pieces of tabular black slate which have on each surface lightly incised designs and a human face, the whole representing a possible clothed human figure. These come from the uppermost levels of the great Uyak Bay site, and are almost certainly attributable to the ancestors of the modern Koniag (whom the Russians first encountered on Kodiak Island at the time of its discovery in the middle eighteenth century). These two pieces of evidence are in the United States National Museum.

As analyzed by Heizer: the first is five inches long, two inches wide and 3/16 inch thick. The face is simply portrayed by an arch for eyebrows and a vertical line to represent the nose. Two short lines indicate the mouth. Scratches on the cheeks and/or chin is a line with vertical spurs on both obverse and reverse, and on the former an interrupted line of four short vertical bars which could perhaps indicate tattoo marks or a string of beads. Legs and arms are not represented. Rows of spurred lines, arranged vertically on the obverse and horizontally on the reverse might be interpreted as gutskin clothingseams with the usual tufted decorations five inches long, 3-7/16 inches wide and 1/4 inch thick. The obverse and reverse faces are similar to each other as well as to the two in figure one. The obverse of this figure is weathered. Light incisions are so obliterated that only fragments can be made out with certainty. The reverse surface design is somewhat different from the obverse. It is composed of metopes or panels bordered by spurred lines. That these represent a patchwork clothing article is possible, though there are few known ethnographic-archaeologic specimens which bear decorations that specifically resemble those on the slate tablets.

"The most significant feature of these inscribed slate tablets is the treatment of the face, which is so similar to those inscribed on the granite cliffs at Cape Alitak that we may safely infer genetic style relationship," Heizer states. He continues: "The problem of outside relationships may now be approached. Petroglyphs do not seem to be an Eskimo culture trait, and I have not found any references to them from further north. It is improbable, however, that they are completely absent, since some coastal (Western) Eskimos have no doubt had sufficiently close contact with the interior Athabascan Indians to have occasionally been exposed to rock engravings or rock engravers.

It is clear that we should not look to the north for the source of the Alitak petroglyphs, but in another direction. Toward the south in the territories of the Northwest Coast Indians we find an abundance of petroglyphs. Published reports include those by Niblack, Drucker, Keithahn, Paalen, Hoffman, Smith, Boas, and Emmons. Drucker illustrates an outlined face which is decidedly reminiscent of those on Kodiak Island and is even more suggestive of the incised slates. Drucker mentions faces without lines. This would seem to be an aribtrary feature and may therefore be listed as a trait of the petroglyphic complex which affiliates Kodiak with the Northwest Coast. Keithahn shows several petroglyph designs which are exact duplicates of Kodiak glyphs, both the clockwise and counter clockwise spirals, the five pointed "star" with hollow center, and one face whose features are similar to the Kodiak un-outlined faces. Emmons also illustrates, from southeastern Alaska's Tlingit territory, the Kodiak type of non-outlined face, as well as the star, and spiral. This is not an exhaustive comparison, but is sufficient in indicating that Kodiak petroglyph complex is probably derivable from further south on the Pacific coast in territory occupied by the Tlingit, Haida, Tsimshian, and northern Kwakiutl. There is nothing startling in such a conclusion since Pacific Eskimo culture was heavily influenced in the social and material departments by the Indians of the Northwest Coast. The stimulus to indulge in petroglyphic inscription fell on fertile ground since the art of stone-pecking was very well developed on Kodiak as attested by the old and excellent lamp sculpture, and numerous objects (mauls, heavy splitting adzes) made by the stone-pecking technique.

It is quite apparent that the Kodiak rock engravings are linked with those of the Northwest Coast which here includes the coast region as far south as Puget Sound. Even at this southernmost extremity the stylistic resemblances are sufficiently close so that one would unhesitatingly attribute Kodiak and Gulf of Georgia petroglyphs to the same complex. Since most of the Northwest Coast petroglyphs portray more or less directly the distinctive, representative, and symbolic designs of the modern (traditional) art style of this region, and because there is considerable evidence indicating the latter as a recent development, we may infer that the petroglyphs of the North Pacific Coast are also assignable to fairly late times. This conclusion, insofar as it concerns Kodiak, is consistent with that arrived at earlier through other lines of evidence," Heizer states.

Anthropologist Phillip Drucker, however, believes that the earliest inhabitants of the northern coasts — people with whom the ancestors of the modern Kwakiutl and Nootka came into contact (or who may also have been their ancestors) — possessed a culture, if not specifically Eskimo, at least Eskimoid in its essential features. "Theirs must have been the southernmost extension of the highly specialized and ancient circumpolar tradition. That is, the ancestral culture of the Northwest Coast, whether it was specifically 'Eskimo' with all the cultural and ethnic connotations of the term, or, as may have been the case, was a slightly watered-down derived version, nonetheless was based on the essential patterns of ancient Western Eskimo civilization. It was a culture oriented toward the sea, with an emphasis on navigation and the hunting of sea mammals, and a tradition of neat craftsmanship in working wood and bone. If the Eskimoid type of the original Northwest Coast culture is eventually proved, it will go a long way toward explaining the uniqueness of the Northwest Coast in relation to aboriginal cultures of ethnographic times in western North America," Drucker believes. He further states: "An older interpretation of Northwest Coast culture as essentially an extension of that of northeast Asia, contacts with which were disrupted by 'the intrusion of the Eskimo into western Alaska' no longer can be sustained. Investigations of recent years in Eskimo and Aleut archaeology demonstrate that those people have occupied the shores of Bering Strait, southwest Alaska, and the Aleutian Islands continuously since long before the birth of Christ. The Asiatic influences that reached the Northwest Coast must have been transmitted by Eskimo and Aleut, or else formed a part of the ancestral sea hunting culture. In fine, all the light of modern evidence fits the hypothesis that the source of the Northwest Coast Civilization, as we know it from modern ethnography, was a derivation of that of the ancient Eskimo. Those old patterns were modified and adapted to the richer and milder environment in the course of time; then further modified and eventually enriched and elaborated to new heights by the ancestors of the Tlingit, Haida, and Tsimshian, and Salishan-speaking peoples as well, who worked their way down the coast from the interior," Drucker concludes.

Some Alaskan petroglyph designs are more Eskimoid than Totemic. Were they created then, before the advent of the presently identified historic cultures of the Northwest Coast? Did they come from a people neither Aleut, Eskimo or early Indian? Until more precise dating is done; until considerable more new evidence develops we shall not know with a strong degree of certainty who created the Alaska petroglyphs, or why and for what precise purpose they were done. It is a fascinating mystery. The enigma persists.

Of the greatest period, Robert Tyler Davis, has said it well: "The Indians of the Northwest Coast of America developed a culture with a tremendously rich artistic expression. The expressions were sometimes powerful and dramatic, sometimes fine and delicate; but always they were alive. The art is one that had something to say, and what the artist made was not only useful in the material sense but functioned also in telling part of the story of a whole culture. The artist was never content to make an empty or a meaningless decoration. Even when his products were made to serve practical purposes the shapes and decorations were devised to have meaning; and even further, a meaning that would enhance the use of the product.

The objects, in wood, horn, bone (sea shell, native copper, stone) and the other raw materials found along the coast, all have an expansive vitality that is striking. One can feel a deep flow of energy that poured itself out in making the great variety of objects needed by the society: massive heraldic house posts, made to support the beams of a spacious house where several related families lived and where the clan's ceremonies also were enacted; still larger totem poles which stood outside the house to announce the heraldic affiliations of its owner; colossal feast dishes in the form of recumbent human or animal figures (a great hollowed-out log from which a variety of foods could be served to a throng of guests), as well as small carved charms used by the medicine men; graceful and elegant horn spoons carved with the owner's crest; and ingeniously devised dance rattles. These are only a few of the things that were carved and constructed in three dimensions.

Decoration in two dimensions was spread over the planks of house fronts, over Chilkat ceremonial blankets, on the appliqued bead and button-decorated shirts, and on mantles made from trade blankets or of painted buckskin. Flat surfaces were often carved as well as painted, as plain surfaces were avoided except as occasional contrast.

Everywhere there is a feeling that the shapes are easy and appropriate. Techniques may be elaborate and difficult, but the creative impulse seems always sustained by the knowledge that the work was useful and essential. The same conventional motifs were repeated again and again, but fitted with amazing facility to the varied shapes they enliven and decorate. The common stock of designs was adapted with seemingly endless ease and ingenuity to the whole range of surfaces. It is clear that these people were artists of extraordinary creative energy, skill, and ingenuity, working within a culture whose institutions provided generously for using and sustaining their talents.

The people of this cultural area on the northwest Coast were divided into a number of distinct language groups, each with dialects and subdialects. They were as divided, by language and details of customs, as are contemporary Europeans. Yet they show a surprising cultural unity. There are differences in the details of the organization, customs, and interests of the various groups, but they are all closely related in their culture. In the rapid development of their cultural expression during the 1800's they freely borrowed institutions, techniques, and ceremonies across the language barriers. The cultural unity was no doubt the result of the identical environment of all the groups, and all made a similar adjustment to it. All were shut off to the north by the rugged and frigid conditions, to which the quite different race of the Eskimo made another and remarkable adjustment. Back of the coast all were cut off completely from the rest of the American continent by the great mountain ranges as well as the unfriendly woods. To the south, beyond the Columbia River, the more open coast kept them from any but occasional expeditions in the direction. So, enclosed by these physical barriers, developed a singularly homogeneous culture which gave all their artistic expression a definite and indigenous character. A striking characteristic of the work is the unity that pervades it. One can at once recognize a Northwest Coast object, wherever one encounters it. Even if the piece is so unusual as to be unique, one still knows that it belongs unmistakably to the Northwest Coast. Established designs are repeated over and over, never twice the same, but based on a model carried in the maker's mind. These motifs were the heritage of the culture, and although varied by the personal imagination and the ability of the artist, they give that unmistakable unity to the objects which makes recognition inevitable," Davis wrote in part, describing the great Rasmussen Alaskan collection at the Portland Art Museum.

Although there are similarities between Northwest Coast art forms and petroglyphs there are also contradictions and dissimilarities: the glyphs continue to be a provocative enigma. Part of this may be explained by age. Most of the great known ethnographic art objects are historic. They date, mostly from late 1600 to 1900. The oldest of the petroglyphs — in fact most of the great or most significant glyphs appear to be pre or proto historic. They generally predate the flowering, or apex of Northwest Coast art, it would appear. They are that much different from the general style and form or recognizeable Northwest Coast Indian art. Yet the nuances are pervasive!

But the fact remains: a real break-through of all known facts must yet come. These fascinating historic objects, more Eskimoid to some specialists; strongly and clearly totemic to many more experts, and above all unique and exciting in their own right, are part of a vanished heritage. Perhaps some day we may know almost exactly how and why they came into being and by whom. Maybe the mystery and the anticipation — once solved, will be anticlimatic.

Yet the petroglyphs of Alaska just as they are, are worthy of extensive further study and exploration. Every possible effort must be made to preserve and protect these unique antiquities of the Great Land!

Hetta Inlet

6. Petroglyphs
of the Lower Columbia River
and the Dalles Area

Our survey of coastal petroglyphs began with Puget Sound and moved north to the Aleutians, leaving the southern boundary area to the last. We have chosen this order because the Columbia petroglyphs fit somewhat awkwardly into the petroglyph style area and because a discussion of stylistic details will lead us into the following chapter, an analysis of petroglyph designs. As the Northwest Coast culture area extends from Alaska to northern California, a survey of the rock art of the region must include an examination of the lower Columbia carvings. Certainly the Indian inhabitants of the southern area, the Chinook and the Yurok, are Northwest Coast people in most aspects of their cultures. And yet, speaking of the petroglyphs, Cain[1] observed that "Any one familiar with the typical art style of the Northwest Coast is immediately impressed by the complete difference from the petrography of the Columbia River. In no case is it possible to show the slightest connection between the two." Our initial impression was the same as Cain's. Most of our reading had led us to expect a Northwest Coast undercurrent in the petroglyphs of the lower Columbia area, with a strong influence from the interior of the continent, and the two forces interacting to produce a developed Columbia River style: ultimately we found all three, but our first reaction was to agree with Cain.

We came to the Columbia River at Portland, where it flows through the flat coastal rain forest. Long before we reached The Dalles, travelling eastward beside the wide river, the country began to change. At about the Hood River the Douglas fir was being replaced by oak and pine, and all trees had dwindled away when we reached the mountain barrier at The Dalles. There the high barren hills were covered with sagebrush, with occasional willows along the banks of streams. It is colder there in winter and hotter in the summer. The winds, channelled by the Columbia valley, blow so fiercely that wind warning signs have had to be posted along the highway. There were sand drifts beside the road. To us, after two years of searching for petroglyphs on the rain coast, this was different country indeed. We had left the wet forest behind us and the petroglyphs also were no longer the same.

Through hundreds of tributary rivers and creeks the waters of the high plateaus drain into the awesome Columbia River. All this water must plunge to the coast plain through the gap at The Dalles. Before the completion of the Dalles Dam in 1961, the river descended eighty-one feet through a narrow twelve-mile slot. The great river was literally turned on edge. The narrows at

The Dalles

Seuferts and Big Eddy were only about 140 feet wide at the narrowest point. The violence of the plunging, foaming river caused powerful currents. Fuller[2] describes how the river could tear rocks from its basalt bed, hoisting them ninety feet or more out of the holes in the bed of the river and hurling them over the rim. This roaring, deafening place of crashing waters was once also one of the continent's most important petroglyph sites. There were over four hundred carvings in four main groups. Of all this, almost nothing survives.

Today the massive silent dam stands firmly, taming the river. Behind the concrete wall the placid waters of the new Lake Celilo cover the Long Narrows, the ancient fishing sites, and the petroglyphs. Wrenched from their original settings and lying now against the dam wall, forty-six stones were salvaged before the lake level began to rise. In many private collections of the district there are rubbings and photographs. Foremost in preserving a record of the petroglyphs were Malcolm and Louise Loring, whose collection of rubbings is now safely stored in the Oregon Historical Society museum. The publication of

their work will one day provide us with as complete a record as we can have of the designs of the petroglyphs. But we shall not see again the awesome narrows of the Columbia where they were carved, which was also the greatest salmon fishery of the continent.

Ivan Donaldson[3] compares the six to ten million salmon caught in the lower Columbia at the present time to the catch of 42,000,000 in 1883. It is estimated that before the smallpox, malaria and measles brought by the Europeans destroyed about 80% of the Indian people, there were approximately 50,000 Indians living in the area, a dense population. The fishing season attracted thousands more Indian people from both the coast and the interior. The region of the Long Narrows must then have been like a huge fair during the summer, with so many Indians mingling, trading, gambling and peaceably sharing the fisheries which could yield more than they all needed. Where the spawning salmon rested in the eddies and pools after fighting through the strong currents and violent rapids, they were easily taken by the fishermen, with dipnet and spear.

How are the petroglyphs related to all this? No evidence survives to give us a precise answer to this question. This was a fantastically powerful place and an extremely rich source of food and here were carved over four hundred petroglyphs. We may only guess at the relationship of place and petroglyph. Were they carved to mark ownership of specific pools, or the right to fish in the river? Were they tribal symbols used to mark the presence of far ranging interior peoples, as the Coltons[4] have described the use of petroglyphs to record the dangerous journey for salt in Arizona? Did they give power to catch fish? Or power for the hunt, since more than a third of the petroglyphs represent animals of the plateau and there is only one fish? Were they associated with the quest for spirit power so much a part of Chinook life, as elsewhere on the Northwest Coast? Were they carved near dangerous spots to placate the spirits of the river? Or were all of these reasons valid?

The rich salmon resource which brought the Indians from far and near made The Dalles an important trading centre. From the cold interior winters of the Plateau came fine glossy furs. There was jade from the Fraser River, mountain-sheep horn (which the Chinook people fashioned into bowls), basketry, woven robes, dentalia from the Nootkan region, kerfed wooden boxes from the Coast Salish and the Nootka, and a brisk trade in slaves. The Chinook had a variety of canoes but the most popular model seems to have been the Nootkan. Lewis and Clark reported men wearing the finely woven conical basketry hats with spiked knob, whaling scenes along the brim, obviously traded from the northern coast. In winter the Chinook might choose to wear a rabbit-skin robe from the Plateau or a woven rain cape made by the Puget Sound Salish. From 1792 onwards, European ships became part of the commercial scene. They found that the elk hides they could get in trade for guns or axes at the Columbia were much in demand further north and could profitably be exchanged for otter. Drucker[5] suggests that even Indian slaves were taken aboard the sailing ships, to be exchanged for otter skins up the coast. When we consider the ramifications of this trading activity in terms of the spread of designs, articles and ideas, we see the ease with which design motifs could be transferred (although their meanings could have altered in the move) and the unlikelihood of independent invention of designs.

If we plot on a map the occurrence of that strange design feature, the line running down from the eye like a tear drop, we find it from Kodiak Island to The Dalles.

At The Dalles, Northwest Coast and Interior cultures meet. How do the petroglyphs reflect this encounter? Earlier petroglyph observers generally divided the Lower and Middle Columbia River petroglyphs into two groups. Cressman[6] found a) an early style "evidently related to the elaborate stone carvings of the lower Columbia and Willamette rivers" and b) petroglyphs which show "rather striking resemblances to the Great Basin style" (the Great Basin being part of the high interior plateau area). Strong and Schenck[7] state firmly that the Lower River petroglyphs are not stylistically connected with the type at The Dalles and speak of the lower river petroglyphs as the "Old Type", possibly assigning greater age to the lower river carvings because they associate them with "exceedingly crude faces" pecked on boulders on the Columbia River shore opposite the mouth of the Willamette River (which do not seem to have been recorded and cannot be found). They observed that Lower River carvings are often cut quite deeply, that the designs are circular and often there are

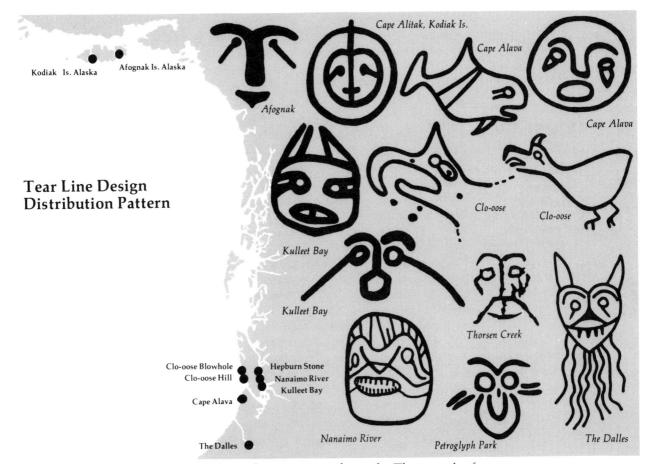

**Tear Line Design
Distribution Pattern**

Kodiak Is. Alaska

Afognak Is. Alaska

Afognak

Cape Alitak, Kodiak Is.

Cape Alava

Cape Alava

Clo-oose

Clo-oose

Kulleet Bay

Kulleet Bay

Thorsen Creek

Clo-oose Blowhole
Clo-oose Hill

Hepburn Stone
Nanaimo River
Kulleet Bay

Cape Alava

The Dalles

Nanaimo River

Petroglyph Park

The Dalles

smoothly sculptured holes, sometimes with connecting channels. They speak of up-river examples of this old type and name the stone from Wallula, now on display outside the City Hall in Portland. Like Cain, they relate the petroglyphs at The Dalles (their second and more recent type) to the Great Basin area. Hedden[8] does not separate the petroglyphs into a Down River style as opposed to those at The Dalles, as Cressman, Strong and Schenck appear to do, but he does distinguish two styles. The first is the curvilinear pattern of anthropomorphic or zoomorphic images with large faces and strongly emphasized eyes, which he suggests may represent survivals or adaptations of ancient mask designs found as far north as Kodiak Island in Alaska. He saw eyes without other features (which we have observed so frequently further north on the coast) and formalized rib patterns as evidence of a relationship with the Northwest Coast. Possibly the eye petroglyphs have simply not survived the flooding of the river, for we failed to find them. As for the rib motif, we saw

The Dalles

The Dalles Damsite

only a few petroglyphs with this device, including the all-over herringbone pattern on two petroglyph sheep which may be derived from the x-ray rib device and ribbed "Water Devil". Hedden's second style, dominant in number at The Dalles, is generally linear (in contrast to his curvilinear first style) and makes use of geometric patterns with occasional recessed surfaces. The designs include quadrupeds, human stick figures, sunbursts, rakes, zigzags. He links this style to the interior of the continent.

In our turn we examined the petroglyph sites of the lower Columbia and the surviving evidence at The Dalles, and were content to divide the carvings into a Down River style (with Northwest Coast connections) and The Dalles style (a distinct Columbia River style plus petroglyphs showing Interior connections). The Down River group is characterized by two dominant elements: the round holes we shall call "pits" and the concentric circles. The pitted boulders were at Fisher's Landing, Underwood, Camas, Garrison Eddy and Gentry's Landing. At this last site there appeared an amazing patterning of zig-zag and lineal designs which fitted somewhat awkwardly into our category. The only similar design on the Northwest Coast is at the Harewood Plain site near Nanaimo, a site which also has many round pits. The round concentric circle designs are conspicuous on the Garrison Eddy stone and on the stone from Wallula, a beautifully carved boulder which seems to be an anomaly in its original location so far east along the Columbia. We observed that the stones which fall into our Down River category are all found on the north shore of the Columbia River below The Dalles (with the exception of the Wallula stone) and that they are found near the water's edge. This suggests that they must have been carved at a time when the river was at the same level as it is now. Excavations have shown that cultural remains are found below the present water table, which would lead us to think that the petroglyphs are not associated with the earliest occupation. Thus these petroglyphs seem to belong to a period of occupation when the people along the north shore were different from those on the south, when the river was at the same level as it is now, and when there was some cultural connection extending to Wallula. Future archaeological research may throw some light on the problem.

In our second style, at The Dalles, we observed the strong Plateau influences mentioned by Cain, Cressman, Strong, Schenck and Hedden. We saw:

a) small realistic animal figures (and animal footprints)

b) stylized birds. Where we were able to examine animals and birds on the same rock we could see no difference in technique or erosion. The use of solidly pecked areas appears in both. Stylistically the Skamania "owl" fits with the "Spedis owls" at The Dalles rather than with the other sites of the Lower River.

c) stylized many-legged creatures; turtle and lizard-like creatures

d) human stick figures, whose poses differ from Northwest Coast positions

e) sun "headdresses", at Cape Horn, Miller's Island and The Dalles, which differ greatly from the rays emanating from heads on the Northwest Coast petroglyph. The Dalles Headdresses are large curved semicircles, large in proportion to stick figures and frequently appearing with an associated human figure.

f) three anthropomorphic faces (Spearfish stone, Black Rock Point boulder and Tsigaglalal).

In what ways do these two styles relate to the Northwest Coast? We have already suggested that the pits, concentric circles and parallel curving lines express such connections, and we have detailed the occurrence of the diagonal-line-from-eye device. Although we failed to find eyes alone, or an extensive use of the rib motif, we observed a few petroglyphs which seemed familiar to our Northwest Coast eyes. But the differences make a long (and undoubtedly incomplete) list:

a) stick human figures have different posture, with no examples of the familiar "frog" position

The Dalles

b) solidly pecked out areas (i.e. nose of Spedis owl)

c) Spearfish and Tsigaglalal mouth with square "tongue"

d) triangular eye (Black Rock Pt., Tsigaglalal, Spearfish stone)

e) owl with horns or ears

f) semi-circular headdresses

g) high percentage of quadrupeds

h) infrequent use of x-ray rib device

i) no emphasis on eyes

j) absence of disproportionately large heads

k) mythical animals are turtle or insect-like, not the marine creatures of the Northwest Coast petroglyph.

l) absence of fish petroglyphs (one exception)

m) rake hands

n) pointed head

o) hunting scenes

p) lizards

q) parallel zig-zag lines

It is true that we have observed only a fragment of the original wealth of carvings. We were allowed to examine and photograph (but not make rubbings of) the forty-six stones at The Dalles, and we saw the Miller's Island stones at Maryhill Museum. We also examined petroglyph casts in the Oregon Museum of Science and Industry (and have used some pictures of these). Of Hedden's estimated four hundred petroglyphs we have seen less than a quarter. As we have observed only a fraction of the original carvings we shall now refer to the study done under the sponsorship of the National Park Service and the University of Washington in 1956 by Cole and Hegrenes[9] as part of the conservation work done before the flooding of the sites. Their report gives us a list of the design subjects at six locations in The Dalles area, and an approximate idea of how frequently each occurs:

human figure	11
quadrupeds	43
sunbursts	10
concentric circles	6
circle & quadrangle	4
connected circles	1
dot series	1
snakes	2
rakes	4
winged figure (owl)	8
many legged figure	6
anthropomorphic figures	10
tailed figure	3
butterflies	1
herringbones	1
crescents	1
cross	1
train	1
TOTAL	114

In this list we note that quadrupeds account for 38% of the designs: mountain sheep, goats, deer and elk, buffalo, dogs, horses. On the Northwest Coast as a whole the percentage of quadrupeds would be very low. Many of the figures on this list are not represented elsewhere along the coast.

Cole and Hegrenes noted that some petroglyphs appeared to be quite recent with sharp cut lines, whereas others showed a great deal of weathering. They write that some of the rocks were covered by "stain" and in some instances petroglyphs had been cut through this stain while other carvings were underneath it. We failed to observe these differences on the surviving petroglyphs piled against the dam. The Cole and Hegrenes list includes a train, which does not appear to have survived the flood. They report that this petroglyph was found near the Seattle, Portland and Spokane Railroad tracks. Whether this obviously recent carving indicates a young age for other petroglyphs of the area we cannot know. However, the dated antler carving (Late Period 1600 - 1800 A.D.)[10] shown in Chapter One suggests an approximate date for certain other petroglyphs, and further archaeological research may date other stylistic elements, enabling us to determine the age of petroglyphs with similar design elements.

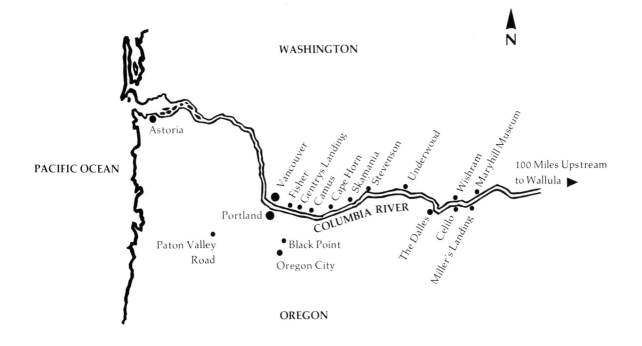

PETROGLYPH SITES: Lower Columbia and The Dalles Area

Patton Valley Road

On a sloping hillside about seventy five feet above the valley is a panel of figures cut into a very soft red sandstone outcrop. The panel measures about sixteen feet by five feet. There are four crude anthropomorphic figures and a canoe-like design. Eye sockets are one to two inches deep. In laboriously scraping off the moss, we discovered how easily this stone can be marked. Vandals have left their initials.

The stick figures do not seem to fit with other rock pictures of the coast and it is possible that they are not aboriginal work. However, the emphasis on the eyes and the rays from the heads are familiar Northwest Coast traits and we have therefore included this site.

4'HIGH

Black Rock Point, near Oregon City   35-03-BP

The petroglyph site is on the east side of the Willamette River, below the falls at Oregon City, about one hundred feet west of the Publishers Paper Company buildings. In excavating for a footing on a new fishway around the falls in 1966, workers discovered the face carved on a basalt boulder and it was arranged that city authorities would haul the rock out. It now rests at the Oregon City Museum, where we examined it. We discovered a smaller faced carved into the other side of the boulder.

There are other petroglyphs cut into the cliff at the Black Rock Point site, a few feet above normal water level but inundated during floods. The sketch of the circular figures on the cliff is drawn from photographs and may not be accurate.

At the time the petroglyph boulder was moved, Stuart Mockford of Oregon City told the Enterprise Courier[11] that the Indians used to camp at Willamette Falls during the annual salmon run. He also said that when the original lock was built, a huge stone frog was found on the west bank of the river. According to Mockford the stone frog "spooked" the Indian workers and they quit their jobs. The frog was removed and Mr. Mockford did not know what became of it. Another frog-like stone is to be found near Fisher's Landing on the north side of the Columbia.

10" x 1'2"

1'3" x 1'3"

Fisher's Landing

According to Malcolm Loring there are more than 400 pits in this single large boulder near the edge of the Columbia River. Back from the beach, in a private garden near Fisher's Landing, is a turtle-like stone with a deep bowl. The figure has four ribs on each side, four-fingered "paws" and measures five and a half by three feet. The bowl has a fifteen inch diameter and is six inches deep.

West about a quarter mile along the beach from Fisher's Landing and imbedded in the sand is a stone with notches cut along a curved spine. At approximately the same place C.A. Gauld found another carved stone in 1927. This stone may now be seen in front of the Public Library Building in Vancouver, Washington.

Gentry's Landing

Also known as Ten-mile Tavern, this place is a half-mile east of Fisher's Landing on the north shore of the Columbia River. The petroglyphs are on a series of fifteen to twenty boulders extending for approximately two hundred yards along the very edge of the river. The stones near the Gentry's Landing Marina have only pits, but the nine stones to the east of them were covered with intricate figures.

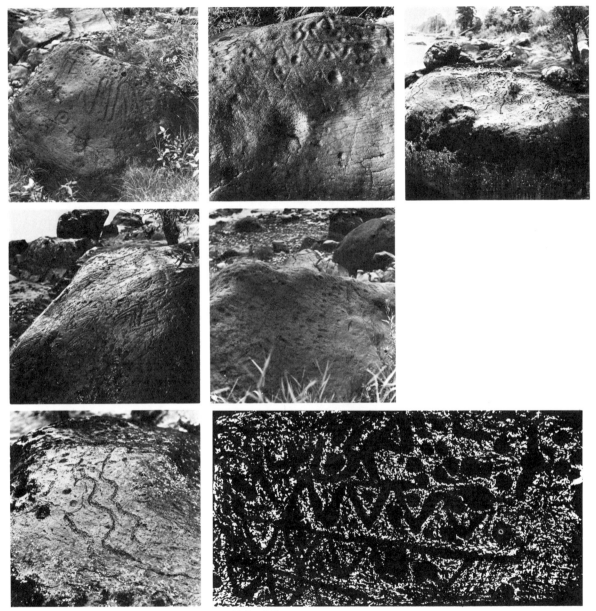

3'4" x 1'9"

Gentry's Landing

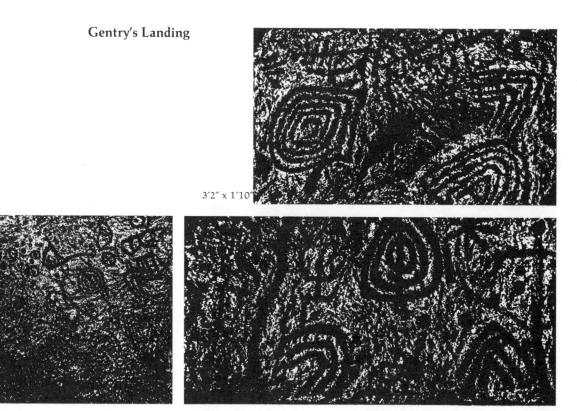

3'2" x 1'10"

7'10" x 5'6"

4'2" x 2'0"

Skamania

45-SM-2

6'6" x 5'6"

Underwood

Underwood is an Indian village at the mouth of the White Salmon River. Below the houses, at the edge of the river, are a few pitted boulders.

Camas

45-CL-11

At this site there are boulders with pit petroglyphs.

Garrison Eddy

45-SM5

This 8′ x 12′ carved boulder has been moved from its original location on the north shore of the Columbia at Garrison Eddy to the Courthouse Annex at the city of Stevenson. It has also been listed as the North Bonneville petroglyph.

Cape Horn

45SM-1

The tiny white marks in the photograph of the eroded basaltic cliffs at Cape Horn are the rubbings shown on this page. We were unable to find a small anthropomorphic figure and have drawn a sketch of it from a picture supplied by the Lorings. There are rock paintings as well as petroglyphs at Cape Horn, the furthest west of the painted figures along the river. To find the Cape Horn petroglyphs you must walk along the railroad to the east entrance of the railroad tunnel, then descend to the shore and look carefully along the basalt cliff west of the tunnel entrance a hundred yards or more.

1'3" x 1'9"

1'2" x 1'10"

The Dalles

The map shows the river's course before the construction of the dam, but we have not attempted to relate the surviving petroglyphs to specific sites. This complex task must be done by someone who worked in the area before the dam. Malcolm and Louise Loring are foremost among the many enthusiasts who made rubbings of the petroglyphs and their important collection is at present stored in the Oregon Historical Society. We have here reported only what we were able to see of the surviving petroglyphs.

We examined but were not allowed to make rubbings of the forty six stones at The Dalles dam and the first nineteen pictures were taken of some of these stones. Because we were unable to move the stones, we do not know what other carvings may be there. We saw some petroglyph casts at the Oregon Museum of Science and Industry in Portland. There were two petroglyphs at the Chamber of Commerce office at The Dalles and three stones at the two museum in Vancouver, Washington. In situ we saw only Tsigaglalal and the one fish petroglyph of the area, which survived because it was so far above the water on the basalt wall of a small canyon west of Horsethief Lake State Park.

present waterlevel

1 - 17: Photographs of some of the surviving petroglyphs on boulders stored beside the dam wall.

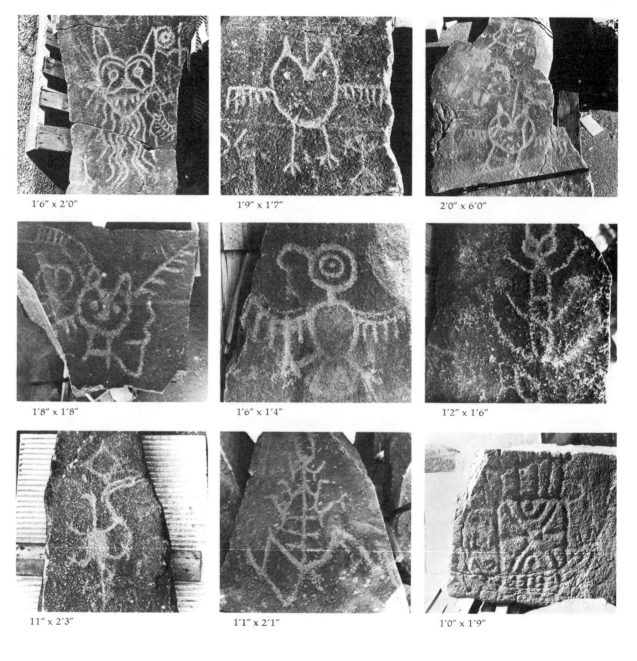

1′6″ x 2′0″

1′9″ x 1′7″

2′0″ x 6′0″

1′8″ x 1′8″

1′6″ x 1′4″

1′2″ x 1′6″

11″ x 2′3″

1′1″ x 2′1″

1′0″ x 1′9″

7" x 1'3"

20" x 4'0"

1'2" x 1'0"

1'7" x 2'8"

1'4" x 1'7"

The Dalles

18: This picture is shown upside down as that seems to be the way the petroglyph has been installed, on a stone base, near The Dalles Dam

19 and 20: A Comparison of one of the petroglyphs at the dam site with a cast of the same carving in the Oregon Historical Society.

1'4" x 1'10"

21 - 26: Petroglyph casts from the Oregon Museum of Science and Industry, Portland, Ore.

1'9" x 2'1"

10" x 1'4"

3'0" x 3'2"

1'3" x 3'5"

The Dalles 27 and 28: Boulders now standing near the Chamber of Commerce Office.

1'7" x 1'11"

30: Found on the basalt wall of a small canyon west of Horsethief Lake State Park, this is the only fish petroglyph of the area and one of the few petroglyphs surviving in situ.

31: Tsigaglalal, "She Who Watches". This well-known petroglyph of the Columbia River used to look down over the famous Long Narrows, one of the finest fishing sites of the coast, but now she surveys the waters of Lake Celilo. The petroglyph appears to have been rubbed with red ochre.

1'3" x 1'3"   26" x 2'6"

Miller's Island

This island was about three miles long and used to lie near the mouth of the Deschutes River. It is now submerged beneath Lake Celilo. The four boulders with petroglyphs were saved from the flooding of the site and may be seen at the Maryhill Museum, on the north shore of the Columbia River near the Highway 97 bridge.

Miller's Island

2'8" x 2'6"

4'0" x 2'0"

Wishram

The ancient Indian village of Wishram was at the head of the Long Narrows and about ten miles downriver from the present village of Wishram. The painted petroglyphs are on the cliffs above the present railway centre named Wishram. Thus the rock art site once overlooked one of the finest fishing sites on the river, at Celilo Falls. Robert Stuart's Journal[12] recorded in 1812 that in the height of the fishing season "the operator hardly ever dips his net without taking one and sometimes two salmon so that I call it speaking within bounds when I say that an experienced hand would catch at least five hundred daily." Seaman speaks of "hundreds of petroglyphs" on the rocks of Celilo Falls.

Nothing survives of that site. However, on the cliffs high above the new lake is a rock art site with both pictographs and petroglyphs, and a painted petroglyph as well. It is somewhat difficult to distinguish each in the photographs. The clear white lines of the designs on the right are pictographs in white paint. The petroglyphs are on the left side of the panel. The rubbing shows one of the petroglyph figures.

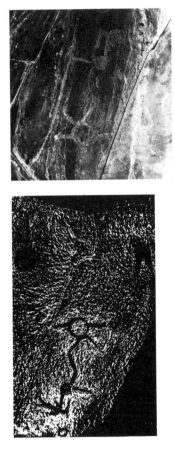

Petroglyphs (left side of panel) and pictographs (white figures at right side of panel) and painted petroglyphs at the bottom of the panel.

2′4″ x 3′8″
Rubbing of petroglyph figure

Painted Petroglyph

Painted Petroglyph

261

Wallula Petroglyph

According to Seaman,[13] the huge carved boulder was found about five miles west of Wallula on the right-of-way of the O.R. & N. Railroad, about thirty feet south of the track. It was discovered in the spring of 1897 when an engineering party sat on the boulder to eat their lunch. The boulder has been mounted in an upright position in its present location at the City Hall in Portland, but in its original position it lay flat, with the carved designs on the flat surface planes. Seaman tells us that the top of the rock was entirely covered with a short moss or lichen, but the engineers noticed a bit of carving and started to scrape off the moss. Soon all joined in and cleaned the entire top of the rock. Later, arrangements were made to move the ten ton stone to Portland.

According to Indians questioned by Seaman, the rock was used in the training of young men. The Indians spoke of the training of youths at puberty to attain strength and courage. They said one test of courage was to send a lad to a marked spot far from the village and in the direction of unfriendly neighbours, where he must stay for a day and a night. The carved stone marked such a spot. The Indians told Seaman that the carvings had not been made by the young men who stayed there, but "had been made ages ago and were known to the Indians in that region". This tells us something about the use of the stone by Indian people of the last generations, but gives us no clue as to the meaning of the carvings. The petroglyph figures, out of place amid the rock art of the upper Columbia, resemble the carvings on the Garrison Eddy stone, many miles to the west.

7. Design, Distribution and Interpretation

In our survey of the rock carvings of the lower Columbia River we examined the different style and motifs appearing on the boundary of our petroglyph province. Now it is our task to re-examine the petroglyphs of the coast to define the basic style elements and trace their distribution. What, precisely, enables us to speak of a Northwest Coast petroglyph art? It is the similar stylistic conventions and motifs of a geographically elongated body of carvings which may occupy ten thousand years of time. We must observe both similarities and variations. "Since any moment of time, be it ten thousand years in length, is still only part of an endless stream, and since the locale of any art impinges on the territory of another style, and as artists are individuals reacting in unique ways to their cultural environs, we can accept that there is wide variation of style in an artistic period."[1]

We shall begin by listing the motifs and attributes which are widespread through the Northwest Coast cultural area. The ubiquitous round pit must be at the head of the list. Though single pecked depressions are very common, boulders covered with hundreds of pits are not found so frequently. The Fisher's Landing boulder on the Columbia River and the Cape Mudge boulder at the north end of the Gulf of Georgia come immediately to mind, and the McMullen Point stone has many depressions in association with a petroglyph face. We do not know the meaning of the pits. At the sites on the Venn Passage most of the hundreds of tiny pits are grouped into small three-hole non-outlined faces. Pits with circles, circles alone, and concentric circles are frequently found along the coast, and there are two further developments of these: first, the frequent representations of paired depressions, circles, or pits

Douglas Channel

Nanaimo River

Nanaimo River

Wrangell

Douglas Channel

Wrangell

264

and circles as eyes; secondly, the use of the dot and circle as a whole body or head. The petroglyph observer quickly becomes aware of the prevalence of anthropomorphic figures and faces. The human figure is usually portrayed in a frontally oriented pose with the knees bent or drawn up in a "frog" position, and the arms bent upwards, a pose with the tense energy of a dance. The hands and fingers are usually carefully delineated but the feet are frequently ignored or given little attention. Heads are proportionately large. Heads with rays, haloes or projections are very common, as is also the portrayal of ribs or other internal parts. Another common feature of petroglyph faces is a projection below the mouth which may represent the labret, an ornament worn through a slit usually below the lower lip although among the Kodiak Island people paired labrets were worn on either side of the upper lip. Though anthropomorphic subjects dominate the petroglyphs, there are also carvings of fish and birds. Quadrupeds are found less frequently. There are many representations of monsters or mythical animals. A list of the characteristic attributes of the Northwest Coast petroglyphs must therefore include:

1. pits; pit and circles; circles; concentric circles

2. eyes

3. pit and circle as whole body or head

4. dominance of anthropomorphic figures and faces

5. anthropomorphic figures usually in a "frog" position

6. hands and fingers delineated but feet of little importance

7. proportionately large heads

8. heads with rays, haloes or projections

9. labret-like projections

10. x-ray rib style

11. zoomorphic figures are fish or birds — few quadrupeds

12. mythical animals frequently represented

In their distribution, these motifs and design elements are not limited to the Northwest Coast, but they are characteristically found here. With regard to the head with rays, which they term the "solar figure", Romas and Joan Vastokas[2] observe that it does not appear in the Palaeolithic art of Europe. "On the basis of available evidence, the image appears to be a predominantly American Indian and Siberian motif". They demonstrate, furthermore, that it is a motif that is "supremely shamanistic in character and meaning." From many sources, such

Return Channel

265

Noeick River

The Dalles

Venn Passage

Agate Pt.

Jump Across Creek

Denman Island

Return Channel

Port Neville

Kulleet Bay

Clo-oose Blowhole Site

Port Neville Narrows

Petroglyph Park

as the description of Christ's disciples at Pentecost and Castaneda's account of the shaman Don Juan, we are familiar with the haloes, flames and emanations of light associated with trance and hallucinatory experience. There can be little doubt that the heads with rays represent a figure seen in a visionary experience. Further, since the spirit quest of the shaman is an arduous training for just such a trance vision, it is quite likely that the heads with rays are associated with Northwest Coast shamanism.

The heads with tall ears, horns or other projections probably have a similar connotation. The shaman figure in the Trois Freres cave art of the Late Palaeolithic has antlers, and the horned shaman, the Master of the Animals, is an ancient shamanistic figure in Europe and across Siberia. Horned figures are widespread in North America and Mallory notes that horns are used by the Ojibwas to represent shamans.[3]

The characteristic posture of Northwest Coast figures is a frontally oriented pose, with the knees bent and the arms bent upwards. Those who have had the opportunity to watch West Coast Indian dancing will recognize this as a dance position. The association of rattles with some of the figures further suggests both the dance and also the connection with shamanism. The figures from the southern coast tend to be less rigid and more realistic than the stylized "frog" figures from the northern part of the coast.

Douglas Channel

Cape Alitak, Kodiak Is.

Thorsen Creek

Myers Passage

Douglas Channel

Douglas Channel

East Carolina Is.

Elcho Harbour

Metlakatla

Whaling Station Bay

Clo-oose

Ford Creek

Chrome Is.

Holden Lake

The Dalles

The Dalles

A large number of petroglyph faces have projections below the mouth which suggest labrets. Alternatively the projection could represent a long tongue. I prefer the first interpretation because the projection usually is below the mouth and separate from it, but it is possible that some are labrets, others are tongues. Krause[4] in 1885 described the wearing of labrets by women of the Tlingit area and wrote that as soon as the first signs of maturity appear in a girl her lower lip was pierced and a bone point inserted. After marriage a larger ornament was pressed through the opening. As the opening enlarged through the years, ever larger labrets were worn. Krause observed that a lip plug "worn by a very distinguished lady" was fully five inches long and three inches wide."

Shuyak Is.

Hetta Inlet

Cape Alava

Thorsen Creek

Douglas Channel

Thorsen Creek

Petroglyph Park

Helen Point

Douglas Channel

Although Barnett states that labrets were not worn by the Coast Salish, a recent excavation in the Gulf Islands produced six labrets at one site, in a variety of shapes and sizes.[5] As Barnett did not observe Coast Salish labrets and as the Gulf Islands excavation referred to is thought to belong to the Marpole phase of the Gulf of Georgia area (about 500 B.C. to A.D. 500), we may ask whether the many petroglyph faces with labret-like projections could be associated with this earlier period. The Kodiak petroglyph faces have a small pit on either side of the upper lip, which may be identified as two small labrets because such labrets are known ethnologically in the area.

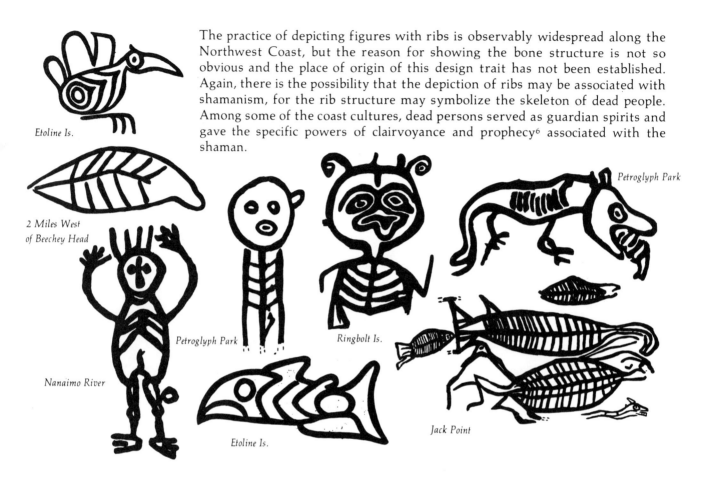

The practice of depicting figures with ribs is observably widespread along the Northwest Coast, but the reason for showing the bone structure is not so obvious and the place of origin of this design trait has not been established. Again, there is the possibility that the depiction of ribs may be associated with shamanism, for the rib structure may symbolize the skeleton of dead people. Among some of the coast cultures, dead persons served as guardian spirits and gave the specific powers of clairvoyance and prophecy[6] associated with the shaman.

Etoline Is.

2 Miles West of Beechey Head

Petroglyph Park

Nanaimo River

Petroglyph Park

Ringbolt Is.

Etoline Is.

Jack Point

The large number of petroglyph birds must also be noted in connection with shamanism, for the bird is an ancient symbol in this association. At 30,000 B.C. in France, in the cave of Lascaux a human figure with bird mask was painted. Siberian shamans sometimes had bird costumes and a picture of a Siberian shaman's coffin shows bird figures on the posts. The bird is a symbol of the human soul and birds are sometimes receptacles for the souls of the dead. Jenness[7] relates that a Salish old couple thought that ghosts often assumed the shapes of owls and haunted their old homes or the places where, in their former lives, they had obtained guardian spirits. A unique group of figures with bowls, found in the Salish area of North America and probably associated with shamanistic practices, includes several in which the human figure (probably the shaman) has bird attributes and two in which the bird has replaced the human.

270

Wrangell

Douglas Channel

Wrangell

Noeick River

Etoline Is.

Clo-oose

Clo-oose Blowhole Site

Petroglyph Park

Nanaimo River

Nanaimo River

Nanaimo River

The Dalles

The Dalles

271

Jung[8] states that both a bird and a shaman are common symbols of transcendence and often are combined. This is not to say that all the petroglyph birds should be interpreted as symbols of transcendence, for some in the northern area are undoubtedly crest symbols or associated with myths.

Both the Jack Point legend and the Tlingit story of Raven and the spring salmon have been discussed in an earlier chapter to show how the fish petroglyphs may have functioned. The assemblage of sea animal petroglyph designs enables us to compare the more realistic style of the south with the stylized fish of the Kwakiutl and Tlingit areas. The petroglyph sea animals from Kodiak Island are recognizably whales and some are pecked in a style unusual on the coast, an intaglio style with fish-shaped indentations.

Cape Alitak, Kodiak Is.

Cape Alitak, Kodiak Is.

Cape Alitak, Kodiak Is.

Cape Alitak, Kodiak Is.

Cape Alitak, Kodiak Is.

Near Beaumont Is.

Return Channel

Return Channel

Return Channel

Return Channel

Etoline Is.

Return Channel

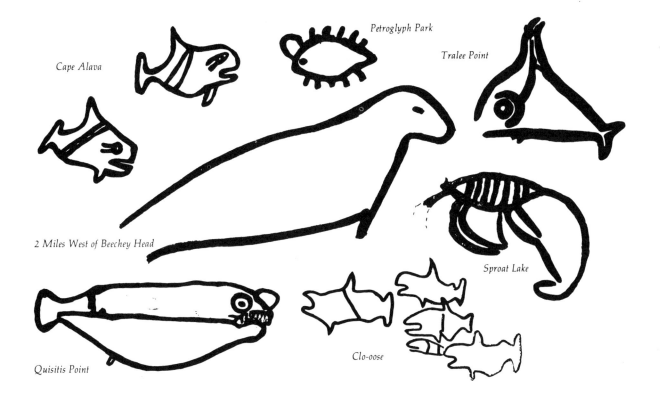

Cape Alava

Petroglyph Park

Tralee Point

2 Miles West of Beechey Head

Sproat Lake

Quisitis Point

Clo-oose

As Drucker observed, monsters are indeed numerous on the North Pacific coast,[9] and not all petroglyph mythical animals can be identified. Smith[10] learned from Captain Schooner of the Bella Coolas that petroglyphs at the Noeick River possibly represented the Haohao, a mythical bird with a long beak and teeth, and the sniniq, an animal like a large grizzly bear but with short front legs ending in eagle's talons. Newcombe[11] reported that the Eneti petroglyph was the thunder-bird. He also thought that one of the Sproat Lake figures had a close resemblance to the mythical snake called the Haietlik by the Clayoquots. It was said that when the thunderbird wished to kill a whale, he hurled the Haietlik at it, and the snake speared the whale like a harpoon. In another paragraph the Haietlik is described as like an alligator, a long creature with huge mouth and teeth and in every other respect like a serpent. This description fits the strange creatures at Petroglyph Park and the dragon-like monster at the Nanaimo River site. Indians called the Dogfish Bay figure a seawolf. The petroglyph is near a spring and Emmons noted that the guardian spirit of fresh water, the mythical Kun-nook, sometimes took the guise of a wolf. Keithahn[12] called a petroglyph at Wrangell a "Sea-Grisly" and another

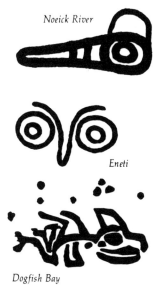

Noeick River

Eneti

Dogfish Bay

273

petroglyph sea monster is compared to the Haida "Wasgo" which was part killer-whale and part wolf. In this petroglyph at Hetta Inlet the dorsal fin is present, the recognition feature of the killer-whale, as well as the prominent teeth and long tail of the wolf. The monster at the Nanaimo River site may also be a southern version of Wasgo for it is quite similar to the Edensaw painting from Boas[13] which shows the Wasgo with a wolf's body and large ears and in the picture the Wasgo also has a human head between his jaws.

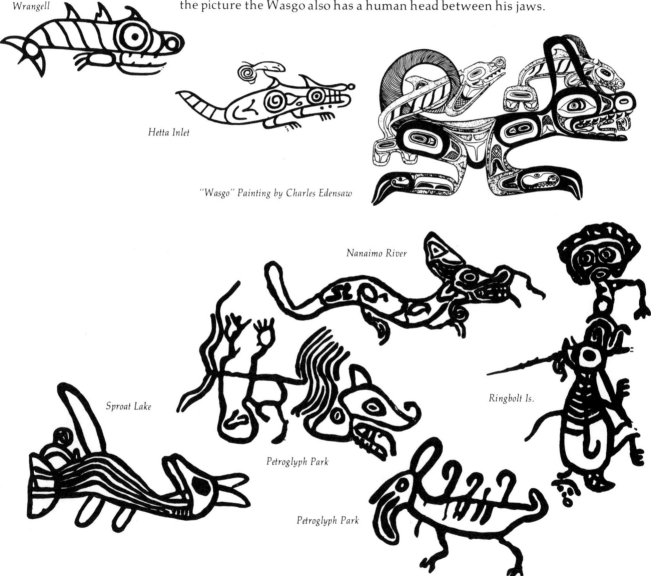

Wrangell

Hetta Inlet

"Wasgo" Painting by Charles Edensaw

Nanaimo River

Sproat Lake

Petroglyph Park

Ringbolt Is.

Petroglyph Park

Of the petroglyph features which have a limited distribution in our petroglyph province, one of the most interesting is the different treatment of left and right eyes. Gjessing[14] assumes that this indicates a blind eye. He finds the blind eye motif in Europe, Siberia, through the Pacific, along the Northwest coast of North America, in the West Indies and on the Northeast coast of South America. The one-eyed gods are ancient: Odin gave one of his eyes in exchange for wisdom and a knowledge of things to come. In an interesting parallel, a spirit with one eye named Lqwalus, in a Spirit Canoe Ceremony in the Puget Sound area is purported to have said "Now look at me! I have only one eye and with it I can see everything."[15] The widespread occurrence of this distinctive feature does not necessarily indicate anything precise in terms of the transfer of ideas or people. The blind eye motif may be an example of Rands'[16] view that "Stylistic factors have empirically proven more reliable than motifs as criteria for tracing precise time-space relationships." Motifs diffuse more easily than integrated art styles. However, the blind eye motif appears to be associated with the idea of spiritual power and hence the spread of the feature may represent the diffusion of a religious concept.

Nanaimo River

Return Channel

East Carolina Is.

Campbell River

Thorsen Creek

Thorsen Creek

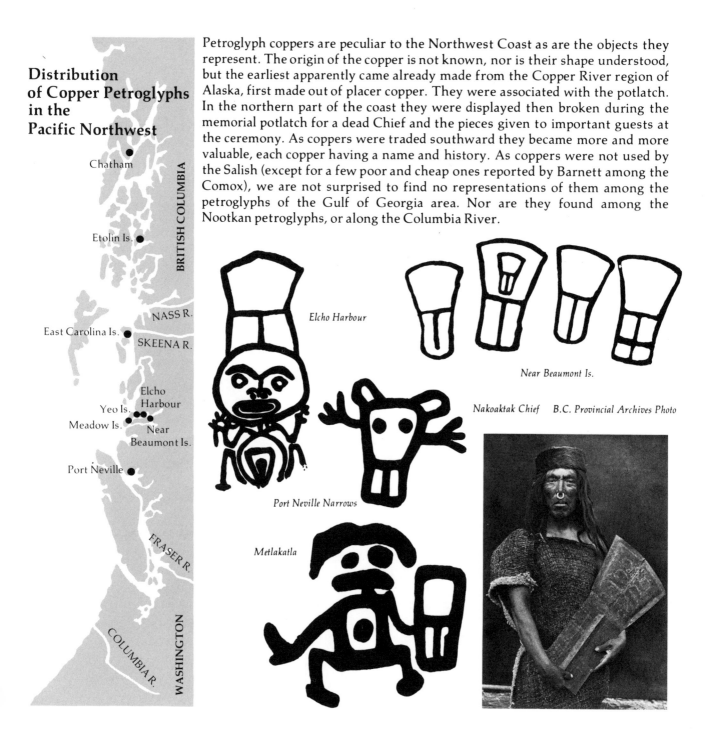

Distribution of Copper Petroglyphs in the Pacific Northwest

Chatham

BRITISH COLUMBIA

Etolin Is.

NASS R.

East Carolina Is.

SKEENA R.

Elcho Harbour

Yeo Is.

Meadow Is.

Near Beaumont Is.

Port Neville

FRASER R.

COLUMBIA R.

WASHINGTON

Petroglyph coppers are peculiar to the Northwest Coast as are the objects they represent. The origin of the copper is not known, nor is their shape understood, but the earliest apparently came already made from the Copper River region of Alaska, first made out of placer copper. They were associated with the potlatch. In the northern part of the coast they were displayed then broken during the memorial potlatch for a dead Chief and the pieces given to important guests at the ceremony. As coppers were traded southward they became more and more valuable, each copper having a name and history. As coppers were not used by the Salish (except for a few poor and cheap ones reported by Barnett among the Comox), we are not surprised to find no representations of them among the petroglyphs of the Gulf of Georgia area. Nor are they found among the Nootkan petroglyphs, or along the Columbia River.

Elcho Harbour

Near Beaumont Is.

Nakoaktak Chief   B.C. Provincial Archives Photo

Port Neville Narrows

Metlakatla

276

Another petroglyph motif with a limited distribution is the diagonal line from the eye, and the similar motif, the triangular shape at the corner of the eye, illustrated in Chapter 6.

A circle to mark joints appears only a few times among Northwest Coast petroglyphs, but as it is important in the wood carving complex of the northern area and as the device appears in some art of eastern Asia, it is worthy of mention here. Many anthropologists have pointed out the use of the "hocker device" (anatomical joints articulated by decorative devices) as evidence of connections with Northeast Asia, a subject which is outside the range of our petroglyph survey. However we may remark here that, considering the importance of this device in the wood carving art of the northern coast and its rarity in petroglyph carvings, the carving of many petroglyph figures may antedate the use of the hocker device in wood carving. The petroglyph site where the device is most conspicuous on petroglyphs, the Nanaimo River site, has some of the most complex and sophisticated of petroglyph designs. Also, the Nanaimo River site is an unexplained distance from the coastal peoples who made so much use of the hocker device.

Nanaimo River

Wrangell

Hetta Inlet

Nanaimo River

A design feature with a very limited distribution may represent a mythological shaman of the Tlingit region. A petroglyph face near Hydaburg Creek was recognized by an informant[17] as the duplicate of one at Karta Bay supposed to represent "Shin-quo-klah" or "Mouldy End", a high caste Tlingit boy who gained favour with the Salmon Chief by making a slave eat dried salmon that had been kept too long and was mouldy. The soul of the salmon was thereby released to return to his own country at the bottom of the sea and Shin-quo-klah subsequently acquired great power and became a shaman. Similar faces at Wrangell, Etoline Island and Ringbolt Island may therefore be other representations of Shin-quo-klah.

Ringbolt Is.

Wrangell

Etoline Is.

The owls of the lower Columbia form a distinctive group. There is also an owl petroglyph at Nowish Island but in style it differs greatly from the "Spedis" owls. The hooked-nosed birds with crests are found only at the petroglyph sites of the Nootkan area. This is also true of the petroglyph carvings of ships, which is certainly logical as the vessels with the high sails would have been first sighted by people living on these shores.

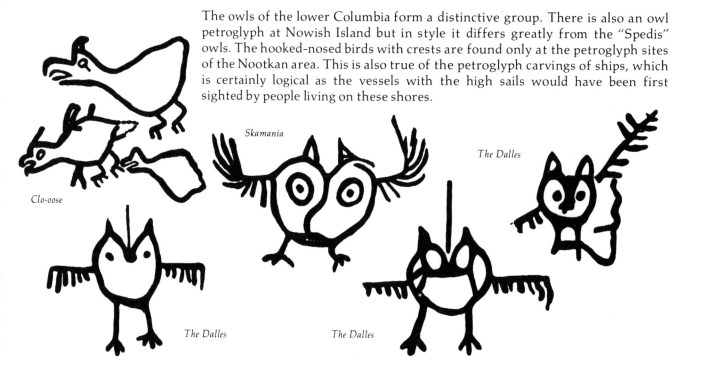

Clo-oose

Skamania

The Dalles

The Dalles

The Dalles

278

Either representing individual artists reacting in unique ways to their culture or the specific cultural concerns of a group, some petroglyph designs are found at one site only. The halibut of Petroglyph Park is an example. No other anthropomorphic figures have such detailed treatment as the three from Jump Across Creek, with the probable depiction of face paint, costume, and ear rings. Nowhere else did we see an object like the one resembling a hand bag, held by one of these figures. The distinctive Jump Across Creek style of nose is found at

Jump Across Creek

Petroglyph Park

Jump Across Creek

Ringbolt Is.

one other site on the coast, Ringbolt Island. Jump Across Creek site has a petroglyph canoe; although canoes are common in painted rock pictures, they are rarely found among the petroglyphs. The Ringbolt Island animal figures are found only at that site. The one horse and rider is found at Clo-oose, but the

Meadow Island

Meadow Island

Jump Across Creek

Clo-oose

Cedar-by-the-sea

rider's top hat is matched by one at the North Return Channel site. Meadow Island has several unique designs: the dumb-bell shaped objects, the incised double-cross figure, and the large square bowl cut into the main panel of petroglyphs. Sun disks are fairly common, but the only crescent moon is at the site near Carmanah Point. Two figures with spears were found, at the Carmanah Point site and at Cedar-by-the-sea, but the figure at the latter site is unique in that the quarry appears to be lying at the hunter's feet. The Clo-oose

Clo-oose

Clo-oose

Hill site has two unique carvings: a copulation and the representation of a figure apparently holding a trophy head. We could extend this list, but probably the examples given are sufficient to demonstrate the wide variations within the Northwest petroglyph province.

We have observed that certain elements are widespread and are the distinguishing stylistic features of the petroglyph area as a whole, that other motifs have a more limited distribution, and that there are local variations. We may make the further general observation that the petroglyphs of the southern part of the area tend to be more realistic and less rigid in style than the more stylized northern petroglyphs. There appears to be a division between the petroglyphs of the Salish/Nootkan area on the one hand and the Kwakiutl and northern acreas on the other. The Columbia petroglyphs are a third section. It is interesting to note that the petroglyph style of the Nootkan area support de Laguna's[18] unwillingness to recognize an "Eskimoid" style in Nootkan culture. The whale-hunting Nootkan people have been regarded as long established on the Northwest Coast and their culture linked to the old Bering Sea culture,[19] yet the petroglyphs of the Nootkan area fit stylistically with those of the Salish area. Further archaeological research may throw light on this question. The more stylized northern petroglyphs seem to reflect the greater stress on rank among the northern groups. The right to use certain crests or carvings was a very important possession of a high-ranking northern person, and this stress on crests probably promoted the growth of Northwest Coast art. The petroglyphs of the northern area frequently have crest functions, denoting ownership of territory, a use probably not associated with the petroglyphs on the southern part of the Northwest Coast.

Another difference between north and south is the greater emphasis on sexual symbolism in the Salish/Nootkan area. Phallic representations are more conspicuous generally. The Clo-oose Blowhole site has a female figure utilizing a deep natural fissure of the rock and portraying the breasts as elongated depressions, a most unusual representation. A short distance away, the Clo-

Clo-oose

oose Hill site has a petroglyph carving of a copulation. The Carmanah Point site a few miles to the south along Vancouver Island's west coast has a figure with a divided oval appendage and a design in the middle of the abdomen which may represent a pregnancy. Another figure at a nearby site also has a small figure within the body of a larger figure. The divided oval, which resembles female fertility symbols from many other parts of the world, is a conspicuous element at the Cape Alava site at the southern periphery of the Nootkan area. In the Pachena Point Cave to the north along the coast of Vancouver Island there is a rock carved with probable female symbols and a single fish. Giedion[20] has

Cedar-by-the-sea

Near Camanah Point

Cape Alava

Pachena Pt.

observed that the bisexual nature of the universe is sometimes expressed in primitive art by the juxtaposition of male and female symbols and gives as examples first the conjunction of a phallus in the form of a fish with a diamond-shaped vulva on an engraved antler from Lorthet in France, and secondly the combination of the same two symbols on Mesopotamian cylinder seals. It is difficult to know how to interpret the sexual imagery of the petroglyph sites. Eliade has described the erotic elements associated with Siberian shamanism but there is no evidence for such aspects of shamanistic practices on the West Coast.

The petroglyph sites themselves must be described in this context. The work of Leroi-Gourhan and Laming has taught us to examine the sites of prehistoric art as places with sexual and sacred significance, the two aspects of art being inseparable. The earth as the female entity, the sky as male, is a concept familiar to us in mythology and the cave as a symbol of the female has frequently been noted. Romas and Joan Vastokas[21] describe the Peterborough petroglyph site, a flowing white bedrock with narrow crevasses and apertures and an underground stream, as "an ideal feminine symbol; it is a symbolic uterus and a means of access for the shaman to the hidden power or sexual energy of nature upon which he can draw for the benefit of mankind." The Clo-oose petroglyph site is on the coast, on sandstone with holes and fissures, above an oval beach enclosed by two rock points which almost meet, so that the rising tide pours in through a narrow gap, filling and emptying the basin with every change of tide.

The Pachena Point site is a cave. The Cape Alava site is a rocky point dominated by a sheer pinnacle rising several hundred feet above the petroglyph site. Thus the site itself can be viewed as having sexual connotations.

In this chapter we have frequently passed from the observation of the nature and distribution of various petroglyph designs to a consideration of their meaning, and in earlier discussions of economics and religion there was the same tendency. Now it is our task to bring together the scattered references and formulate some general conclusions about the function of petroglyphs.

8. Some General Conclusions about the Function of Petroglyphs

To the Pueblo Indians breathing is an act of prayer. If a physiologist were to define the function of breathing, he would undoubtedly discuss oxygen and the circulation of the blood. I suspect that it is equally difficult for us to understand the function of the petroglyphs in terms of the people who made them.

In our search for understanding, guidance comes from four sources. First there were the Indian people of many years ago who still knew or remembered why the petroglyphs were carved. Although anthropologists frequently echo Emmons[1] who wrote in 1908 that "the present generation, even the oldest natives, have no knowledge of their origin", the Indians have, in fact, left us much information which has been detailed in preceding chapters. Next there are the voluminous writings of the anthropologists and ethnologists. Then we must listen to the Indians of today who hold firmly to the old ways; Frank Waters and Carlos Castenada are examples of the writers who can teach us how to see with different eyes. Finally, there is much to be learned from those people who have attempted to apply modern psycho-analytical insights to the study of the origin of man; Lommel's "Shamanism: the beginnings of art" is an example of such an approach. We shall need wisdom from all four sources if we are to interpret the petroglyphs.

In a brief chapter on this complex subject, let us first review the functions of the petroglyphs as revealed to us by the Indian people themselves and by the anthropologists who heard them speak, and then discuss the psycho-analytical approach which can give us insights into our origins. As the interpretive comments of coastal people and their recorders have already been noted with the appropriate sites and discussions of earlier chapters of this book, we shall only refer to them briefly here.

An important function of West Coast petroglyphs is in gaining supernatural power over the inhabitants of the sea. A Haida Indian told Keithahn[2] that the old people said the petroglyphs were for the purpose of causing rain. Indian people told Eels[3] that if the Eneti stone were shaken, rain would fall. The Kulleet Bay stone was named the "rain god". As the returning salmon wait for a rise in water levels caused by rain before entering the streams to spawn, the Indians were probably telling us that the petroglyphs were carved as a way of influencing the spawning salmon to come to the waiting nets and spears. Boas[4] reported that if the fish didn't come, the "Nootka wizard" would put an image of a fish into the water and would pray to the fish. There is also the evidence from the Jack Point[5] petroglyph site, where the shaman rubbed red ochre on the fish carvings and burned four substances in front of the stone. Keithahn[6] expressed the view that the petroglyphs were placed where the tide would submerge them in order that the fish would hear the message of the carved figures, and the Tlingit legend of Raven[7] and the stone with the carved face probably described a function of petroglyphs. The Shin-quo-klah[8] story concerned a shaman who had power from the salmon and certain petroglyphs were identified by the Indians as representations of this legendary figure. Makari,[9] one of de Laguna's informants, told her that the whale hunters made the petroglyphs in secret places to bring them luck.

However, when we say that some petroglyphs were carved to call the fish, we must then look for the deeper meaning and try to understand the way in which the Indian was imbedded in the world around him, a humble element in it. Giedion[10] says "what is so difficult for us to grasp is the inseparable interlocking of matter with its spiritual content." On the 5th Thule Expedition, when Knut Rasmussen was in conversation with Aua, an Eskimo shaman, Aua said to him, "We fear the souls of dead human beings and of the animals we have killed . . . the greatest peril of life lies in the fact that human food consists entirely of souls."[11]

The Bella Coola people told McIlwraith[12] that the Tastsquam petroglyph site was a meeting place for a secret organization and an uninitiated person would have been killed for trespassing there. Smith[13] was told that the Bella Coola petroglyphs were carved by a family while secretly singing sacred songs. We can infer a ritual or religious function for these petroglyph sites, but it is easy to say "ritual function" and difficult indeed to understand what those words meant in terms of the Indian culture.

de Laguna[14] was told by Tlingit people that petroglyphs were sometimes made as a record of slaves sacrificed at potlatches. Both the Boas[15] report of the Fort Rupert ceremonial slave killing, and the information from Cape Mudge in Charles Smith's[16] letter to H.I. Smith (describing a flat rock with a head carved on it which the Indians said was the place where prisoners were killed) related to the same function of petroglyphs. McIlwraith[17] recorded that if a chief gave an important ceremony, he or one of his friends carved a petroglyph of a man or of an animal connected with the ceremony, to recall the event. He adds that as no carvings have been made within the life-time of any living person, there may have been a further significance, no longer known. It is this deeper meaning we must seek. What is the significance of the terrible act of eating, or pretending to eat, human flesh? And what exactly is the relationship of the petroglyph to this ceremonial event? Boas says that the face carved represents a spirit, but that is only the beginning of the answer. Although the limitations of both this author and this book preclude an investigation of these matters, the questions must be asked.

Eyes dominate the petroglyphs of the Northwest Coast, peering at us from the past. Keithahn[18] says that "spirits are sometimes portrayed as eyes, sometimes complete faces particularly if the space was large." What is the further meaning of eyes with a different treatment of right and left eye? We have already mentioned the ancient theme examined by Gjessing,[19] relating how, like Odin's bargain, the eye could be exchanged for wisdom and clairvoyance, and we have observed the Salish Spirit Canoe ceremony in which the spirit Lqwalus says: I have only one eye and with it I can see everything.[20]

Captain Schooner[21] identified certain petroglyphs at Noeick River as specific mythological animals, and we must consider the possibility that another function of the petroglyphs is the recording of myths. The best example of this is the petroglyph Emmons[22] saw in 1888 at Baranof Island. A very old Indian chief showed him a hidden carved rock near the mouth of a stream, a short distance above the high-tide mark. He saw a picture made up of five principal figures, which told the story of the creation of the world. The legend, well-known on the Northwest Coast, tells that the world in the beginning was a dark chaos but a spirit known as Yehlh, who had many forms but often

Baranof Is.

appeared as a raven, created man and wrested light, fresh water and fire from the other spirits, then governed the winds and gave to men all these benefits. The petroglyph panel shows Yehlh in bird form, and a spiral which Emmons' interpreter named "where the sunlight comes from". The bill of the raven holds a stick-like form which could be the fire Yehlh stole from the sun. Joined with the raven is a figure made of three concentric circles which represents the earth. Directly above is a form identified as Hoon, the north wind. The last figure is Kun-nook, the guardian of fresh water, frequently represented as a wolf, from whom Yehlh stole fresh water.

The fortuitous discovery and interpretation of this petroglyph occurred in 1888, but even at that date the petroglyph was old: "Age and the elements have almost effaced some of the grooves and possibly others are wholly lost". This ancient stone is eroded and faint even though it is above the high tide line a short distance, and therefore would not have suffered sea erosion at present sea levels.

The mythological animal who was the ancestor of a group became a crest symbol, and these were sometimes used to mark boundaries. de Laguna[23] states that the Coast Salish told H.I. Smith that they carved petroglyphs to mark the boundaries of family hunting territories. She was told by a Tlingit person that the petroglyphs could be "read like totem poles" and were a record of territorial claims. The Observatory Inlet[24] stone was said to mark fishing rights. In *Men of Medeek,* Wright[25] tells how Neas Waias put his mark on the place to which he would return to make a new village.

As for the association of petroglyphs with the spirit quest and with shamanism, there is some evidence from the Northwest Coast, and much more to be said in a general way. We have already mentioned some petroglyph examples showing connections between shamanistic practices and power over the fish, such as the Jack Point shaman's ceremony using ochre, the "Nootka wizard", and other instances, but there is less to connect petroglyphs with the power quest itself. This is not surprising as the shaman's experience was a very private ordeal occurring in a remote place, whereas the fishing ceremonial was a public affair involving the entire band. de Laguna[26] was told that paintings were done by people training to be shamans, and that some figures represented the familiars of shamans. Though she did not see the rock picture at Agattu Island, she was told that it was a picture of female genitals and had been made by a shaman. Newcombe[27] wonders if the carving of the Sproat Lake figures had something to do with the prolonged period of solitary training of the candidates for admission to secret societies "during which they sometimes had to illustrate, as well as they were able, the spirits with which they held communion."[28] The Interior Salish recorded the trance experiences of their spirit quest and "making the picture was supposed to help in the attainment of supernatural power". We have described the possible shamanistic associations of the Kulleet Bay pool.

Although we have previously made little use of references to pictograph function, we should like now to refer to the work of J.A. Teit,[29] one of the anthropologists working for many years with the Interior Salish. From twenty years of observations, he reached certain conclusions about rock art. He said first that it was generally found in lonely or secluded places where the Indians "were in the habit of holding vigil and undergoing training during the period of their puberty ceremonials when they generally acquired their manitous. These places were resorted to because they were considered mysterious and were the haunts of "mysteries", from whom they expected to obtain power. The mysterious forces or powers of nature were believed to be in greater abundance and strength at these places and the novices desired to imbibe power and knowledge from these sources to help them in after years." Teit goes on to say that at the end of the training, or sometimes during it, if they had any visions or experiences of extraordinary importance, the novice painted pictures on cliffs or boulders, recording their experiences during training "such as things seen in peculiar or striking visions and dreams, things obtained or partially obtained as manitous or guardians etc., things wished for or desired to be obtained, things actually seen during training or during vigils which were considered good omens, actual experiences or adventures of the novice, especially those in connection with animals etc." The making of the painting assisted them to attain the power, or manitous. Teit also states that adults of any age would make a rock picture "after a very striking dream believed to portend evil, for the purpose of warding off the disaster." Similarly paintings of manitous were sometimes made near villages or "overlooking paths and routes (on land or water), by which enemies might approach" as the manitous helped to protect the route. Another important use of art recorded by Teit: "persons when they saw (or thought they had seen) something supposed to be supernatural or some monstrosity or sóme ghostly thing, drew a picture of it ... partly it seems to protect themselves from possible harm and partly to obtain power from it or obtain it as a manitous." Although he is writing about the Interior Salish and about pictographs, we cannot help thinking of his words when we consider the position of the Fulford Harbour petroglyph, for example, at the seaward end of village site. Other petroglyphs, such as the Clo-oose ships, could be interpreted as frightening objects, possibly supernatural, from which the Indian people required protection or could obtain power.

Teit also observes that people usually made their pictures in secret and alone, and that one person did not know precisely the meaning of a figure made by another because he did not know the other person's trance experience. This is a reminder to us of our limitations in understanding the meaning of each symbol at a site.

Though the evidence connecting petroglyphs with the spirit quest and shamanism is tenuous, we have a few facts and some indirect evidence to support the association, and the work of the psycho-analysts would lead us to infer shamanistic connections. But before we briefly discuss this, there are several further points to be made concerning the interpretation of the petroglyphs.

First of all, though some were undoubtedly done merely to pass the time, this explanation is not satisfactory for most of the petroglyphs. The evidence from the Indians recorded by archaeologists and others, the limited information in myths, and the historical incident described by Boas, all suggest that the prehistoric carver had a purpose and meaning in mind as he worked.

Secondly, even when we understand something of the meaning of a particular glyph in one place, we cannot safely transfer our interpretation to a similar carving elsewhere. For example, although the symbol of a large pit and two concentric circles is identified as the earth by the Emmons[30] informant, we cannot therefore assume that concentric circles elsewhere also represent the earth. In Hawaii, the round pit hole was made to contain the umbilical cord, the ceremony being associated with long life for the infant.[31] Ritter[32] records that, among the Pomo Indians, powdered rock removed from pits was sometimes eaten in association with a search for fertility, pregnancy protection and prenatal sex determination. However, we have no evidence that either of these concepts were part of West Coast life. The meaning of the pit marks of the Northwest Coast rock art is still not known.

Heizer[33] has shown that nearly all the petroglyphs in Nevada occur along deer migration trails, at spots where the animals could be shot with bow and arrow, and he provides additional evidence that the petroglyphs were part of the practice of compulsive magic of the hunt. In discussing whether the carvings are made by the hunter or a shaman, he inclines to the probability that they were made by the shaman, as shamanistic rituals connected with hunting were a widespread Basin practice. Though his findings are valid for Nevada and his research admirable, his interpretations cannot be transferred to the petroglyph animals of The Dalles, for example. Motifs are more easily transferred than the meanings people attach to them.

Similarly the Coltons[34] detail the long journey for salt made by the Hopi Indians, who have traditionally descended into the Grand Canyon by a perilous route involving climbing down a yucca rope tied from a rock pinnacle where the traveller would hang over a drop of thousands of feet. Moreover, the Indians believed that the spirits of the dead Hopi lived in the shadowed canyon, so that the journey was a descent into the Underworld. On a boulder by the salt trail generations of men have cut their clan symbols into the stone. Though the Hopi carved petroglyphs as part of a perilous journey, we cannot transfer this interpretation to carvings elsewhere, and, in fact, we do not know the full meaning of the salt journey petroglyphs: did they invoke the ancestral spirit of their clan for protection in the ordeal to come, or did they carve the glyph on the way back as a proud symbol of their achievement?

Competent archaeologists have been justifiably reluctant to offer petroglyph interpretations, for the meanings and the functions of art symbols are little understood. Consider our "Peace" symbol: several thousand years hence, unless he were informed of its meaning, an anthropologist would be likely to note its resemblance to female fertility symbols and would have no way of reading the meaning as "Peace". However, when all the precautions and limitations are kept in mind, and when the illusive nature of symbols is understood, there is still much to be said about the function of petroglyphs and much to be learned from the work of those who study the origins of man using psycho-analytical methods.

Jung[35] writes of the symbol-making propensity of man, who unconsciously transforms objects or forms into symbols, thus giving them a power. They are powerful because man thinks they are powerful. "The intertwined history of religion and art, reaching back to prehistoric times, is the record that our ancestors have left of the symbols that were meaningful to them." McCully[36] assumes that prehistoric art had a psychological function and that "it contains imprints from the psychology of its creators." Symbols, often emerging from fantasy visions, are created to represent the inner experience. They are an objectification of a subjective experience.

In discussing possible theories for the origin of art, Giedion[37] sees the source of artistic creation in man's anxiety and fear. Art gives form to the inner life of man; "symbolism arose from the need to give perceptible form to the imperceptible", such as the frightening difference between life and death. In studying this aspect of prehistoric cultures, archaeological research is a clumsy tool indeed and the interpretation of petroglyphs presents serious problems to the archaeologist.

The key may well be the further study of shamanism. The psychological process by which shamanistic powers are acquired is still poorly understood, but it would seem that both visions and artistic creation are a part of it. What kind of men are shamans? Why are they valued? They are men who, by virtue of unusual qualities, achieve a recognized power. They are somehow able to use powers inherent in nature for the benefit of their fellow men. Lommel[38] writes that "Shamanism may be an intensification of the world view of the early hunting cultures. Yet it is also a psychological technique for bringing to life the mythological images of the group and thus giving potency to the collective psyche. To this end the images must be conceived, formed, displayed and transmitted."

Although we cannot relate these views precisely to specific petroglyphs, we will examine rock art more intelligently if we have some insights into the attitudes of those who produced the carvings. Grahame Clark[39] observes that "the idea that because archaeology depends on material traces it must be limited in its reconstructions to the material aspects of prehistoric life is, as we have already seen, fallacious ... religion is reflected in the graphic arts, of which indeed it was commonly the main if not the only inspiration."

But, as Waters reminds us, the Indians do not have a word for religion, for they themselves are part of the life force that pervades all nature. Indeed, the use of the word "religion" to describe a separate category of human experience is a misunderstanding of the nature of the Indian world and the petroglyphs produced by the peoples of the coast.

With respect and reverence we have recorded the petroglyphs. Archaeologists have been apprehensive about the publication of this book because of the threat of vandalism. We can only appeal to you the readers to recognize the petroglyphs as a priceless inheritance and to help enforce the laws that protect them from desecration.

For underlying the functions of the petroglyphs as supernatural aids in attracting salmon or hunting whales, in "recording" myths or events such as the ceremonial killing of slaves, or in marking ritual places, or the probable connection of some petroglyphs with shamanism, is a profoundly wise world view that does not separate man from the matrix of the living earth, that recognizes the unity of all things and substances and animals, including man. Possibly our growing interest in ecology reflects our search for the wisdom of the petroglyphs.

Addenda

Site Numbering Schemes

In this book we have arbitrarily given each site a geographic name, but the scientific designation of the site follows the accepted Canadian and United States systems as outlined below.

In the United States, archaeological sites have a three-part symbol. The first part is a number representing the STATE, the second is a two-or three-letter abbreviation of the COUNTRY, and the third is a number assigned in sequence to a specific site. Thus the petroglyph site at Cape Horn is numbered 45 for Washington State, SM for Skamania Country and 1 as the first designated site in this area: 45-SM-1.

Such a system could not be applied to Canada because of the lack of county divisions or the equivalent. Dr. Charles E. Borden in 1952 devised a scheme which has been adopted for the designation of sites in Canada. He used latitudinal and longitudinal co-ordinates for defining basic unit areas, and within the areas the sites are then numbered in sequence as they are identified. As thousands of archaeological sites are being identified in different parts of the country and by various archaeologists and institutions, this admirable scheme is preventing chaos.

Site List

1. Agate Point 45 KP 15
2. Agate Pass
3. Miami Beach
4. Victor 45 MS 49
5. Eneti
6. Hartslene Island 45 MS 28
7. Eld Inlet 45 TN 6
8. Tacoma
9. Youngstown
10. Lake Whatcom
11. Bellingham
12. Whiterock DgRr 7
13. Crescent Beach DgRr 9
14. Hastings Mill
15. Aldridge Point DbRv 5
16. Large Bedford Island DbRv 6
17. Two miles west of Beechey Head DbRw 1
18. Beechey Head Islet DcRv 40
19. Half mile west of Otter Point DcRw 18
20. Point No Point DcRx 1
21. Otter Point DcRw 26
22. Cape Alava
23. Clo-oose, Blowhole site DdSf 1
24. Clo-oose, Hill site DdSf 2
25. Near Carmanah Point DdSe 2
26. Near Carmanah Point DdSe 3
27. Pachena Point DeSq 7
28. Pachena Point DeSq 8
29. Quisitis Point DfSj 2
30. Hesquiat DiSp 5
31. Fulford Harbour DeRu 45
32. Helen Point DfRu 33
33. Thetis Island DfRw 6
34. Georgeson Bay DfRu 24
35. Parminter Point DfRv 6
36. Hilarius Farm DgRw 30
37. Degnen Bay DgRw 2
38. Kulleet Bay pool DgRw 36
39. Kulleet Bay "Rain god" DgRw 37

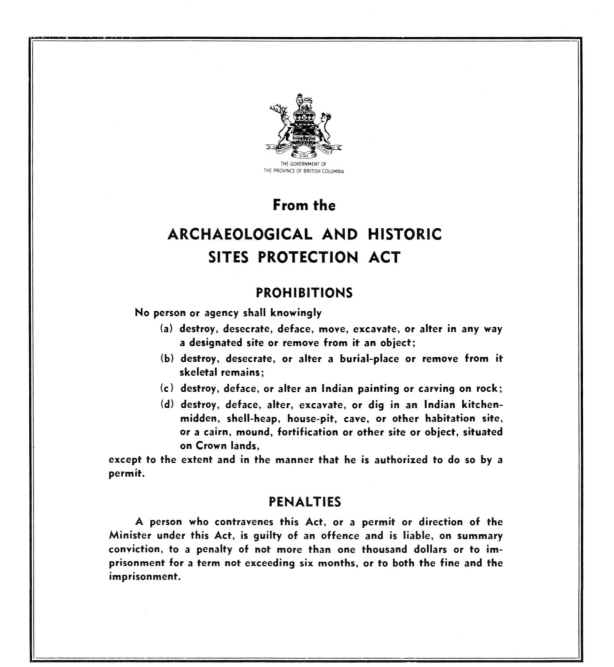

THE GOVERNMENT OF
THE PROVINCE OF BRITISH COLUMBIA

From the

ARCHAEOLOGICAL AND HISTORIC SITES PROTECTION ACT

PROHIBITIONS

No person or agency shall knowingly

    (a) destroy, desecrate, deface, move, excavate, or alter in any way a designated site or remove from it an object;

    (b) destroy, desecrate, or alter a burial-place or remove from it skeletal remains;

    (c) destroy, deface, or alter an Indian painting or carving on rock;

    (d) destroy, deface, alter, excavate, or dig in an Indian kitchen-midden, shell-heap, house-pit, cave, or other habitation site, or a cairn, mound, fortification or other site or object, situated on Crown lands,

except to the extent and in the manner that he is authorized to do so by a permit.

PENALTIES

A person who contravenes this Act, or a permit or direction of the Minister under this Act, is guilty of an offence and is liable, on summary conviction, to a penalty of not more than one thousand dollars or to imprisonment for a term not exceeding six months, or to both the fine and the imprisonment.

Archeological Sites Protection Act of Alaska, U.S.A.

LAWS OF ALASKA

<u>1971</u>

Source

HCSSB 119 am H

Chapter No.

<u>130</u>

AN ACT

Relating to historic preservation.

BE IT ENACTED BY THE LEGISLATURE OF THE STATE OF ALASKA:

* Section 1. AS 41 is amended by adding a new chapter to read:

CHAPTER 35. ALASKA HISTORIC PRESERVATION ACT.

Sec. 41.35.010. DECLARATION OF POLICY. It is the policy of the state to preserve and protect the historic, prehistoric and archeological resources of Alaska from loss, desecration and destruction so that the scientific, historic and cultural heritage embodied in these resources may pass undiminished to future generations. To this end, the legislature finds and declares that the historic, prehistoric and archeological resources of the state are properly the subject of concerted and coordinated efforts exercised on behalf of the general welfare of the public in order that these resources may be located, preserved, studied, exhibited and evaluated.

Sec. 41.35.020. TITLE TO HISTORIC, PREHISTORIC AND ARCHEOLOGICAL RESOURCES; LOCAL DISPLAY. (a) The State of Alaska reserves to itself title to all historic, prehistoric and archeological resources situated on land owned or controlled by the state, including tideland and submerged land, and reserves to itself the exclusive right of field archeology on state-owned or controlled land. However, nothing in this chapter diminishes the cultural rights and responsibilities of persons of aboriginal descent or infringes upon their right of possession and use of those resources which may be considered of historic, prehistoric or archeological value.

Sec. 41.35.200. UNLAWFUL ACTS. (a) It is unlawful
for a person to appropriate, excavate, remove, injure, or
destroy, without a permit from the commissioner, any
historic, prehistoric or archeological resources of the
state.

(b) It is unlawful for a person to knowingly possess,
sell, buy or transport within the state, or offer to sell,
buy or transport within the state, historic, prehistoric
or archeological resources taken or acquired in violation
of this section or 16 U.S.C. 433.

(c) No person may unlawfully destroy, mutilate,
deface, injure, remove or excavate a gravesite or a tomb,
monument, gravestone or other structure or object at a
gravesite, even though the gravesite appears to be
abandoned, lost or neglected.

(d) An historic, prehistoric or archeological
resource which is taken in violation of this section shall
be seized by any person designated in sec. 220 of this
chapter wherever found and at any time. Objects seized
may be disposed of as the commissioner determines by
deposit in the proper public depository.

Sec. 41.35.210. PENALTIES. A person who violates
a provision of this chapter is guilty of a misdemeanor,
and upon conviction is punishable by a fine of $1,000, or
by imprisonment for not more than six months, or by both.

Archeological Sites Protection Act of Washington, U.S.A.

Archeological Legislation

Citation. Wash. Rev. Code, Sections 27.44.00 through 27.44.020 (1964);
Wash. Rev. Code, Section 27.48.010 (1964).

Principal Provisions. Willfully removing or injuring a cairn or grave or a
glyptic or painted record of any prehistoric tribe is prohibited, unless the record
from such shall be destined for exhibit or perpetual preservation in a recognized
manner and permission has been granted by the president of the University of
Washington or Washington State University or a designated faculty member.

Chapter References

CHAPTER 1

1. Newcombe 1907, p. 2
2. Cox and Stasack 1970
3. Heizer 1959
4. Colton 1931
5. Strong and Schenck 1925, p.79
6. Boas 1895, p.439
7. Leechman 1952
8. Bremerton Sun Sept. 7, 1968
9. McIlwraith 1948, p.178
10. Meade 1971, p.10
11. Shepard 1964
12. Keithahn 1940
13. Emmons 1908, p.222
14. Butler 1957b, p.160

CHAPTER 2

1. Petersen, J. 1973
2. Drucker, P. 1955a
3. Barnett, H.G. 1955, p.141
4. Gunther, E. 1972, p.49
5. McFeat, T. 1966, p.29
6. Robinson, W. 1962, p.55
7. Drew, F.W.M. 1969, p.17
8. McFeat, T. 1966, p.45
9. Emmons, G.T. 1908, p.225

CHAPTER 3

1. Boas, F. 1890, p. 569
2. Drucker, P. 1965, p. 84
3. Keithahn, E.L. 1940, p.132
4. Swanton, J.R. 1909, pp.3-5
5. Boas, F. 1890a, p.108
6. Barnett, H.G. 1955, p.89
7. Keithahn, E.L. 1939
8. Barnett, H.G. 1955, p.89
9. Barnett, H.G. 1955, p.94
10. Barnett, H.G. 1955, p.104
11. de Laguna, F. 1956, p.105
12. Heizer, R.F. 1947, p.288
13. Teit, J.A. 1900, pp.378, 381
14. Leechman, D. 1954

15. Jenness, D. 1955
16. Barbeau, M. 1958, p.39
17. Lommel, A. 1967
18. Malouf, C.
19. Newcombe, C.F. 1931
20. Hoebel
21. Duff, W. 1964, p.100
22. Barnett, H.G. 1955, p.293
23. Boas, F. 1895

CHAPTER 4

1. Leechman, D. 1952. p. 267
2. Hunt, H. 1916. v. 1. p. 21
3. Smith, M.W. 1946. p. 314
4. Bremerton Sun, Sept. 7, 1968
5. Mallory, G. 1893. p. 214
6. Alcorn, R. 1959
7. Cheeka, J. 1973. Pers. Comm.
8. McBride, D. 1974. Pers. Comm.
9. Hunt, H. 1916. v. 1. p. 21
10. Smith, M.W. 1946. p. 315
11. Newcombe, W.A. 1928
12. Jenness, D. 1955. p. 91
13. Daugherty, R.D. 1974. Pers. Comm.
14. Higgins, D.W. 1905
15. McKelvie, B.A. 1925
16. Shinabarger, J.J. 1928
17. Barrow, F.J. n.d.
18. Newcombe, C.F. 1931
19. Keithahn, E.L. 1939. p. 22
20. Leechman, D. 1952
21. B.C. Provincial Museum files
22. B.C. Provincial Museum files
23. Barrow, F.J. 1942
24. National Museum Files
25. Vancouver Daily Province, May 1926

26. Newcombe, C.F. 1907
27. National Museum files, Ottawa
28. National Museum files, Ottawa
29. Barrow, F.J. 1942
30. Emmons, G.T. 1908. p. 224
31. Barrow, F.J. B.C. Provincial Museum files
32. Boas, F. 1895
33. Newcombe, W.A. 1928
34. Smith, H.I. 1925
35. Drucker, P. 1943
36. Drucker, P. 1943. p. 92
37. Smith, H.I. 1925. p. 136
38. Smith, H.I. 1924a. p. 50
39. McIlwraith, T.F. 1948
40. Smith, H.I. 1924a. p. 49
41. McIlwraith, T.F. 1948
42. Smith, H.I. 1924a. p. 50
43. MacDonald, G.F. 1970
44. Drucker, P. 1965. p. 120
45. Inglis, R. 1972. p. 15
46. Smith, H.I. 1936
47. Meade, E. 1971. p. 11
48. Walker, D.R. 1974. Pers. Comm.
49. Will Robinson. B.C. Provincial Museum files
50. Vancouver Sun, Aug. 24, 1919
51. Museum Notes. 1927
52. Harry Kemp, National Museum files, March 1930
53. Drew, F.W.M. 1969. p. 17
54. Rushbrook, C. 1938
55. Barbeau, M. 1935. p. 223
56. Gessler, N. 1973
57. Newcombe, C.F. 1907
58. Gessler, N. 1972. B.C. Provincial Museum files
59. Leechman, D. 1952

CHAPTER 6

1. Cain, H.T. 1950. p. 49
2. Fuller, G.W. 1931.
3. Donaldson, I. 1971.
4. Colton, M.R.F. 1931. p.32
5. Drucker, P. 1965.
6. Cressman, L.S. 1937.
7. Strong, W.D. 1925.
8. Hedden, M. 1957.
9. Cole, D.L. 1953.
10. Butler, H.R. 1957b.
11. Oregon City, 1966.
12. Seaman, N.G. 1967 p. 87
13. Seaman, N.G. 1967 p. 119

CHAPTER 7

1. Rands, R.L.
2. Vastokas, J.M. 1973. p. 61
3. Mallory, G. 1893. p.577
4. Krause, A. 1956. p.98
5. McCauley, R. 1973.
6. Barnett, H.G. 1955. p.148
7. Jenness, D. 1955. p.84
8. Jung, C. 1964. p.149
9. Drucker, P. 1965. p.84
10. Smith, H.I. 1925. p.86

11. Newcombe, C.F. 1907.
12. Keithahn, E.L. 1940. p.131
13. Boas, F. 1927. p.159
14. Gjessing, G. 1948.
15. Waterman, T.T.
16. Rands, R.L.
17. Keithahn, E.L. 1940. p.130
18. de Laguna, F. 1964. p.210
19. Drucker, P. 1955. p.68
20. Giedion, S. 1962. p.210
21. Vastokas, J.M. 1973. p.89

CHAPTER 8

1. Emmons, G.T. 1908: 221
2. Keithahn, E.L. 1939: 22
3. Mallory, G. 1893: 214
4. Boas, F. 1890z: 108
5. Barnett, H.G. 1955: 89
6. Keithahn, E.L. 1940: 132
7. Swanton, J.R. 1909: 3-5
8. Keithahn, E.L. 1939: 22
9. de Laguna, F. 1956: 105
10. Giedion, S. 1962: 290
11. Giedion, S. 1962
12. McIlwraith, T.F. 1948
13. Smith, H.I. 1924a: 50
14. de Laguna, F. 1956: 106

15. Boas, F. 1895: 439
16. Smith, H.I.
    National Museum files
17. McIlwraith, T.F. 1948: 178
18. Keithahn, E.L. 1943: 62
19. Gjessing, G. 1948
20. Gjessing, G. 1948
21. Smith, H.I. 1925: 86
22. Emmons, G.T. 1908: 223
23. de Laguna, F. 1956: 106
24. Rushbrook, W.F. 1938
25. Robinson, W. 1962: 55
26. de Laguna, F. 1956: 106
27. Newcombe, D.F. 1907
28. de Laguna, F. 1956: 106
29. Teit, J.A. 1918
30. Emmons, G.T. 1908: 223
31. Cox, J.H. 1970: 56
32. Ritter, D.W. 1970: 56
32. Ritter, D.W. 1970: 408
33. Heizer, R.F. 1959
34. Colton, M.R.F. 1931
35. Jung, C.G. 1964: 232
36. McCully, R.S. 1973
37. Giedion, S. 1962
38. Lommel, A. 1967
39. Clark, G. 1939: 232

Bibliography

ACKERMAN, Robert E.   1965   "Art or Magic: The Incised Pebbles from Southern Alaska" in *The Michigan Archaeologist* Vol. II, Numbers 3-4, Sept. - Dec. pp. 181-8.

ALASKA PACKER'S ASSOCIATION   1917   "Petroglyphs on Kodiak Island, Alaska" in *American Anthropologist* Vol. 19, pp. 320-2.

ALCORN, Rowena L. & ALCORN, Gordon D.   1959   *Mystery rock at Victor keeps it secret.* Tacoma Sunday Ledger-News Tribune, Tacoma. March, 15, 1959, p. 6.

ANONYMOUS   1925   Note under "Anthropology: An Act to Provide for the Preservation of Historic Objects" in *Report of the Provincial Museum of Natural History*, p. C9, Plates I, II and III.

BARBEAU, Marius   1935   *Volcanoes on the Nass.* Canadian Geographic Journal, 10: 215-225 May.

     1958   *Medicine-men on the North Pacific Coast.* National Museum of Canada, Bulletin 152, Anthropological series 42. Ottawa.

BARNETT, Homer G.   1955   *Coast Salish of British Columbia.* University of Oregon, 1955.

BARROW, Francis J.   n.d.   *Petroglyphs, Notebook 1.* Manuscript in the B.C. Provincial Museum, Victoria.

     1942   "Petroglyphs and Pictographs on the British Columbia Coast" in *Canadian Geographical Journal*, 24:94-101, February.

BLAND, Laurel L.   1972   *Special Historical and Cultural Inventory of Imuruk Basin, Final Report, Phase II*, February.

BOAS, Franz   1890   Second general report on the Indians of British Columbia. in: British Association for the Advancement of Science. Report on the northwestern tribes of Canada. 6th, 1890. v. 1, pp. 10-163.

     1891   *Felsenzeichnung Von Vancouver Island.* Verhandlungen der Berliner Gesellschaft fur Anthropologie, Ethnologie und Urgeschichte, Ausserordenteliche Sitzung am. 14. Feb. 1891.

     1895   *The Social Organization and Secret Societies of the Kwakiutl Indians.* U.S. National Museum. Annual Report 1895. Washington.

	1896	Sixth report on the Indians of British Columbia. in: British Association for the Advancement of Science. Report on the northwestern tribes of Canada. 11th 1896 v. 2, p. 1-23.
	1927	*Primitive art.* Harvard University Press.
BORDEN, C.E.	1952	*A uniform site designation scheme for Canada.* Anthropology in British Columbia no. 3 p. 44.
	1968a	*Prehistory of the Lower Mainland.* Lower Fraser Valley: Evolution of a Cultural Landscape, B.C. Geographical series no. 9, pp. 9-26. Department of Geography, University of British Columbia.
	1968b	*New evidence of early cultural relations between Eurasia and Western North America.* Proceedings of the International Congress of Anthropological and Ethnological Sciences Congress s-11, Northern Eurasia and Northern America, pp. 331-7.
BRETZ, J.H.	1924	*The Dalles type of river channel.* Journal of geology v. 32, p. 139.
BREMERTON SUN	1968	*Contractor find stone carved by Indians in Kitsap tidelands.* Sept. 7, 1968.
BUREAU OF LAND MANAGEMENT, U.S. DEPARTMENT OF THE INTERIOR	1969	"Technical Note: The Care and Repair of Petroglyphs" issued December 5. Filing code 6231 (D-370).
BUTLER, Robert B.	1957a	*Dalles Reservoir prehistory: a preliminary analysis.* Washington Archaeologist v. 1, No. 8, p. 3.
	1957b	*Art of the Lower Columbia valley.* Archaeology v. 10, No. 3, p. 158.
CAIN, Thomas H.	1950	*Petroglyphs of Central Washington.* University of Washington Press. Seattle.
CLARK, Donald W.	1960	*Archaeology Report: Kizhuyak Bay Excavation.* Kodiak and Aleutian Islands Historical Society, Kodiak, Alaska, August.
	1964	"Incised Figurine Tablets from Kodiak, Alaska" in *Arctic Anthropology,* Vol. 2, Number 1, pp. 118-134.
	1971	"Petroglyphs on Afognak Island, Kodiak Group, Alaska". *Anthropological Papers of the University of Alaska,* Vol. 15, Number 1, pp. 13-17.
CLARK, Grahame	1939	*Archaeology and society.* Methuen.
COE, Ralph T.	1972	*Northwest coast art.* American Indian art: form and tradition. Dutton.

COLE, David &
HEGRENES, Jack R. Jr.
    1953   *Report on the petroglyphs of The Dalles Reservoir.* Unpublished report. U.S. Department of the Interior. National Park Service. San Francisco.

COLTON, M.R.F. &
COLTON, H.S.
    1931   *Petroglyphs, the record of a great adventure.* American Anthropology. V. 33, No. 1, p. 32.

CORNER, John
    1968   *Pictographs in the Interior of British Columbia.* Wayside Press, Ltd. Vernon, B.C. Canada.

COX, J.H. &
STASACK, E.
    1970   *Hawaiian petroglyphs.* Bishop Museum Press, Honolulu.

CRESSMAN, L.S.
    1937   *Petroglyphs of Oregon.* University of Oregon, Eugene.
    1960   *Cultural sequences at The Dalles, Oregon.* American Philosophical Society, V. 50, Pt. 10.

THE DAILY ALASKA EMPIRE
    1929   "Petroglyphs are Found By Kashevaroff" in *The Daily Alaska Empire,* Saturday, October 12, p. 8.

D'ANGLURE, Bernard Saladin
    1963   "Discovery of Petroglyphs near Wakeham Bay" in *The Arctic Circular,* Vol. XV, Number 1, pp. 6-13.

deLAGUNA, Frederica
    1934   *The Archaeology of Cook Inlet, Alaska.* Philadelphia; the University of Pennsylvania Press, p. 149, Plate 2, Plates 61-68.
    1947   *The Prehistory of northern North American as seen From the Yukon.* Memoir 3, Society for American Anthropology.
    1956   *The Archaeology of Prince William Sound, Alaska.* University of Washington Press, Seattle, pp. 102-109.
    1960   *The Story of a Tlingit Community.* Smithsonian Institution, Bureau of American Ethnology Bulletin 172, pp. 70-79.
    1964   *Archaeology of the Yakutat Bay area, Alaska.* Bureau of American Ethnology, Bulletin 192.

DONALDSON, Ivan &
CRAMER, Fred
    1971   *Fishwheels of the Columbia.* Binfords.

DREW, F.W.M.
    1969   *Totem poles of Prince Rupert.* F.W.M. Drew, P.O. Box 742, Prince Rupert, B.C.

DRUCKER, Philip
    1943   *Archaeological survey of the Northern Northwest Coast* Bulletin of the Bureau of American Ethnology, Bulletin 133. Anthropological papers no. 20, pp. 17-132.

	1948	*The Antiquity of the Northwest Coast Totem Pole.* Journal of the Washington Academy of Sciences. V. 38, no. 12, pp. 389-397.
	1955a	*Sources of Northwest Coast Culture.* In: New Interpretations of Aboriginal American Culture History, 75th Anniversary Volume of the Anthropological Society of Washington, D.C. pp. 59-81.
	1955b	*Indians of the Northwest Coast.* Anthropological Handbook No. 10. American Museum of Natural History. McGraw-Hill.
	1965	*Cultures of the North Pacific Coast.* Chandler Pub. Co. San Francisco.

DUFF, Wilson

| | 1956 | *Prehistoric stone sculpture of the Fraser River and Gulf of Georgia.* Anthropology in British Columbia, No. 5. Victoria. |
| | 1964 | *The Impact of the white man.* The Indian History of British Columbia. V. 1. Anthropology in British Columbia memoir no. 5. Victoria. |

EIDSON, Rex

| | 1961 | *Last days of Petroglyph Canyon.* Science of Man, V. 1, No. 6, p. 184. |

EMMONS, George T.

| | 1908 | *Petroglyphs in Southeastern Alaska.* American Anthropology (N.S.) V. 10, No. 2, p. 221. |
| | 1930 | *The Art of the Northwest Coast Indians,* Natural History, V. 30, pp. 282-292. |

FOSTER, Mrs. W. Garland

| | 1926 | *Stone images and implements and some petroglyphs.* Vancouver Art, Historical and Scientific Association Museum and Art Notes, V. 1, No. 3, pp. 14-16. |

FULLER, George W.

| | 1931 | *History of the Pacific Northwest.* Knopf. |

GARFIELD, Viola E.

| | 1950 | *Tsimshian and their neighbors.* In: The Tsimshian Indians and their Arts. University of Washington Press, Seattle. |

GESSLER, N

| | 1973 | *Petroglyphs near Kiusta, Queen Charlotte Islands, B.C.* Unpublished report. B.C. Provincial Museum. |

GIDDINGS, James L.

| | 1941 | "Rock Paintings in Central Alaska", *American Antiquity* 7(1): 69-70. |

GIEDON, S.

| | 1962 | *Eternal present: The Beginnings of art.* Pantheon Books, New York. |

GJESSING, Gutorm

| | 1948 | *Auden med det ene oye.* Saertryk Au Viking Tidskrift for Norden Archaeologi, Oslo. |
| | 1952 | *Petroglyphs and pictographs in British Columbia.* In: |

Sol Tax (ed.) Indian tribes of Aboriginal Amerca. International Congress of Americanists, Proceedings or Selected Papers, 29, Volume 3, p. 66.

1958 *Petroglyphs and pictographs in the Coast Salishan area of Canada.* In: Miscellania Paul Rivet. Publaciones del Instituto de Historia, Primera Serie, No. 50, p. 270. Mexico City.

GRANT, Campbell 1967 *Rock art of the American Indians.* Crowell.

GUNTHER, Erna 1972 *Indian life on the Northwest Coast of North America, as seen by the early explorers and fur traders during the last decades of the eighteenth century.* University of Chicago Press. Chicago.

HAEBERLIN, Hermann & GUNTHER, Erna 1930 *The Indians of Puget Sound.* University of Washington Press. Seattle.

HEDDEN, Mark 1957 *Petroglyphs: art of prehistoric man carved on the cliff walls of Oregon's Columbia River.* Craft Horizons V. 17 (September) p. 281.

1958 *Surface printing as a means of recording petroglyphs.* American Antiquity. V. 23, No. 4, Pt. 1, p. 435.

HEIZER, R.F. 1947 *Petroglyphs from S.W. Kodiak Island, Alaska.* Proceedings of the American Philosophical Society, V. 91, No. 3, August 1947.

1952 "Incised Slate Figurines From Kodiak Island, Alaska" in *American Antiquity,* Vol. 17, number 3, p. 266.

HEIZER, R.F. & BAUMHOFF, Martin A. 1959 *Great Basin petroglyphs and prehistoric game trails.* Science V. 129, No. 3353, p. 904.

HEYERDAHL, Thor 1953 *American Indians in the Pacific.* Rand McNally.

HIGGINS, David William 1905 *The Passing of a race and more tales of western life.* W. Briggs, Toronto.

HOEBEL, Edward A. 1966 *Anthropology: the study of man.* McGraw-Hill.

HOFFMAN, W.J. 1884 "Remarks on Aboriginal Art in California & Queen Charlotte Island" *Proceedings of the Davenport Academic Society,* 4: 105-122.

HOLE, Frank & HEIZER, Robert F. 1965 *An introduction to prehistoric archaeology.* Holt, Rinehart and Winston.

HOLM, Bill 1965 *Northwest Coast Indian art, an analysis of form.* University of Washington Press.

HRDLICKA, Ales   1944   *The Anthropology of Kodiak Island,* 67, 105-110, fig. 15-18. Philadelphia, Wistar Institute.

HUNT, Herbert   1916   History of Tacoma, V. 1. S.J. Clarke Publishing Co. Chicago.

INGLIS, Richard   1972   *Archaeological project in the Prince Rupert harbour, 1972.* In: The Midden, Volume IV, No. 5, December 1972.

IRVING, William N.   1961   "Field work in the Western Brooks Range", *Arctic Anthropology,* I(1), pp. 76-83.

INVERARITY, Robert B.   1967   *Art of the Northwest Coast Indians.* University of California Press.

                                  197.   *Observation on Northwest Coast Indian art and similarities between a few art elements distant in time and space.* In: Barnard N. ed. Early Chinese art and its possible influence in the Pacific Basin, V. 3.

JENNESS, D.   1928   "Archaeological Investigations in Bering Strait", National Museum of Canada. *Annual Report for 1926,* bulletin Number 5, pp. 71-80.

                                  1955   *The Faith of a Coast Salish Indian.* Anthropology in British Columbia, No. 3. Victoria.

JOCHELSN, Waldemar   1925   *Archaeological Investigation in the Aleution Islands,* Carnegie Institution, Washington, D.C.

JORGENSEN, G.M.M.   1970   *A comparative examination of Northwest Coast shamanism.* Unpublished thesis. University of British Columbia.

JUNG, C.G   1964   *Man and his symbols.* Doubleday.

KEITHAHN, E.L.   1939   *Secret of the petroglyphs.* Alaska Sportsman. March 1939.

                                  1940   *Petroglyphs of Southeastern Alaska.* American Antiquity V. VI, p. 123.

                                  1943   *Monuments in cedar.* Reprinted 1963 by Superior Publishing Co. Seattle.

                                  1953   "About Slate Figurines" *American Antiquity,* Vol. 19, Number 1, July, p. 81.

                                  1953   "The Tools of the Petroglyph Mason" Abstract in *Proceedings of the Fourth Alaska Science Conference,* pp. 750-2.

                                  1962   "Stone Artifacts of Southeastern Alaska" in *American Antiquity,* Vol. 28, Number 1, July, pp. 66-77.

                                  1966   *Alaska for the Curious: Alaska Centennial Edition 1867-1967:* Superior Publishing Company, Seattle, Washington.

KRAUSE, Aurel   1885   *Tlingit Indians.* Reprinted University of Washington Press 1956.

LEECHMAN, Douglas   1952   *The Nanaimo petroglyph.* Canadian Geographical Journal, V. 44, p. 266.
                                       1954   Some pictographs of Southeastern British Columbia. Transactions of the Royal Society of Canada, XLVIII, series III, sec. 2, p. 77.

LEROI-GOURHAN, A.   1967   *Treasures of prehistoric art.* Harry N. Abrams Inc. New York.

LEVINE, M.H.   1957   *Prehistoric art and ideology.* American Anthropologist, V. 59, p. 949.

LOMMEL, A.   1967   *Shamanism: the beginnings of art.* McGraw Hill, New York.

McCAULEY, Robin   1973   *Artifact classification and description, with reference to site DfRu 4 assemblage, Ganges Harbour, Saltspring Island.* Unpublished report. B.C. Provincial Museum.

McCULLY, Robert S.   1971   *Rorschach Theory and Symbolism.* Williams & Wilkins Co. Baltimore.
                                       1972   *A Psychologist looks at Prehistoric Art.* Art International, V. 16, p. 63. November 1972.

McDONALD, George F.   1970   *Preliminary culture sequence from the Coast Tsimshian area, British Columbia.* In: Current Archaeological Research on the Northwest Coast, a symposium presented at the 22nd Annual Northwest Anthropological Conference.

McFEAT, Tom   1966   *Indians of the North Pacific Coast.* McClelland and Stewart, Toronto.

McILWRAITH, T.F.   1948   *The Bella Coola Indians.* 2 vols. University of Toronto Press, Toronto.

McKELVIE, B.A.   1925   *S.S. Beaver's romantic story.* Sunday Province, April 12, 1925, Vancouver.

MALLERY, G.   1893   *Picture writing of the American Indians.* Tenth Annual Report, Bureau of American Ethnology. Washington, D.C.

MALOUF, Carling   1970   *Review of 'Shamanism: the beginnings of art'.* Current Anthropology V. 11, No. 1.

MATTILA, Marlys   1971   "Messages from the Past", *Ketchikan Daily News,* Ketchikan, Alaska, December 28.

MEAD, George R.   1968   *Rock art north of the Mexican-American border: an annotated bibliography.* Colorado State College, Museum of Anthropology.

MEADE, Edward   1971   *Indian rock carvings of the pacific Northwest.* Gray's Publishing Ltd., Sidney, B.C.

MEGAW, J.V.S.   1967   *Art styles and analysis.* Mankind, V. 6, No. 9, p. 393.

NEWCOMBE, C.F.   1907   *Petroglyphs in British Columbia.* Victoria Daily Times, Sept. 7.

     1931   *Annual Report.* B.C. Provincial Museum. p. 6.

NEWCOMBE, W.A.   1928   *Annual Report.* B.C. Provincial Museum.

NIBLACK, Albert P.   1890   *The Coast Indians of Southern Alaska and Northern British Columbia* Annual Report of the United States National Museum: 1888; pp. 225-386, Plate 20.

OKLADNIKOV, A.P.   1971   *Petroglyfi Nezhnego Amura.* Ezdatelstvo "Nauka", Moskva.

OSBORNE, D.   1954   *Pictographs and petroglyphs: what, who, when and why.* Northwest Mineral News, V. 1, No. 4, P. 17. Portland.

OSGOOD, Cornelius   1937   *The Ethnograpny of the Tanaina,* Yale Publications in Anthropology, Number 16, pp. 117-18, New Haven.

PETERSEN, Lance   1971   "Ancient Aleut Rock Paintings: The Clam Cove Pictographs", in *The Alaska Journal,* Vol. 1, No. 4, Autumn, pp. 49-51.

PETERSEN, James   1973   *A reverent connection with the earth: a conversation with Frank Waters.* Psychology Today, May 1973 V. 6, No. 12, p. 66.

PETTYJOHN   1971   "Alaska's Ancient Red Cave Paintings" in *The Alaskana,* Vol. 1, No. 10, November, pp. 10-12.

RANDS, R.L.   1957   *Comparative notes on the hand-eye and related motifs.* American Anthropologist V. 50, No. 2, p. 247.

RAY, Dorothy Jean   1966   "Pictographs near Bering Strait, Alaska" in *Polar Notes, Number VI, June, pp. 35-40.*

RITTER, Dale W.   *1970*   *Sympathetic magic of the hunt as suggested by petroglyphs and pictographs of the Western United States.* Valcamonica Symposium.

ROBINSON, Will | 1962 | *Men of Medeek,* as told by Walter Wright. Northern Sentinel Press, Kitimat.

RUSHBROOK, W.F. | 1938 | *Stone Totem very unique.* The Evening Empire, June 22, 1939, p. 2. Prince Rupert, B.C.

SAPIR, Edward | 1915 | *The Social organization of the West Coast tribes.* Proceedings and transactions of the Royal Society of Canada, 1915. Series 3, V. 9, Sec. 2. In: McFeat, T. Indians of the North Pacific Coast, p. 29.

SEAMAN, N.G. | 1967 | *Indian relics of the Pacific Northwest.* Binfords and Mort, Portland.

SHEPARD, Francis P. | 1964 | *Sea level changes in the past 6000 years: possible archaeological significance.* Science V. 143, p. 574.

SHINABARGER, J.J. | 1928 | *The very first Pacific steamship.* Peninsula Daily Herald, July 26, 1928. Monterey, Calif.

SMITH, H.I. | 1907 | *Archaeology of the Gulf of Georgia and Puget Sound.* Memoirs of the American Museum of Natural History, V. 4, pt. 6, p. 303.

1909 | *"Archaeological Remains on the Coast of Northern British Columbia and Southern Alaska",* American Anthropology, 11: Number 4, 595-600.

1923 | *An album of prehistoric Canadian art.* Canada, Dept. of Mines, Geological Survey. Victoria Memorial Museum Bulletin, Ottawa, 37, Anthropological Series, V. 8.

1924a | *The end of Alexander Mackenzie's trip to the Pacific.* The Canadian Historial Association Annual Report.

1924b | *The petroglyph at Aldridge Point, near Victoria, B.C.* American Anthropology (N.S.) V. 26, No. 4, p. 531.

1925 | *A prehistoric petroglyph on the Noeick River, B.C.* Man 25, p. 136.

1926 | *Cement casts of petroglyphs.* Science Dec. 24, 1926.

1927 | *A list of petroglyphs in British Columbia.* American Anthropologist XXIX No. 4, p. 605.

1936 | *The man petroglyph near Prince Rupert, or the Man who fell from Heaven.* In: Essays in Anthropology presented to Alfred Louis Kroeber. University of California Press. Berkeley. p. 309.

SMITH, Marian W. | 1943 | *Columbia Valley art style.* American Anthropologist V. 45, p. 158.

1946 | *Petroglyph complexes in the history of the Columbia-*

		Fraser region. Southwestern Journal of Anthropology 11, No. 3, P. 306.
SOLECKI, Ralph S.	1952	"A Petroglyph in Northern Alaska" *American Antiquity,* Vol. 18, Number 1, July.
STEWARD, J.H.	1929	*Petroglyphs of California.* University of California Press.
STRONG, Emery	1959	*Stone age on the Columbia River.* Binfords and Mort. Portland.
	1973	*Archaeological evidence of land subsidence on the Northwest Coast.* The Ore Bin, Vo. 35, No. 7, July 1973. Dept. of Geology and Mineral Industries. Portland, Oregon.
STRONG, William Duncan & SCHENCK, Egbert W.	1925	"Petroglyphs near the Dalles of the Columbia River" in *American Anthropologist,* Vol. 27: 76-90, January.
STRONG, W.D., SCHENCK & STEWARD, J.H.	1930	*Archaeology of the Dalles-Deschutes Region.* University of California Publications in American Archeology and Ethnology. V. 29, No. 1, P. 1-154. Berkeley, California.
STRONG, W.D.	1945	*The occurrence and wider implications of a 'ghost cult' on the Columbia River, suggested by carvings in wood, bone and stone.* American Anthropology 47, P. 244.
SWANTON, J.R.	1909	*Tlingit myths and texts.* Washington, Government Printing Office.
SWARTZ, B.K. Jr.	1963	"Aluminum Powder: A Technique for Photographically Recording Petroglyphs" in *American Antiquity,* Vol. 28, Number 3, pp. 400-401.
TAYLOR, Herbert C. Jr. & DUFF, Wilson	1956	*A post-contact southward movement of the Kwakiutl.* Research Studies, State College of Washington V. XXIV, p. 56.
TEIT, J.A.	1900	*The Thompson Indians of British Columbia.* American Museum of Natural History, Jesup North Pacific Expedition, V. 1, p. 163.
	1918	*Notes on rock painting in general.* Unpublished paper. B.C. Provincial Museum.
	1928	*The Middle Columbia Salish.* University of Washington Publications in Anthropology. V. 2, No. 4. Seattle.
UCKO, P.J. & ROSENFELD, A.	1967	*Palaeolithic Cave Art.* World University Library, Weidenfeld & Nicolson. London.

VANCOUVER ART,
HISTORICAL AND SCIENCE
ASSOCIATION

1927   Museum Notes, V. 2, No. 1. February 1927. Vancouver.

VASTOKAS, Joan M. &
VASTOKAS, Romas K.

1973   *Sacred art of the Algonkians.* Mansard Press, Peterborough.

WATERMAN, T.T.

1930   *The paraphernalia of the Duwamish "Spirit Canoe"* ceremony. In: Indian notes, Museum of the American Indian, Heye Foundation. V. 7, No. 4.

WINGERT, Paul S.

1951   *Tsimshian sculpture.* In: The Tsimshian Indians and their arts. University of Washington Press. Seattle.

Index